WOMEN WORLD LEADERS PRESENTS

Kingdom LeadHERship

STEPPING JOYFULLY INTO GOD'S CALLING

VISIONARY AUTHORS

STACY JO COFFEE-THORNE

DEANN ALAINE

Kingdom LeadHERship: Stepping Joyfully Into God's Calling
Copyright ©2026 Women World Leaders

Published by World Publishing and Productions
PO Box 8722, Jupiter, FL 33468
Worldpublishingandproductions.com

ISBN: 978-1-957111-56-8
Library of Congress Control Number: 2026904200

Scripture quotations marked AMP are taken from *The Amplified® Bible,* Copyright © 1954, 1958, 1962, 1964, 1965, 1987, by the Lockman Foundation. Used by permission. (www.Lockman.org.) All rights reserved.

Scripture quotations marked CSB have been taken from the Christian Standard Bible®, Copyright © 2017 by Holman Bible Publishers. Used by permission. Christian Standard Bible® and CSB® are federally registered trademarks of Holman Bible Publishers.

Scripture quotations marked *ESV® Bible are taken from (The Holy Bible, English Standard Version®),* Copyright © 2001 by Crossway, a publishing ministry of Good News Publishers. Used by permission. All rights reserved.

Scripture quotations marked KJV are taken from the King James Version. Public Domain.

Scripture quotations marked NASB are taken from the New American Standard Bible®, Copyright ©1960, 1962, 1963, 1968, 1971, 1972, 1973, 1975, 1977, 1995 by the Lockman Foundation. Used by permission.

Scripture quotations marked NIV are taken from THE HOLY BIBLE, NEW INTERNATIONAL VERSION®, NIV® Copyright © 1973, 1978, 1984, 2011 by Biblica, Inc.® Used by permission. All rights reserved worldwide.

Scripture quotations marked NIRV are taken from the Holy Bible, NEW INTERNATIONAL READER'S VERSION®. Copyright © 1995, 1996, 1998, 2014 by Biblica, Inc.®. All rights reserved worldwide. Used by permission.

Scripture quotations marked NKJV are taken from the New King James Version®. Copyright © 1982 by Thomas Nelson. Used by permission. All rights reserved.

Scripture quotations marked NLT are taken from the *Holy Bible,* New Living Translation, copyright © 1996, 2004, 2015 by Tyndale House Foundation. Used by permission of Tyndale House Publishers, Inc., Carol Stream, Illinois 60188. All rights reserved.

Kingdom leadHERship Declaration

I declare that I am a daughter of the Most High God—

Set apart, chosen, and called for such a time as this.

I release the fear, doubt, shame, and striving

That once held me back from fully walking in purpose.

I surrender my timeline, my comfort, and my control—

And I say YES to the plans of heaven.

I receive the identity that heaven has spoken over me:

I am bold. I am anointed. I am equipped.

I am not too much, and I am not too late.

God's hand is upon me, and His Spirit lives within me.

I will lead with humility and courage,

Serve with love and authority,

And steward the gifts I've been given—

Not for applause, but for impact in the kingdom of God.

I fix my eyes on Jesus,

The author and perfecter of my faith.

I seek first His kingdom and His righteousness,

And I trust Him to lead every step.

From this day forward,

I will step joyfully and boldly into my God-given calling.

I will rise, I will lead, and I will not look back.

In Jesus' name,

Amen.

Contents

Introduction

God's calling on your life is far greater than you could ever imagine. He is waiting with overflowing excitement to honor and empower *you* as you joyfully step into His invitation to be a kingdom leadHER. Allow this reality to awaken something within you!

Being a kingdom leadHER does not begin with a title; it begins with a stirring, an awareness that God placed something valuable inside you, something meant to influence and impact the world. The incredible truth is that God desires to strengthen and lead you even more than you long to honor and serve Him.

Every woman carries influence. Most of us impact those in our own homes, and some ignite and sway others in boardrooms or ministries. We have opportunities to affect people in our neighborhoods, creative spaces, and communities. Sometimes we lead with a strong voice, and at other times, our quiet spirit can shift the atmosphere despite never stepping onto a platform. No matter the expression or means, leadHERship in God's kingdom always begins with a Jesus-centered heart.

The Lord reminded us of this truth when He told Samuel, *"The Lord does not look at the things people look at. People look at the outward appearance, but the Lord looks at the heart"* (1 Samuel 16:7 NIV). God sees beyond experience and position to the posture of your heart. He recognizes the marks of kingdom leadHERship in His daughters as they willingly strive toward purity, compassion, and humility.

Kingdom LeadHERship: Stepping Joyfully Into God's Calling is a collection of voices of women who have said yes to God in various seasons and circumstances. Each story and teaching is unique, yet they all share a common thread: a life beautifully shaped by the Holy Spirit. Some authors discovered leadHERship early, and others stepped into their calling after unexpected life events. They experienced character-strengthening deep healing, boldly released old hurts, grew through mentorship, and followed the quiet leading of God—one small step at a time.

As you turn these pages, you will discover that becoming a leadHER for God's kingdom is a journey that often requires healing, which God will provide as we allow Him to touch those places that hold fear and disappointment or old memories that no longer serve our future. You will also learn that joyful and wise leadHERship calls for us to release the weight of unforgiveness so our hearts can move freely in clarity and peace.

> *Bear with each other and forgive one another if any of you has a grievance against someone. Forgive as the Lord forgave you* (Colossians 3:13 NIV).

This anthology is not about being a perfect leadHER; it is about being willing to give your heart to God and lead others toward Him and His kingdom. These authors have chosen faith over fear, answering a call to reveal their stories in order to bring light into the world. They have learned that God does not waste any part of our journey—He shapes every triumph and trial into purpose.

No matter where you find yourself today, know that God has a plan for your life!

> *"For I know the plans I have for you," declares the Lord, "plans to prosper you and not to harm you, plans to give you hope and a future"* (Jeremiah 29:11 NIV).

God promises to anchor you as you step joyfully into His plan. His promise is not limited to certain personalities or backgrounds—it is for every daughter of the King who desires to walk in obedience.

As you read these pages, we know that the Holy Spirit will come alive and move within you—encouraging, strengthening, and inspiring you to trust God as you follow His call to be a leadHER for His kingdom. We pray you will feel connected to this sisterhood of women who are walking out their God-given assignments with grace. Listen closely as the Holy Spirit whispers to your heart, reminding you that your story matters and your calling is real.

You are a kingdom leadHER.
God has chosen *you* to influence others.
He has, is, and will always equip you.

So step joyfully and confidently into your calling!

This is your moment to step into *Kingdom LeadHERship!*

Stacy Jo Coffee-Thorne

Stacy Jo Coffee-Thorne is a best-selling author, speaker, and kingdom-centered entrepreneur with a passion for helping people step boldly into God's purpose. She is the founder of Freedom Support Solutions, a financial concierge and bookkeeping firm equipping individuals and business owners with clarity, organization, and guidance so they can steward life with confidence.

In 2021, she founded the Association of Christian Business Women (ACBW), a thriving community where women gather for prayer, leadership development, and Christ-centered connection.

Alongside her husband, Allen, Stacy Jo co-leads Reviving Recovery: Unbound, cultivating a Spirit-led environment for healing and renewal. Together, they also host the *Faithfully Invested* podcast, sharing transparent conversations on marriage, leadership, faith, and stewardship.

A mother of four adult children, Stacy Jo treasures her family and carries a deep commitment to philanthropy. She serves on the board of Hearts for Moms and CareBag, organizations devoted to uplifting vulnerable communities. Her mission is to see women rise with courage and unwavering trust in God as they step into their unique callings.

To connect with Stacy Jo, contact her at stacyjo@stacyjocoffeethorne.com

www.acbw.org
www.thefreedompros.com
www.faithfullyinvested.com
https://www.facebook.com/stacy.coffeethorne/

Redeemed to Lead

By Stacy Jo Coffee-Thorne

I grew up in a little country church. My family had a rhythm on Sunday mornings: attend church and sit in the same pew, me right between my parents and grandparents. Church wasn't a negotiation. It was steady; it was home. Church was where I learned that Jesus loved me and where I thought the ground under my feet would never move.

Then life happened. My mom had a massive stroke, my parents ended up divorcing, and the ground did move. The pew felt different. The air felt heavier. I was still that little girl with a bow in her hair and a soft heart, but the lightness in me dimmed. I wasn't the happy, fun-loving, joyful kid everyone knew anymore. I got quiet and learned to smile on cue. And inside, I started to believe something that was not true, but felt true at the time: I didn't matter, I was not enough, and I would never be enough.

The Lord is close to the brokenhearted and saves those who are crushed in spirit (Psalm 34:18 NIV).

Looking back, I can see God's nearness, but during that time, I only felt the crushing. Little did I know that, though there was more pain to come,

God had destined me to lead for His kingdom—just as He has for all His children.

Middle school and high school came, and I did what a lot of girls do—I filled my calendar: youth group, band, cheerleading, chorus—anything to keep me occupied. I laughed at the right moments, stayed late, came early, and kept the energy up. From the outside, I looked like I was holding it all together. On the inside, I was a girl with a secret: I didn't think I fit in. I thought leadership was for the prettier girls, the popular girls, those who always knew what to say, who the boys all liked, and who didn't cry in their bedrooms at night.

As he [a man] thinketh in his heart, so is he (Proverbs 23:7 KJV).

What I thought about myself shaped everything: what I said yes to or turned down, who I followed, and who I let speak over me. I didn't realize how powerful that inner agreement was.

By my late teens, the lie had grown legs. I got my first real job in a restaurant, and instead of standing where God placed me, I followed people who weren't following Him. I stepped into rooms that were exciting for a moment and empty the next. I found myself drawn into the drug and alcohol scene, and I gave pieces of my heart away through promiscuity, confusing chemistry with connection and attention with love. I want to be clear: God spared me from addiction; although I became wrapped up in how the drugs and alcohol made me feel and the false sense of confidence they gave me, by His mercy, they never owned me. God set a boundary I could not see, and by His grace, I walked away from that life.

For the wages of sin is death, but the gift of God is eternal life in Christ Jesus our Lord (Romans 6:23 NIV).

I was headed toward death in a thousand little ways; God put life in front of me a thousand and one times.

I'll never forget waking up in the driver's seat of my car, parked on the street, while blue-and-red lights bounced off the windows. Police were surrounding me. I didn't even know how I'd gotten there. With the taste of cotton in my mouth, fear and shame settled over me like a wet blanket. Thankfully, my keys were not in the ignition, so the police allowed me to exit the vehicle and go inside my friend's house without receiving a DUI charge. That should have been the moment I turned everything around. Instead, the enemy used it to whisper: "See? Worthless. You'll never be anything." And I continued to believe him.

Let me pause here and talk to the woman who knows that shame. You've looked at yourself in a mirror and wondered if God has anything good left to say about you. Sister, that voice is not your Father's. The Father's voice convicts to heal; the enemy's voice condemns to paralyze. God's Word says that He is near the brokenhearted. He was near me, and He is near you— right now, in this very moment.

After waking in my car to the flashing lights, there came an even darker night.

A "friend" I had known and trusted for many years crossed a line. Being violated ravages in ways language can't name. It rips, ushering in a silence that roars. In the storm of shame and confusion, I tried to end my life. I just wanted the noise to stop—the blaming, the bargaining, the *maybe if I had...* I was not trying to get God's attention. I was trying to escape. But God had already written something different for me.

Your eyes saw my unformed body; all the days ordained for me were written in your book before one of them came to be (Psalm 139:16 NIV).

God had days on His calendar for me that I hadn't seen yet, and He would not let my story end there. The enemy does not get the final word.

After several breakups with the one I believed to be the love of my life—the one my heart always circled back to, I made a decision out of exhaustion: I married someone else. He was ten years older. I thought maturity would translate to security. I thought marriage would fix the dissonance in me. I assumed people who said they loved Jesus actually lived like it. I was extremely naïve. That marriage wasn't a covenant under God; it was me trying to outrun myself. It didn't heal me. It hollowed me.

And yet—God. Out of that first marriage came four of the greatest blessings of my life: my children. Those babies were mercy swaddled in skin. I didn't know what I was doing, and I certainly wasn't always the example I wanted to be, but I knew their eyes were on me and their hearts needed me. That's when it clicked—leadHERship wasn't optional; it was in the room calling me by name. I learned that leadHERship isn't about perfect speeches; it's about faithful presence. It's showing up when you're trembling and trusting God to fill your empty hands. *Children are a heritage from the Lord, offspring a reward from him* (Psalm 127:3 NIV). God had given me four reminders that He still trusted me with something precious.

If you're reading this and you feel like you've already failed your kids, please hear me: God's grace is bigger than your failure. God loves your children even more than you do. He can trace His redemption through the places you wish you could redo. Don't let guilt write your parenting story. Bring the whole thing to Jesus. He's not afraid of the mess.

That marriage ended. The next one did too. Two divorces, a lot of rubble, and me standing in the middle of it with four children and a heart full of questions. The old lie, "You'll never be enough," kept trying to take up the whole room. But even there, God stitched Romans 8:28 into my days like a hidden hem: *And we know that in all things God works for the good of those who love him, who have been called according to his purpose* (NIV). God will weave good from what was never good to begin with.

I packed the car and my kids and left Ohio for Florida. I was leaving everything—family, friends, familiar streets, the place where I had spent my entire life. I can still feel the steering wheel under my fingers as I crossed Route 26, my palms slick, shoulders tight, heart drumming, *What if you fail again? What if this is the wrong move? What if you're dragging your kids into another mistake?* I pulled the car over to gain my composure, breathing prayers that were more like exhales: *Jesus, help. Jesus, be here. Jesus, don't let go.*

One month in, things seemed to be looking up. I had just gotten a great job in a local law firm doing what I loved. The kids had just started school. And then the unthinkable happened: my mom passed away back in Ohio. Grief bent me in half.

If you've known that kind of loss, please know the God of comfort is not a theory. *Praise be to the God and Father of our Lord Jesus Christ, the Father of compassion and the God of all comfort* (2 Corinthians 1:3 NIV). *"So do not fear, for I am with you... I am your God. I will strengthen you and help you; I will uphold you with my righteous right hand"* (Isaiah 41:10 NIV). These weren't just verses to me; they were oxygen. On days I couldn't stand, God held me up.

Florida turned out to be more than a new address; it was a new assignment. God started pulling lies out by their roots and peeling back the labels I'd worn—failure, disqualified, too much, not enough. He whispered the truth, reminding me I am chosen, loved, His daughter, called. He also began writing the pages of my love story, not just with the "love of my life," but with the "Lover of my soul." My heart, which had been a battlefield for so long, started to feel like a garden again. *But you are a chosen people, a royal priesthood, a holy nation, God's special possession* (1 Peter 2:9 NIV). I didn't feel royal. I felt recycled. But God doesn't recycle—He resurrects. He called me out of darkness and into His light, and when you stand in His light long enough, your name begins to sound different in your own ears.

Slowly, being a leadHER grew in me like a sunrise. At work, God kept sending people to my desk—women who needed courage, men who needed clarity, coworkers who needed someone to tell them, "You can do this. God's put something in you." I trained, encouraged, gently corrected, and loudly celebrated. LeadHERship was staying late to help someone, praying in the bathroom stall, writing Scripture on sticky notes, and choosing holiness in small decisions no one would ever see. Jesus taught, *"Whoever can be trusted with very little can also be trusted with much"* (Luke 16:10 NIV). He was teaching me stewardship in the unseen.

And then He said the thing I didn't feel qualified to hear: "Start your own business."

I looked at my past and then at His face. "Me, Lord? The girl with the police lights in her story? The girl who tried to end it? The woman with two divorces, four children, and a thousand reasons to sit down quietly in the back row?"

He didn't stutter. He didn't flinch. He is the God who calls things as He sees them, not as we do.

> *Commit to the Lord whatever you do, and he will establish your plans* (Proverbs 16:3 NIV).

> *Being confident of this, that he who began a good work in you will carry it on to completion* (Philippians 1:6 NIV).

So I said yes—hands shaking, knees knocking, heart steadying under His hand.

That yes turned into a hallway of yeses—one door opening to another. Clients came who I didn't have the "right" résumé to impress. Wisdom showed up in conversations I didn't script. God used my voice to call order out of chaos and dignity into places where shame had lived for too long. That's leadHERship—serving people like Jesus does in whatever space He plants you. Sometimes there's a microphone. Often there's a spreadsheet. Either way, His Spirit is the difference.

God does not ask for a spotless record; He asks for a surrendered present. The blood of Jesus really is enough. *Because of the Lord's great love we are not consumed, for his compassions never fail. They are new every morning* (Lamentations 3:22–23 NIV). New mercies. Today. For you.

I want to honor the testimonies God has written in me, not as headlines but as holy ground:

—The night in the car with police lights could have ended my life; God spared it.

—The night I tried to die after being sexually assaulted could have silenced my purpose; God breathed on embers and called me back.

—The move to Florida looked like exile; God made it an entrance.

—The passing of my mother felt like abandonment; God held me closer than my own breath.

—The years that looked like wandering were years He used to pull me into wonder.

—The season that could have grown into addiction became a testimony of His protection and power; He spared me, and by grace I walk free.

If you're carrying an "I should have been dead by now" story, or an "I should have lost everything" story, or even an "I don't know how to be a mom/wife/leadHER" story, welcome. You are exactly the kind of woman God loves to anoint. *For we are God's handiwork, created in Christ Jesus to do good works, which God prepared in advance for us to do* (Ephesians 2:10 NIV). Prepared in advance—before the police lights, before the tears on Route 26, before the moving boxes and the phone call about my mother, before the courtroom papers, before I learned how to pronounce the word *survivor.* He prepared good works for me.

There are moments I still think about driving across Route 26. I can feel the wheel, hear the kids rustling in the back, see miles of road that felt like a question mark. I remember bargaining with God: "If You'll steady me, I'll go. If You'll help me lead these babies, I'll show up. If You'll tell me who I am, I'll stop trying on everyone else's names." And He did. He steadied, He helped, He named. He's still doing it.

When I think of leadHERship now, I don't think of the spotlight first. I think of the woman who refuses to bow to the old lie, the mother who gets back up after a hard day and blesses her children while they sleep, the business owner who tells the truth in a world that rewards cutting corners, and the daughter of God who walks into a room and changes the atmosphere by carrying peace. LeadHERship looks like obedience at scale—your "yes" lived out loud. It's less about being "in charge" and more about being *in Christ.*

And if you're wondering whether your past disqualifies you, let me say it plain: it doesn't. Jesus settled that. If anything, your past becomes the platform where His mercy stands taller.

I used to think my story was too messy for ministry. Now I know my story is exactly where ministry starts—at the intersection of my need and God's kindness. The places I thought disqualified me are the same places people lean in to understand when I speak.

So here I am: I grew up in church, lost my way, believed a lie about who I was, chased feelings that felt like freedom, and found chains disguised as comfort. I should have been the statistic people whisper about, a cautionary tale. But God had other plans. He called me daughter when I still felt like a runaway. He put leadHERship in my mouth when my lips were used to apologizing. He gave me four beautiful children and taught me that presence beats perfection every time. He walked me across state lines and through grief and into purpose. He redeemed what I didn't think could be redeemed.

And now I step—joyfully—into His calling. Not because I'm fearless, but because I'm His. Not because I've done it all right, but because Jesus did. Not because I have the best strategy, but because I have the right Shepherd. *"For I know the plans I have for you," declares the Lord, "plans to prosper you and not to harm you, plans to give you hope and a future"* (Jeremiah 29:11 NIV). I believe that for me. I believe that for you.

If you need someone to tell you it's time to rise, consider this your confirmation. Break your agreement with the old lie. Ask Jesus, right now, "What do You say about me?" Then write down what aligns with His Word, and let that be the new thought you think about yourself. Let your heart say it until your life starts to sound like it: "I am chosen. I am loved. I am forgiven. I am called. I am a leadHER because Christ lives in me."

And when the enemy tries to pull you back with reruns of your worst day, remind him of your Savior's best day—the day the stone was rolled away, death lost, and your future stood up alive. Your story isn't headed toward darkness; it's marching into light. *"But you are a chosen people... that you may declare the praises of him who called you out of darkness into his wonderful light"* (1 Peter 2:9 NIV).

Sister, I bless you to step into your assignment with joy: Mother with grace. Build with integrity. Forgive courageously. Worship honestly. Work excellently. Lead humbly. Carry Jesus everywhere—into boardrooms, kitchens, car lines, church foyers, hospital rooms, and courtrooms. Know the nearness of the God who stayed when others left. Live like mercy is new each morning—because it is.

I was redeemed to lead, no longer the little girl who lost her laughter, I'm the woman who found her voice. And by His grace, I use it now to speak life over my family, my work, my community, and over you. This is *Kingdom LeadHERship* to me: saying yes to Jesus, again and again, until the echo of that yes sounds like joy.

DeAnn Alaine

DeAnn Alaine, known widely as the General of Joy, is a multifaceted leader in the Christian entrepreneurial community and the creative arts. She is a dynamic musical comedienne whose signature songs "Mama Trauma", "Keep Your Clothes On", and "It Takes Courage to Age" bring healing through humor and faith. DeAnn is also a contributing writer in Voice of Truth, a faith-based women's magazine, and the co-author of *Kingdom LeadHERship: Stepping Joyfully Into God's Calling.*

As the creator, director, and producer of the award-winning sitcom *Fade Away,* DeAnn continues to expand her influence in media with her upcoming Christian sitcom, *Stilettos and Pearls,* celebrating sisterhood, faith, and shoes.

Through her powerful program, General of Joy: Developing Joy as a Strength, DeAnn's mission is clear: teaching women to walk by faith, fight from victory, and lead with unshakable joy. Whether on stage, on screen, or in print, DeAnn Alaine stands as a vibrant, joyful force dedicated to equipping women to rise into their God-given identity with courage, confidence, and contagious joy.

The Company We Keep

By DeAnn Alaine

I am a Christian comedienne with a mandate from the Lord—to bring joy to the world. I am being very intentional with this first sentence, to prepare you for what you're about to read! Comedians tend to go through difficult life situations and then turn those situations into laughter for others. So, as you are reading this chapter and the teaching lessons throughout this book, please extend all the mercy and grace that this sanctified, Holy Ghost-filled, comedienne truly needs!

As a teenager, I was naive. One evening, I asked my parents if I could spend the night at a girl's house whose family attended our church. My parents said, "Yes." I packed an overnight bag and arrived at this girl's home. We didn't know each other well, and I was eager to get to know someone new!

After dark, she wanted to go for a walk. We walked for quite a while and arrived at an outdoor sitting area where there were a couple of soda machines. She asked me if I had any change, and I told her, "No." I then went to the nearby restroom, telling her I would be right back. When I came out, a police officer was shining a flashlight in my face! I was scared stiff.

The officer asked me to empty my pockets, so I did. Of course, there was nothing in them. It turned out that the girl I was with had invited her boyfriend to meet us there, and apparently, the two of them had broken into the soda machines. Thankfully, the owner didn't press charges! However, that didn't matter to me, because my dad—an Air Force officer, and my mother—with her black belt degree in Woop Yo Tush, would be notified of the situation. That was going to be faaaaaar worse than any punishment from a judge.

When we returned to the girl's house, it was as if nothing wrong had occurred! Her mom said, "Well, you're teenagers and no harm was done."

Even I felt horrified at the situation, and I was innocent! I told the woman, "When my parents find out, I'm gonna get it!!!"

She said, "You have no reason to be afraid because fear is of the devil."

I replied, "My parents eat the devil for lunch! They bully him around!"

I didn't sleep at all that night. I got picked up the next day; it was as silent as the grave in our minivan. The Bible says, *Do not be afraid of the terrors of the night* (Psalm 91:5 NLT), but it doesn't say nothin' 'bout the fear of Mom and Dad by day!

We arrived home and, as I was heading to my room, my mother calmly asked, "What were you thinking?"

I told her the truth about what happened. While she was still very upset, she passed me and entered her room. Then there was a knock on my door. All I said was, "Yes, Dad?"

He came in peacefully angry with his belt in his hand. "What on Earth were you thinking!" I shared the same story with him, and he said, "I'm going to spank you now, and you're going to write a letter to the county judge apologizing for hanging out with the wrong people! Had charges been pressed, you would have cost us money to appear in his courtroom, wasting his time and ours. AND, you're grounded for the next 75 years!"

Okay, he said, "six months." And though I thought my life was going to end that day, by sundown, I still had a pulse.

Do not be deceived: "Bad company corrupts good morals" (1 Corinthians 15:33 CSB).

The one who walks with the wise will become wise, but a companion of fools will suffer harm (Proverbs 13:20 CSB).

Several years later, I had another run-in with bad company.

I was checking out guys on an online dating site (mistake #1). One of my matches had a nice face and bio, so we began to chat. After a while, chatting online led to talking on the phone. He was extremely funny, which helped me during a difficult period after my brother's passing. Anyway, I remember asking him, "What kind of accent do you have?" It was unique, and I couldn't quite place it. He gave a vague answer, and I wasn't troubled about it.

We decided to meet at a mall during the day, which seemed safe enough. I told him my vehicle type and which store to meet outside of. As I drove around the parking lot, I noticed a man waving like he was hyped up on Red Bull and Cocoa Puffs! I wondered out loud, "Why is that guy waving at me?" Then it hit me, that was *him!* Girls, he didn't look like his photo, but I had already waved back (mistake #2)!

He was thrilled, and I was stunned. When you're getting to know someone on the phone, certain details should probably come up in conversation, like "DeAnn, you have a great sense of humor. By the way, I'm 3'2", and don't have any arms." Well, he left that part out. Before you toss this book in the trash, you need to know that I also have special needs that I overcome every day. Had he been honest with me, I would have been even more thrilled to meet him and ask him all the questions that I've always wanted to ask!

I got out of my car, trying to gather myself. The accent I'd heard earlier wasn't actually an accent; it was a speech impediment. And yes, he really didn't have arms. With as much grace as I could manage, I told him I wasn't laughing at him, I was just shocked. With a grin, he said, "So, what do you think of my flippers?!" Then he started impersonating a penguin!!! Girls, I couldn't help it, I burst out laughing with that deep, can't-breathe, tears-streaming-down-your-face laughter. He was laughing too, which only made it worse! Especially since I had just taken a drink of my fruit punch/Sprite mixer! Yes, it went everywhere!

Thank God we were going to see an animated film because I needed that time in the dark theater to collect myself! He asked for my forgiveness for lying, so I forgave, and we became buddies (mistake # 3).

He was a headhunter, and a couple of months later, he told me about a company hiring for a work-from-home position. I filled out all the forms and was excited when they scheduled an interview. When I arrived at the address, nothing was there. I called him... no answer. Hours later, he called me and told me that it wasn't a real job, and he had planned on stealing my identity, but he changed his mind, because I was so nice to him! Nice to him??? I was not the General of Joy yet!

Even though I was yelling at him, I forgave him and then called a 3-letter agency to report him for fraud! He was charged with a federal crime! I wouldn't want to be him in prison! The Lord protected me all the way!!!

Both these stories highlight the kind of company we *don't* want to keep. I've learned a lot since then!

Alright, let's go to the Word. In Ruth chapter 1, we see that Naomi and her family moved from Bethlehem in Judah to Moab because of famine. She was married to Elimelech, who then died. Her sons, Mahlon and Kilion, married two Moabite women; one was named Orpah and the other Ruth. About 10 years later, Naomi's sons also died.

> *This left Naomi alone, without her two sons or her husband. Then Naomi heard in Moab that the Lord had blessed his people in Judah by giving them good crops again. So Naomi and her daughters-in-law got ready to leave Moab to return to her homeland* (Ruth 1:5-6 NLT).

The three women were on the road when Naomi told her daughters-in-law, *"Go back to your mothers' homes. And may the Lord reward you for your kindness to your husbands and to me. May the Lord bless you with the security of another marriage." Then she kissed them goodbye, and they all broke down and wept* (Ruth 1:8-9 NLT).

Here's the kicker: Orpah returned to her homeland, but Ruth knew the company that she *wanted* and *needed* to keep. Although she had no idea what she would encounter on the road, let alone in Naomi's hometown as a foreigner, Ruth knew Naomi well. And she had determined in her heart that there was no way she was going to part ways with her!

> *Ruth replied, "Don't ask me to leave you and turn back. Wherever you go, I will go; wherever you live, I will live. Your people will be my people, and your God will be my God"* (Ruth 1:16 NLT).

Settled into their new home, Ruth knew they needed to eat, so she asked her mother-in-law if she could glean—gather fallen grain behind the harvesters in the fields; Naomi gave her blessing (Ruth 2:2 NIV). Are you familiar with the epic love story that follows? There are so many amazing tidbits to this story, but I don't want to take us down a rabbit hole. (DeAnn, focus!)

I'll just put it this way: Besides Naomi, Boaz soon became part of the company Ruth kept. The Lord will always bring us the right company if we follow His lead! Here's the Cliff Notes version of what happened because of Ruth's obedience: Ruth had baby Obed, Obed's wife had Jesse, and Jesse's wife had baby David, and David's family line led to the son of God. That's the kind of company I wanna keep!

When I was younger, my parents showed me how to love and welcome other people into our home. What I didn't know, though, was that the phrase, "The more, the merrier!" is only appropriate at certain times. We cannot live a consecrated life if we welcome anybody and everybody as the company we keep. I'm talking about people we receive into our lives to offer counsel.

I'm going to expand a personal story here that you're going to read a little more about in one of the teachings later in the book.

My heart was breaking. I loved the church I attended. I was closely woven with the priceless women I did ministry with. I sang and played keyboard on the praise team and was writing a blog. (Is blog writing still a thing? Just curious.) I worked as a part-time nurse, lived on my parents' farm, and was about to start my senior year in Bible college. The company I kept was fabulous! I was so satisfied, and I would say very blessed. Then, within nine weeks, the Lord changed everything.

In the military, one of the orders given is "Dismissed!"; that's exactly what happened in my life. God dismissed me from my life! Y'all, it was so painful. God called me to surrender my job, my girlfriends, my church family, and my own family. All without any explanation... because the Lord owes no one an explanation.

There I was, trying to explain something I had no idea how to explain to loving parents who didn't know what was going on with their daughter! I didn't know what was going on with me; I just knew that I had to obey the Lord, "Drive, pray, and listen." He told me on several occasions, "I will restore you to a place you've never been. I will restore you to your family. You will breathe without the weight, and you will have so much fun."

He has been faithful to accomplish His promises to me!

My husband and I drove all over the eastern seaboard, from Maryland to Florida. It took me months to stop weeping for what I had lost and learn to weep for those who were lost. When I say lost here, I'm talking about two different things: lost as in they hadn't met the Savior, and a church's mission and identity in Christ being lost. We prayed for both. The Lord was loving, careful, and very brutal in stripping me of what I thought He wanted me to do and who He was calling me to be. After that, I had the adventure of living with my in-laws for 18 months. If that's happened to you, then you understand how humbling that can be. And I thank God for every day we were there.

I know the Lord is so gracious, and we can ask Him questions like "Why?" and "What are you doing to me?" But I made the decision that I wasn't going to ask Him those questions, even though I knew He would love me through my raw emotion. I wanted to dare to trust Him, and I knew that would take a lot of restraint on my part. As we were on the road, He would ask us, "Do you trust me?" Over and over, He'd ask, "Do you trust me?" We would both say, "We trust you, Lord." Girls, I had to work to learn how to trust Him!

Why is this so important? Because the company He wanted me to keep was Himself! It took beating the tar outta me to know that He *can* keep me. He *can* keep my mind, will, and emotions in unison with Him—if I will let Him.

The real question I had to face was, *Do I just want Jesus?* Or did I want the evidence of my own good works (which is a lie in the first place), to keep me comfy cozy in DeAnn's Egocentric Fan Club? Now that just sounds... ew!

Had the Lord not called me to Himself in a very small space with my new husband for 2.5 years, I would have never been prepared to serve Him and people the way He desires. Being set apart requires seasons of isolation!

The backside of my wilderness set the stage for "Kingdom University." If I didn't learn how to trust God with my safety, food, and shelter, how would I trust Him as a kingdom leadHER of a ministry or with the company He wants me to keep?! I needed to learn that He *can* keep me and *wants* to keep me so I know how to keep the right company.

Jesus kept the right company, especially when he invited Judas to walk with him. I think I just opened a can of whoop dee doo! Jesus was willing to keep His betrayer in His company. So who decided to teach people to pray, "Lord keep the Judases away!"? I've heard prayers like that. That person walks in fear and fatigue. Has God got us or not? That's the stuff a kingdom leadHER has developed through surrender!

What do you do when the Lord places you in the middle of a mess, and you don't get a choice about the company you keep?!? Think about Joseph being betrayed first by his brothers, then by Potiphar's wife, and thrown into prison! I am convinced that all those experiences prepared him for the real test: Serving the Lord God among people who practiced polytheistic worship and embraced perversion. Joseph didn't get to choose the company he kept, but stayed in a surrendered position of refinement, so he could literally be a kingdom leader.

If you've heard God's voice and you know He is calling you to lead in some capacity, I strongly recommend you get alone with our King. If you are in that season of Kingdom University, isolated for His plan and purpose, *stay the course and don't be in a rush.* God is preparing you for the company you will keep in your next season of victory! You are a G.I.T., General In Training. Refuse early retirement! You are stronger than you think; stay surrendered. (Good gracious, where did all that come from?)

This all brings me to my main point: As we trust God to surround us with the right company, remember He has included joy as part of His plan for your life!

Always be joyful (1 Thessalonians 5:16 NLT).

Every person who knows that life is hard understands that joy is a necessity to keep us all out of prison! Joy really is a serious business. Did you know that comedy is one of the top three genres in film? I know, you're not surprised!

It wasn't until the summer of 2024 that the Lord said to me, "The joy of the Lord is your strength." My reply to him was, of course, "Yep!" Then I really started to think about that, "The joy of the Lord is my strength." How did that happen? God began to take me through different sections of my life, from childhood into adulthood, showing me how He's preserved me, and taught my heart and brain how to be washed clean with His Word.

It's true, I have been brainwashed... several times... every time I open my Bible, it happens again!

I am generally a joyful person. God just flipped it on me and called me His General of Joy!

Having joy is necessary in this long-distance race that we're running—gargantuan, beautiful, heaping tons of sustaining joy! If you don't have someone who is full of joy in the company that you keep, then guess what? You get to become that person! Every leadHER is called to lead with the joy of the Lord. This is possible by trusting God to lead *us* every step of the way. What can be more joyful than following in the footsteps of the One who knows exactly where He is going and is leading you to pastures greener than you could ever imagine?

Keep showing up for God. Keep trusting Him. Keep following in obedience. And keep reading and learning about kingdom leadHERship and surrounding yourself with His people—and you will find that the joy of the Lord is yours for the taking!

Hi! I'm DeAnn Alaine, and I'm here to walk with you as your 4-Star General of Joy!

Leading with Identity

By DeAnn Alaine

I am a wife, mom, comedienne, preacher, speaker, author, and business-woman... so which of those things do I need to focus on today? Which of those identities do I need to give attention to? I can't believe I fell for that trick, believing that *what I do* is my identity. What a lie and a surefire way to be completely confused! It isn't easy to lead when you're not sure which part of your leadership you're supposed to lean into; thankfully, God calls us as leadHERs to lean into our identity in Him first, not the abilities He has given us.

There are all sorts of leaders, but the most dangerous kind of leader is one who doesn't have the proper identity. Leaders without Jesus can be brilliant, empowering, and get the job done. But the leadHER who knows Jesus is able to lead 1000 times better because her identity is in Christ.

But what happens if you know Jesus and you say, "I don't know who I am or what my identity is supposed to be. I wear a lot of hats. Which one do I choose?" It's easy to get confused when we tie our identity to a skill. Asking Him, "Okay, Lord, since seasons change, which skill set do you want me to lean into now?" is a wonderful question, but not as it relates to identity! It's wild to me how difficult we make things that aren't supposed to be difficult at all.

How can you know that you are leading with the right identity? First of all, know your identity isn't tied to what you do, but who you know! Jesus told us, *"Remain in me, as I also remain in you. No branch can bear fruit by itself; It must remain in the vine. Neither can you bear fruit unless you remain in me. I am the vine; you are the branches. If you remain in me and I in you, you will bear much fruit; Apart from me you can do nothing* (John 15:4-5 NIV).

Do we understand that apart from God, we don't have the proper identity, and the fruit that we bear as leaders can really harm others? *Be sober-minded; be watchful. Your adversary the devil prowls around like a roaring lion, seeking someone to devour* (1 Peter 5:8 ESV). We have the very sobering responsibility of leading as Christ did, with His identity; and we are called to lead those around us to do the same.

The more I get to know Jesus, the more I know who I am.

How can I know that my identity is truly wrapped up in Jesus? We are all fruit bearers, but whose fruit do we share? God's or our own? Are we living sacrifices? We can know if our identity is found in Christ because, when it is, there will be evidence. *Therefore, brothers and sisters, in view of the mercies of God, I urge you to present your bodies as a living sacrifice, holy and pleasing to God; this is your true worship* (Romans 12:1 CSB). My hubby and I are always saying, "Lord, we don't want our way." That's the evidence of His identity working in us as we can become more like Him!

Several years ago while in the company of my then fiancé, he would say with such assurance, "I know who I am in Christ, I'm the righteousness of God revealed through Christ Jesus!" (see 2 Corinthians 5:21 ESV). What an example of the right kind of identity, especially when many of us find our identity in our jobs. Our only soul tie is the one to Jesus; anything else we tie ourselves to will be a distraction and ensure that we do not lead as Christ calls us to, with HIS identity.

What evidence shows that your identity is in Christ? Go ahead and be a fruit inspector! That's being a kingdom leadHER.

. . . .

Diana Miret

Diana Miret is a self-proclaimed *corporate fugitive* who traded in boardrooms for her true calling—serving God by helping business owners steward their finances with clarity and purpose. A wife, mom, and proud grandma, Diana brings both wisdom and warmth to everything she does.

With over two decades in executive finance roles, Diana now serves as a Fractional CFO and Certified Profit First Professional, guiding small business owners to turn confusion into confidence and cash flow into freedom. Her mission? To help kingdom-minded entrepreneurs build businesses that thrive financially and align with God's design for stewardship.

A marathoner with 11 races under her belt, Diana knows the value of endurance and discipline—qualities she brings to her work and her walk with Christ. Her story is one of bold pivots, grace-filled grit, and the relentless pursuit of kingdom impact.

Through KingdomLeadHERship, Diana shares not just financial strategy, but the heart behind it: that profit is provision, and when we honor God with our business, peace and purpose follow.

A Case of Mistaken Identity

By Diana Miret

Me?

Have a calling?

You must be mistaken.

I'm not smart.

I'm too old.

I've made too many mistakes.

If people knew all the bad things I have done, they would not take me seriously.

God calls "good" people to do important things. Sure, maybe those people were bad for part of their lives, but they turned things around spectacularly. He calls people who used to be sick or lost—He cleans them up and gives them a megaphone.

But I am not spectacular.

God's calling? That's for other people.

Deep down, I always wanted to be special. I longed to be called, to have a purpose. Feelings of worthlessness have plagued me for as long as I can remember.

My earliest memories are of constantly being criticized and called names while receiving little praise and existing in isolation. From a young age, I was told I was stupid, slow, unattractive, evil, and did not have a heart.

My grades were never good enough, and my room was not tidy enough. A ballet teacher told my mother I had no talent, so she should find something else for me to do. Mom seemed relieved—my brothers had athletic skills, and she needed to drive them to baseball and football practice. More time for them, I guess.

Teachers said I had potential, but I didn't apply myself. That angered my parents because it meant I wasn't trying hard enough. How could I explain that there was a constant hum in my ears that caused my brain not to focus? I couldn't articulate that fear of being ridiculed paralyzed me, keeping me from raising my hand in class. I didn't want to ask questions; that would only confirm to others what I believed they thought of me—that I was dumb. School was a constant reminder that I did not measure up.

The only time I felt free was when I was reading my beloved books, stories of beautiful girls with shining curls and pretty dresses. Some had ponies, most had doting parents. That was the world I wanted. My favorite books were fairy tales and Nancy Drew mysteries. Nancy Drew was a beautiful detective who solved mysteries to much acclaim. She was smart and talented. I dreamed of being Nancy Drew and hoped that someday I would solve a mystery or a problem, and people would finally see I was smart enough.

The world gives us identities as we grow, labeling us "smart" or "ugly." Our parents, in an attempt to motivate us, compare us to others, which emphasizes our shortcomings. "Why aren't you more like your brother?" "Why can't you get good grades or behave like that girl?"

School teachers give grades, which can turn into our identity. "She is a C student. She should try harder."

Labels. Identities.

Adolescence brought pimples and a flat chest. I was thin, so I didn't look like the other girls—gawkiness and braces on my teeth added to my feelings of being not-enough. Middle school was the worst; I was no longer a child, but not quite a cool teenager. My few friends either had looks or a talent that gave them standing.

My one friend, Danila, was intelligent and had straight A's. She always looked tidy and put together—her shiny hair braided perfectly. She was the ideal student in her school uniform, complete with her blue knee socks and blazer. One time, I went to her house for a sleepover. Her home was clean and tidy, with her books lined up by height. I did not sleep a wink for fear I would drool or do something gross to mess up her perfect bed, but instead lay awake all night in dread of my own body. After that, Danila never invited me back to her house. Looking back, I was likely not much fun. When you are afraid, you are not fun.

More labels. And by that point, my identity was firmly established.

Nuns told me I needed to take communion so I could be right with God; I had sinned, and only Jesus could save me. It was not clear to me how Jesus could do that, but one thing I knew for sure was that He likely thought I was a waste of time, too.

At night, I frequently looked out of my window towards the sky. I constantly prayed to God and asked for forgiveness. I also asked Him why my parents found so much fault with me, and I begged Him to help me be better, do better. I would soak my pillow with tears, certain that I was letting God down. I loved God, but mostly, I feared Him. I was sure He was passing judgment over every little detail in my life. His "tsk tsk tsk" was deafening in my head.

Another identity: Sinner.

My lack of self-esteem was debilitating. It resulted in poor performance at school, anxiety, and loneliness. I become plagued with fear of failure or embarrassment.

Somewhere along the way, I noticed that studying and getting good grades won me favor with my teachers and parents. So, I tried hard at school, and my grades became decent. I had found a place where I felt like I could do something "right."

After high school, I went to business school. I loved the idea of wearing a suit and going to work carrying a leather briefcase. I wanted to be a savvy businesswoman—respected and capable. I studied accounting and finance; the clarity of numbers comforted me. After graduating, I began to work as an accountant for a Fortune 500 company. I was responsible for closing the books every month—I would reconcile columns of numbers, find errors, and correct them. I longed to feel productive and intelligent.

I channeled so much energy into being accepted by everyone that I never found who I was. The need for approval was a powerful tool the enemy used to keep me chasing my tail, so I would not focus on the One who loved me unconditionally.

As time went on, more labels were added to my identity: wife, mother, divorced woman, wife (again), manager, unemployed, employed, star performer, not so star performer, good wife, not so good wife, good mother, lousy mother... divorced (again). It was exhausting to carry all the identities and descriptors that my mistakes, life, and people bestowed.

When I was 32, I was baptized and joined a church that taught the Bible. I took notes every Sunday and Wednesday evening and did my early morning quiet times for decades, trying to learn about God. My Bible was thoroughly underlined, and I had a shelf full of journals with notes.

Still, I scoured God's Word looking for a shred of peace. But the only scriptures my mind would focus on discussed sin and shortcomings. In some ways, those verses made me feel like I was in good company with others who also had a lot of shortcomings. I learned that I could never attain goodness and that I needed God's grace. On the one hand, that was comforting, but on the other hand, I had experienced that in the real world, people don't often extend grace. God's grace was nice, but I couldn't fully grasp how it applied to me.

My thoughts were full of the identities others had given me; "worthless" was perhaps the most present. A never-ending loop played in my head, repeating everything I had ever done wrong and reminding me of why people don't like me. With this heavy load, I gravitated more and more toward isolation. Books, computers, and numbers do not judge. They do not label you. I found safety and peace with my books, my spreadsheets, and my dogs.

Having beautiful children while feeling worthless is difficult. How can you raise children to have healthy self-esteem when you don't have it yourself? I made many mistakes and unconsciously acted out in my marriages. My actions and a nasty divorce turned my parents against me, which resulted in me losing custody of my two beloved sons. That completely broke me.

Another set of labels: loser, deserter, sinner, and not worthy to raise children.

These thoughts tormented me for decades. The first chance I had, I remarried and ran to another country. But no border will separate you from the strongholds in your mind.

Finally, in my 50s, the Lord and I began the process of dismantling the strongholds of these thoughts seared into my mind and soul. It was slow. Painful. I did not yet fully grasp what Jesus had done on the cross for me— He knew all the things I would do before I was born, and He went to the cross for me anyway? No matter how hard I tried, I could not fully accept His gift. I wasn't worthy.

My husband tried to convince me I had worth. He would say nice things, but I was skeptical that he meant them. Inevitably, I would annoy him and he would remark about my shortcomings; inside my head, I heard, *I knew it. I never believed him anyway when he said nice things.* Other people would complement me on something, and I would smile and let it roll off my back. I knew what they were saying wasn't true.

In my 60s, I met Stacy Jo Coffee-Thorne at a networking event. She invited me to attend her church. At that time, I was content not attending church. Thanks to the recent COVID-19 pandemic, I read my Bible and watched countless church sermons on my iPad. I wanted to be left alone to figure things out.

Then, Stacy Jo invited me to attend a conference in California for Christian businesswomen, saying, "It will be fun!" We would stay at the Ritz-Carlton in Laguna Beach and listen to women tell their powerful stories and share their miraculous transformations. She raved about the woman leading the event and how listening to daily sound bites helped her.

Deep inside, I longed for a transformation. A make-over of my mind would be welcomed. And I thought to myself, *I have been working hard on my business. Why not treat myself to a little trip?* I reasoned that if the sessions were boring, I could head out to the beach and make a vacation of it. Somewhat reluctantly, I bought the ticket, booked the flight and hotel, and met my friend at the airport.

I didn't know it, but God was about to change my identity.

The beautiful hotel ballroom was filled with pink flowers, balloons, streamers, and lights. Everything was pink! I didn't even own anything pink, and this was sensory overload! The women, all younger than me, wore pretty dresses and heels. Their hair was perfectly styled, and their fingernails and toenails were perfectly coordinated. They were laughing and hugging each other. Some were praying with each other and holding hands in solidarity. They loved Jesus! I had attended many conferences for work, but had never experienced anything like this. There were beautiful gift bags at every seat, filled with goodies. A pink name plate showed me where I was to sit. Everything sparkled and shined. I was positive I was the oldest woman in the room. Later, I found out I was correct.

I did not know what to do with myself. I had not worn a dress. I wear pant suits—dark pant suits, to be exact—with sensible shoes. (Did I mention I was 64 at the time?) I looked out of place and felt like an outsider. Anxiety bubbled up, and I excused myself from the room. I went outside and texted my 28-year-old daughter that I had made a mistake coming. I told her that everyone was young, slim, beautiful, and bubbly. Did I mention young?

My daughter's response stopped me in my tracks. She said, "Mom, most women do not have the guts to start a business in their 60s. You have, and you are successful. You have every right to be in that room!" Then she called me a rockstar.

I thanked my daughter and went back into the ballroom and sat down. Her words rang in my ears for a long time. For the next three days, I was introduced to something I had never heard of before: God has given each of us an identity. And our identity in God is not like the irritating label on the back of a tee. I thought that the only identity He had bestowed on me was "sinner"; I learned how mistaken I was.

Life said: You are separated from God.
But God calls me His friend.

Life said: You are not special.
But God says I am chosen.

Life said: You are not beautiful or smart.
But God says I am a masterpiece.

Life said: Your body is dumpy.
But God says it is a temple.

Life said: No one really loves you.
But God says, "I love you."

Life said: You're restricted.
But God says I am free.

Life said: You're old.
But God said I have His strength inside me.

I realized that my negative self-identity was a stronghold in my mind. I had chosen to have a victim mindset.

> For as he [she] thinketh in his [her] heart, so is he [she] (Proverbs 23:7 KJV).

I wanted to join the group and surround myself with women who think differently about themselves—women who strive to see themselves the way God sees them. Alas, joining the group was expensive; I would need two new clients to pay the monthly fee. I prayed to God in that ballroom and asked that if this was something He wanted me to do, could He send me a sign?

After lunch, I checked my email; a colleague had quit, and the business owner asked if I had room for *two more clients*.

Boom! Mic drop. I signed up for the group.

In that pink ballroom, I committed to focus on how God sees me and allow His identity to become mine. This called for a complete overhaul of my mind and thoughts. We all know how hard it is to change our thoughts—they are elusive, slippery little twerps that just slither around and around in your head. But I committed to begin thinking of myself the way God does. By surrounding myself with women who believed in God's identity for them, my thoughts slowly began to change. I devoured books written by Christian authors that described my identity in Christ, and little by little, my thoughts became more in tune with what He thought about me instead of what I had believed about myself.

> *Do not conform to the pattern of this world, but be transformed by the renewing of your mind. Then you will be able to test and approve what God's perfect will is—his good, pleasing and perfect will* (Romans 12:2 NIV).

So, what does all this have to do with leadHERship? Everything.

I serve CEOs of small businesses as a financial strategist and fractional CFO. I review their financials monthly and analyze what is working or not working in their businesses. I often look through the Zoom screen into their eyes and point out ways they are limiting their success. The stats on small business success are 50% after five years and 10% after ten years. Most businesses do not survive ten years; the primary reason is a lack of sound financial management. Entrepreneurship is hard.

When I started my CFO practice with my negative mindset, I skillfully identified profit leaks and cash flow issues, but I felt like an imposter. My business was profitable, but somehow my approach felt nitpicky. I did my work well, but inside, I felt like all I did was discourage business owners by pointing out their financial weaknesses. Logic, I had. I was short on compassion. But I didn't stay that way!

You cannot give, as a leadHER, what you do not have for yourself. As I renewed my thoughts on God's Word, I was able to adopt His view on my identity. My labels began to change, and so did I. I gained the ability to give out what I previously couldn't. Isn't it something to realize that the labels we choose to believe are the opposite of what the Bible says about us?

I could finally see that God was using my 35-year successful background in business to help people. One day, a lovely client said I was "her Esther." I didn't know what she meant, so I read the book of Esther and found that when Esther was in a precarious position and was seeking guidance on what to do, she received this wisdom:

> "For if you remain silent at this time, relief, and deliverance for the Jews will arise from another place, but you and your father's family will perish. And who knows but that you have come to your royal position for such a time as this?" (Esther 4:14 NIV).

After receiving that guidance, Esther determined that she would boldly stand up for her people, putting herself in possible harm's way so they could survive. As soon as Esther made this decision, God went before her, paving the path and giving her wisdom on how and when to handle the situation. As a result, Esther's people—God's people—were saved.

Like Esther, God had skillfully, masterfully, and patiently guided me through a lifetime of acquiring valuable skills for His kingdom. He knew His marketplace people needed a marketplace minister, and He graciously led me to a point in my life where I could choose to serve His people or continue to serve myself and be miserable. So, I choose His people.

Now, I can serve business owners with compassion, love, and joy. I continually ask God to bless the work of my hands for His kingdom and bring me those He wants me to serve. My mind is finally at rest, all my labels are clean, and I am living out my calling.

Oh, yeah. And I now own a pink pant suit and glittery sneakers.

Cheryl Phan

Cheryl Phan is an artist, entrepreneur, author, proud grandmother—AKA GiGi to four amazing grandchildren, and mother to two beautiful daughters who inspire her every day. When she's not painting, writing, or mentoring fellow creatives, you'll find her soaking up time with her family, pouring love into her nonprofit, Paint For Children, and serving at the Hand of Hope special needs ministry.

Cheryl runs a thriving decorative painting business and coaches entrepreneurs on how to turn their passions into income by building multiple revenue streams with their existing business. Her heart is to help others believe in themselves, step into their God-given gifts, and create a business that brings freedom and purpose.

After losing her home and business, Cheryl hit rock bottom. But what felt like the end became a divine turning point that reshaped her life. Cheryl knows firsthand how God can use even the hardest seasons for good. She shares her story with the hope that others will find encouragement, faith, and the courage to begin again—no matter where they're starting from. You can reach her at cheryl@cherylphan.com.

Broke, Bankrupt, and Homeless

By Cheryl Phan

I remember the exact moment I hit rock bottom. I was sitting alone in my car on the side of the road with the engine off to save the gas I couldn't afford to waste. Just across the street, people laughed and chatted over lunch at a little café, sipping iced tea and nibbling on salads like life was normal. Like everything wasn't crumbling.

I wasn't part of their world anymore. I reached into my lunchbox and pulled out a ham sandwich I had made earlier that morning. No chips. No snack. Just that sandwich and the ache in my chest.

Tears filled my eyes before I even took the first bite.

I chewed in silence, fighting the lump in my throat, watching strangers live lives I used to know. I used to be the woman who lunched with friends, who dressed in business casual, who ran her own successful business. But that day? I was just trying to gather enough courage to walk door-to-door, selling ads for a local phone directory—something I never imagined I'd be doing. Something I was terrified to do.

The shame was suffocating. The fear was even worse.

The Lord is close to the brokenhearted and saves those who are crushed in spirit (Psalm 34:18 NIV).

I sat there, frozen, whispering quiet prayers with tears rolling down my face.

God, where are You?

How did this happen?

Why did this happen?

Is this my future?

I wasn't angry—just broken. Tired. Embarrassed. Terrified that maybe I had used up all of God's grace and there was nothing left for me.

I stared at the café window, trying to remember what hope felt like. But all I could feel was the weight of failure pressing down on my shoulders like a wet blanket.

That day, I learned what it meant to be desperate—not for money or success, but for peace. For purpose. For a sign that I wasn't abandoned.

And even though I didn't know it then, that moment, right there on the side of the road, was the beginning of something holy.

Not long before everything fell apart, life felt... stable. I had just bought a cute little condo—one I had picked out with such pride. My decorative painting business was thriving. Money was flowing. I had a team. My schedule was booked out for months. Life felt safe. It felt steady. And I finally thought I had made it. I thought I was living in my purpose.

Then came 2008.

The recession swept in like a wave, crashing through families, businesses, and bank accounts without warning. People all around me were losing their homes. Those who managed to hold on weren't spending their money on anything extra, especially not decorative work for their walls. It felt like the world had shifted overnight—and I was standing right in the middle of the collapse.

Work stopped. Completely. My phone became silent. The income I had been relying on vanished. And to make things even more difficult, I was still recovering from a hip replacement I'd had just two months earlier. I wasn't physically or emotionally ready to carry the weight of this storm. But it didn't wait.

I watched the savings disappear—month by month, then week by week. I cashed in my 401(k), praying it would buy me a little more time, a little more hope. But the bills kept coming. And eventually, I couldn't keep up.

The day I had to short-sell my home was one of the hardest days of my life. I remember standing in the empty rooms, touching the walls one last time. Every corner held memories, dreams, and prayers I had whispered when things were good. Now I was walking away, putting everything I owned in a storage unit.

I was broken. Not just financially—but emotionally and spiritually. Filing for bankruptcy felt like the final blow. I cried in silence most nights, feeling embarrassed, ashamed, and painfully alone. I asked God the same questions over and over: *Why is this happening? What did I do wrong? Where are You?*

But even in the silence, He was near. Even when I couldn't feel Him, He was holding me.

I didn't see it then, but God was stripping away everything I had leaned on so I would finally lean fully on Him. He wasn't punishing me—He was preparing me. Not for destruction, but for something deeper. Something sacred.

That season of loss became holy ground. Because in the breaking, God was planting something I couldn't yet see.

After losing everything—my home, my business, my finances—I found myself standing in the wreckage of what used to be my life. But even in that mess, God made a way. A distant friend, someone I hadn't spoken to in years, called me out of the blue and offered me a place to stay.

I wept when I hung up the phone. It felt like a lifeline—a tiny ray of light breaking through the dark clouds. I packed my clothes and moved in with her, grateful for a safe place to land. I began sending out resumes every day, clinging to hope, praying for God to open a door.

Though the day-to-day was grueling, I had hope that this job would finally turn things around for me.

But just six months later, I was laid off.

The internet was replacing printed directories, and once again, I was left holding the pieces of my life. I found myself back on my knees, crying out to God: *Why is this happening again? Lord, where are You? What am I supposed to do?*

That night, after another exhausting job search, I crawled into bed and pulled the covers up, my body heavy with worry. But nothing could have prepared me for what happened next.

As I lay there in the dark, I felt an unseen weight press down on my chest— so heavy I couldn't move. I couldn't lift my arms. I couldn't speak. My entire body was frozen, trapped beneath a darkness that felt unnatural. Terrifying. Evil.

Panic surged through me.

And then I heard it—a still, small voice deep in my spirit: *Say it: "In Jesus' name, be gone."*

> But the Lord is faithful, and he will strengthen you and protect you from the evil one (2 Thessalonians 3:3 NIV).

I couldn't speak aloud at first, but I kept repeating it in my mind: *In Jesus' name, be gone. In Jesus' name, be gone...*

Over and over.

Suddenly, the pressure lifted. I bolted upright in bed, breathless, trembling. But what startled me even more was the sound that tore from my mouth—a guttural, raw, unnatural sound that didn't feel like mine. It was deep and distorted, almost inhuman—like something ancient and angry had been forced out of me.

It wasn't a cry. It wasn't a scream. It was something spiritual—something dark—that had been trying to take root, and the name of Jesus drove it out.

Something had broken in the unseen realm. I knew it. Chains had snapped. Darkness had been defeated. And it wasn't because I was strong—it was because His name is stronger than anything that tries to come against us.

Later, I discovered my roommate was heavily involved in tarot card reading and often communicated with mediums. She tried to tell me it was "spiritual," even "biblical," and that she could speak to the dead and see the future. But everything in me knew that was a lie.

God's Word is clear:

> Let no one be found among you who... practices divination or sorcery, interprets omens, engages in witchcraft, or casts spells, or who is a medium or spiritist or who consults the dead. Anyone who does these things is detestable to the Lord (Deuteronomy 18:10-12 NIV).

That was all I needed to know.

I am a woman of God. I don't follow horoscopes or seek answers from the dead. I seek my Father, the one true living God. And His Spirit had protected me that night. His name alone had broken the grip of darkness.

So, I packed my things. Again.

No job. No stability. No idea where I was going next.

But I knew this: I couldn't stay in a place where darkness was entertained and invited. I chose to trust God—even if I didn't know the next step. Because when He says, *"I will never leave you nor forsake you"* (Hebrews 13:5 NKJV), He means it. And that night, I knew He was fighting for me, even when I couldn't fight for myself.

After that night—when I cried out the name of Jesus with everything in me and darkness was forced to flee —I knew I couldn't go back to life as usual. Something had shifted. God had shown me firsthand the power of His name, and I wasn't about to take that lightly. It was time to make some changes.

The first thing I knew I had to do was surround myself with people who shared my faith, my values, and my desire to walk in truth. No more gray areas. No more spiritual compromise. I moved in with a dear friend I had known for over twenty years—a woman of prayer, faith, and integrity. It felt like safety. Like home.

I started going to church again. Not just attending, but soaking in every word like it was water for my dry, weary soul. I opened my Bible and let God's Word speak louder than my fear. I prayed differently—bolder, more surrendered. I wasn't just *talking to* God anymore; I was listening. And slowly, a new kind of peace started to grow in my heart.

God was rebuilding me—not with money or status, but with truth, trust, and clarity.

And while it didn't happen overnight, I started to feel a holy confidence rise up inside me. I began believing that I hadn't been disqualified, that my past didn't cancel my calling. I started to understand that failure doesn't mean it's over—it often means you're being repositioned for something greater.

One morning, I felt a stirring I couldn't ignore. It was time to step back into the world of art and design—to return to the gift God had placed in my hands. Not to make a name for myself, but to honor the One who gave me the gift in the first place.

I took a leap of faith and reopened my decorative painting business. I told the Lord, "This time, You're the CEO. I'll show up and do the work—but You direct the steps."

That's when things started to shift.

New doors opened—doors I didn't knock on. Opportunities came from places I never expected. Clients started calling. Projects picked up. My calendar filled up again. And this time, I wasn't hustling to make it happen. I was walking in step with the Spirit.

Romans 8:28 echoed in my heart every day: *And we know that in all things God works for the good of those who love him, who have been called according to his purpose* (NIV).

Even in a struggling economy, God's favor surrounded me like a shield. My business thrived—not just because I had talent, but because I had finally surrendered the outcome to Him.

And yet, something inside me still felt unsettled.

My heart was grateful, my days were full, but deep down, I knew I wasn't fulfilling the full purpose He had placed in me. There was something more—a whisper I couldn't ignore.

I remember praying one night, "Lord, thank You for restoring what was lost. But is there more You're calling me to do? Is there someone else I'm meant to help?"

I didn't know that God was preparing to take my gift in a totally new direction. One that would reach beyond walls and paintbrushes.

Sometimes God breaks us not to punish us, but to position us.

For a long time, I didn't know exactly how, but I knew God wanted to use my story—or my talents—in an even greater way. He had pulled me through the fire for a reason, so I kept praying and asking, "Lord, what now?

And then, as He always does, He answered. It was quiet, unexpected, and clear.

I was visiting my daughter. While she was at work, I spent time with my son-in-law—or, as I lovingly call him, my *son-in-love*. He's a firefighter and EMT, a man with a heart to serve. On his days off from the firehouse, he worked a side job transporting children with special needs to and from school—kids who needed medical support and round-the-clock care.

One afternoon, he came home from a transport and began telling me about one of the children he had driven that day. He spoke with such tenderness about this little boy. The child was completely dependent on others—he couldn't walk, talk, or feed himself, and he was hooked up to machines that helped him breathe and live. Only people like my son-in-love, who were trained to respond if the machines ever failed, could transport these children. He was using his gift to serve God's children.

As I listened to the story, something in my spirit shifted. God whispered to my heart: "These are the children I want you to bless."

> *For we are God's handiwork, created in Christ Jesus to do good works, which God prepared in advance for us to do* (Ephesians 2:10 NIV).

I couldn't shake the image of that sweet little boy lying in bed all day, staring at a blank white ceiling. The same four walls. The same sterile environment. I imagined how lonely, uninspired, and forgotten that space must have felt.

And then I thought, *What if I could change that? What if I could give that child clouds to look at? Stars, smiling animals, a ceiling that would make him feel like he is flying through the sky? A room filled with wonder, joy, and color?*

What if I could use my gift to make him smile?

That was the moment God connected all the dots.

Every heartbreak. Every closed door. Every season of waiting. God had been preparing me—not just to start over, but to step into a calling that wasn't about *me* at all.

I launched a nonprofit called Paint for Children, dedicated to transforming the bedrooms of children with special needs into magical, healing spaces. We go into their homes and give them complete room makeovers—murals, colors, custom details—all designed to bring hope, comfort, and joy.

It is one of the most rewarding, humbling, and sacred things I've ever done.

These children can't run and play like others. Many can't even speak. But the moment they see their room—transformed into a space just for them—you can see it in their eyes. You can feel it in the room. It's like heaven touches earth.

And I finally understood...
God didn't waste my pain.
He repurposed it.

He used it to shape a new identity in me—not a woman broken by life, but a woman *rebuilt by grace.*

I'm no longer a victim of my circumstances. I'm a vessel of His love.

My testimony now lights the way for other women who feel like they've lost it all, people who don't see the value in their gifts, and believers wondering if God still has a plan for them. I can tell them, "Yes, you are valued and God has a plan for you. He's not done with you. In fact, He's just getting started."

I am living proof that God truly works all things together for good.

If you've walked through heartache, faced loss or disappointment, or experienced seasons that left you breathless and broken—I want you to know that you're not alone. I've been there. I've cried the silent tears. I've questioned God's plan. I've sat in the stillness, wondering if life would ever feel full again.

But here's what I've learned: God doesn't leave us in the valley. He walks with us through it. And when we're ready—when our hearts are receptive—He will take every shattered piece and begin to rebuild something more beautiful than we could ever imagine.

God's not finished with you.

That dream He placed in your heart? It still matters. That gift you carry? It still has purpose. Your story—no matter how messy or painful—is the very thing God can use to heal someone else.

To the woman who feels forgotten, broken, or unseen—I see you. More importantly, *God sees you.*

You are not done.
You are not too far gone.
You are not disqualified.

Your comeback is already in motion.
Lean in.
Trust Him.
He's writing a new chapter.

And this time?
It will be filled with purpose, passion, and power.

Let Him lead you.
You don't have to have it all figured out—just say *yes.*

Leading with Surrender

By Stacy Jo Coffee-Thorne

For a long time, I believed great leadHERship meant having everything perfectly in place—every answer, every plan, and every detail. I thought strong leadHERs were those who could stay ten steps ahead while managing and keeping everything under control. So, I worked tirelessly to check each box, cover every base, and leave nothing to chance. This approach seemed responsible and diligent, and in many ways, it was. But it left little room for God to move.

When we launched the Association of Christian Businesswomen (ACBW), I had a beautiful, well-thought-out vision. I knew the speakers, schedule, themes, and even décor. I wanted to create something excellent for God—something that would honor Him and inspire others.

Then, one thing at a time, God began to interrupt my plans. Details shifted, speakers changed, dates required rearranging, and connections fell through. I often wondered why things weren't going the way I had envisioned. Each time I tried to fix it, God reminded me that His ways are higher. And every time I surrendered, He showed me something better.

He would send the perfect speaker with the exact message the room needed. He opened doors I hadn't even noticed and connected me with those who were carrying a missing piece of the vision. Over and over, I watched Him orchestrate things I never could have arranged. It wasn't always comfortable, but it was always good. That's when I learned one of the most freeing lessons of my life: Surrender doesn't mean quitting; it means trusting.

Surrender says, "Lord, here's my gift, my influence, my plans, my dreams—they're Yours first." It means leading with open hands, not clenched fists.

When our hands are open, God can place something new in them. When we hold too tightly, we block the very blessings we're praying for.

I will never forget my friend Tori Kruse telling me that she prays for the Lord to "Bless it or block it." Those five words capture the essence of surrender. It is a simple yet powerful prayer that says, "God, if this is from You, bless it and make it flourish. But if it is not, block it and protect me from it." That kind of surrender takes courage because it means trusting God even when His answer looks different than what we expected. It is saying, "Lord, Your will matters more than my plans."

Proverbs 3:5-6 (NIV) says, *Trust in the Lord with all your heart and lean not on your own understanding; in all your ways submit to Him, and He will make your paths straight.* For leadHERs, that can be difficult—we're wired to solve problems and make things happen. But kingdom leadHERship doesn't start with control; it starts with trust.

I have experienced moments when letting go felt like loss. Although those moments stretched me, they also strengthened my faith. Every time I surrender something to God, He multiplies its impact and aligns it more completely with His purpose.

Surrender is a daily decision. It's waking up and saying, "God, this is Your day, Your business, and Your people. Lead me how You want to lead me." It's choosing obedience over outcome and faith over frustration. It's believing that His plan will always bear more fruit than our best efforts ever could.

To me, the best part of leading with a surrendered heart is that the burden no longer rests on my shoulders alone. I don't have to know every answer because I serve the One who does—He already sees the end from the beginning. When I trust Him fully, peace replaces panic and faith replaces fear.

If things aren't going according to your plan right now, take a deep breath. God's delays are not denials. His redirections are often His protection.

Sometimes He closes a door because He's got a better one for you to walk through.

In God's kingdom, the greatest leadHERs are not those who control everything, but those who trust God completely. They lead with peace. They build with faith. And their impact lasts—not because of their brilliance, but because their leadHERship flows from a heart surrendered to our Lord—the best leader ever.

. . . .

Mila Araujo

Mila Araujo is a faith-driven creative visionary, devoted mother, and storyteller who shares messages of hope, renewal, and purpose. Drawing from her journey, she reflects on how God's grace meets us in every season, revealing beauty even in brokenness.

Mila is the founder of Monzon Marketing (est. 2019), which elevates brands and ministries through authentic storytelling and impactful digital engagement. She is the co-creator of Wild Faith Designs, a Christian clothing line born through a creative bond with her daughter, Myah Amor. In 2026, she will launch Monzon Beauty, her purpose-driven makeup brand empowering women with confidence, authenticity, and God-centered worth.

With a foundation in makeup artistry and digital media, Mila uses her creative gifts to reflect Christ's light in everyday life. Whether behind the camera, building brands, or encouraging women, her mission is to help others see themselves as God does: loved, chosen, radiant, and full of purpose.

Mila inspires women to rise with courage and walk boldly in their calling, reminding us that when we surrender our story to God, every chapter becomes something beautiful.

The Surrender
That Started It All

By Mila Araujo

I remember sitting in church next to my daughter during the December 2022 Christmas service. The sanctuary was packed; twinkling lights framed the stage, and the choir's voices filled the air with songs of hope. Families around us held hands, smiling through tears as they celebrated the birth of Jesus. It should have been a moment of peace, a time of joy. But in my heart, I was overwhelmed by sadness, anxiety, and shame.

My daughter, innocent and joyful, didn't know what was weighing me down. She looked up at me with her big brown eyes, excited for Christmas, while I sat silently beside her, trying to hold myself together. I couldn't afford to buy her the gifts she'd asked for. Even simple things—new clothes, toys, a special Christmas meal—felt far out of reach. I felt like I had failed.

Years earlier, I'd made a promise to myself that when I became a mom, I would give my child everything I didn't have growing up in Argentina—a stable, joy-filled, abundant life. I had fought hard to make that dream come true. I followed all the "right" steps: excelling in school, earning scholarships, studying at great universities. I kept building by attending workshops, networking events, and career fairs—doing everything I could to secure a future for us.

I worked two or three jobs at a time, sacrificing sleep, comfort, and community. I went back to school for certifications, believing that surely this next one would open the right door. But despite all my effort, I was stuck. I was a marketing assistant, interviewing two or three times a month with no progress. Each rejection chipped away at my confidence.

My bank account was overdrawn by $297. I didn't know how I would feed us that week. My credit cards were maxed out from trying to keep the lights on. Bills piled up, and the fear of losing our car and home hovered over my every thought, my every move. Most of my family was far away in Argentina; there was no one nearby to call. I was in survival mode... and I was tired.

And I wasn't just responsible for myself and my daughter; I was also caring for my little sister. I had taken her in when she was 16. She needed stability, love, and guidance, and I stepped in without hesitation. I became the provider, the emotional support, the big sister, the second mom. I was raising my child and helping to raise my sister through one of the most critical seasons of her life. Teenagers usually come with teenage problems, and that was also a new terrain for me to navigate. The extra weight (though carried in love) was heavy. I was stretched thin emotionally and financially, holding it all together for both of them while silently battling fear and burnout.

As the collection basket made its way down the row during that Christmas service, I knew I had nothing to give. I was preparing to pass it along when I heard God speak to my heart, not in a loud or dramatic way, but in that quiet, unmistakable whisper: "Look in your wallet. Take the $5 you've been holding onto and put it in. Trust Me."

All I had was a single five-dollar bill that had lived in my wallet for ten years. My dad had given it to me, telling me it was a rare bill that would bring good luck, that it would attract more money as long as I kept it in my wallet.

It had traveled with me through every season, every low moment, every desperate month. That small bill had become a symbol of control, my way of clinging to security.

But in that moment, I knew God was asking me to release it. Not because He needed my money, but because He wanted my trust. With tears in my eyes, I opened my periwinkle wallet, pulled out the bill, and placed it in the offering basket. It wasn't just paper; it was surrender.

Trust in the Lord with all your heart and lean not on your own understanding; in all your ways submit to him, and he will make your paths straight (Proverbs 3:5-6 NIV).

My act of obedience marked the beginning of something new.

Looking back now, I realize that moment wasn't just about money; it was about letting go of my illusion of control. For years, I carried the weight of trying to be my own provider, my own savior. But when I dropped that $5 in the basket, I also dropped my pride. That night, I didn't just give an offering; I gave God permission to be my provider. And when I finally stepped aside, He stepped in.

Shortly after, something began to shift, not just around me but within me. God started to soften my heart, give me clarity, and fill me with peace. Two weeks later, our company's CEO sent an email about a one-time hardship assistance program for employees facing financial difficulty. My first instinct was to ignore it; I didn't want pity from leadership. But that whisper from God was back, and I heard it loud and clear. So, I applied.

To my surprise, I was approved. The check wasn't huge, but it was exactly what I needed. It covered enough bills to let me breathe again. That provision reminded me that God had seen me crying in that church service. He had already prepared a way before I even knew to ask.

And my God will meet all your needs according to the riches of his glory in Christ Jesus (Philippians 4:19 NIV).

In the weeks that followed, I began showing up to church more. I volunteered in the kids' ministry with my daughter, not expecting anything in return. Each Sunday, as I cared for newborns and toddlers—tiny, wide-eyed humans filled with hope and light—I felt my heart healing. Holding them, singing over them, and praying for them restored something inside me.

For the first time in years, I wasn't striving; I was simply serving. There was peace in wiping tiny hands, rocking babies to sleep, and whispering prayers over little lives, reminding me that purpose doesn't have to be loud to be powerful. I began to see how God uses small, unseen moments to restore us. Each Sunday after serving, I left lighter than when I'd come in, making me realize that healing often begins when we take our eyes off our pain and look for how we can meet someone else's need.

Being around the children's joy reminded me of the sacred beauty in simplicity. Every moment I spent sowing love into their lives felt like planting seeds that would outgrow me, giving me purpose when I felt purposeless. My actions and God's response also showed my daughter that giving back and serving in our community is important and life-changing—for both the one being served and the one who is serving.

During this time, I began pursuing God's Word—not out of obligation, like I did in Catholic school, but out of hunger. I needed truth. I needed promises. I needed armor. Slowly, my spirit came alive. The same Word that once felt distant began to breathe new life into me. Scripture gave me strength when depression tried to isolate me and authority when fear tried to reign.

The Lord is close to the brokenhearted and saves those who are crushed in spirit (Psalm 34:18 NIV).

Then one Sunday, I saw a video on the church screen, a story about Hearts for Moms. I watched through tears as God whispered again: "You need help. They are the way."

That whisper felt risky. Asking for help didn't come naturally to me. I was raised to be strong, independent, self-sufficient. My mother, a single mom herself, always said not to rely on anyone, that no one would come to save me. And I believed her. But this time, I knew I had to make a different choice. I had to pave a new path for myself and for my daughter.

I applied to Hearts for Moms, and to my amazement, I was accepted.

Since joining, my life has taken a new shape. I began therapy to face my depression and unpack the years of weight I'd carried in silence. I was paired with a financial coach who helped me confront my debt and build a plan. A career coach helped me see the value in my experience, and because of that, I was promoted twice in one year.

Hearts for Moms didn't just help me financially; it also gave me community. It was the first place I could breathe without pretending to be strong. I met other women who carried stories like mine—women who had fallen, gotten back up, and still believed God had more for them. Together, we laughed, cried, prayed, and grew. For the first time, I wasn't just being poured into, I was being filled. And in that space of grace, I rediscovered who I was: not just a mom, not just a provider, but a daughter of God.

And we know that in all things God works for the good of those who love him, who have been called according to his purpose (Romans 8:28 NIV).

I'm still part of Hearts for Moms. I'm still navigating my debt. Some days are still hard, but now, I have support, accountability, and community. More than that, I have hope.

That $5 bill I dropped in the basket wasn't just an offering; it was the moment I broke the chain that money, fear, and pride had wrapped around me. That simple act of giving opened the door for God to do what I never could on my own.

That moment of surrender became the foundation of how I lead today. Every decision, every new opportunity begins with that same quiet prayer: "God, I trust You." I no longer chase what I think I can control; I chase what He's calling me to build. And that shift from striving to surrender has changed everything. It's how I raise my daughter, how I serve other moms, and how I approach every challenge with faith first.

Today, I use my marketing gifts to give back to the organization that gave me a new direction. I serve Hearts for Moms through social-media strategy and storytelling. I create campaigns for other brands professionally, but this is different; this is personal. This is purposeful. Every caption, every post, every story is my way of giving life to the mission that once gave life back to me.

Beyond my work with Hearts for Moms, I've discovered that my calling is to lead by example, to be a woman who walks in grace, courage, and conviction. God didn't just restore my circumstances; He transformed my heart so that I could help transform others.

I lead my daughter not by what I can give her, but by who I show her God is. Every morning, we start the day with prayer, gratitude, and worship. She's learned that provision doesn't come from a paycheck but from a faithful God who always shows up on time. I watch her pray with confidence and compassion, and I see the reflection of everything I once begged God to make real in me. She's learning that strength isn't loud or prideful, it's trusting God when the outcome is uncertain.

Start children off on the way they should go, and even when they are old, they will not turn from it (Proverbs 22:6 NIV).

That verse has become a daily reminder for me as a mom. My daughter sees the way I worship through struggle, how I serve even when I'm tired, and how I continue to build, dream, and give. I no longer strive to be the perfect mom; I strive to be a present one. A mom whose faith speaks louder than her fear.

At work, I've stepped into leadHERship not by title, but by testimony. I mentor young professionals who are where I once was: ambitious yet uncertain and battling silent doubts. I remind them that rejection isn't failure; it's redirection. I help them see that every closed door can be a setup for divine opportunity. When I sit across from them, I see pieces of my younger self, hungry for purpose, tired of trying to earn worth, and I remind them that they already have value because God gave it to them long before the world ever did.

For we are God's handiwork, created in Christ Jesus to do good works, which God prepared in advance for us to do (Ephesians 2:10 NIV).

In Hearts for Moms, I help with the same principle. I help other single moms, teaching them marketing and SEO, helping them build websites, resumes, and confidence. But what I'm really teaching them is that they are seen. That God hasn't forgotten them. That their story still has power, even in the middle of the mess.

She is clothed with strength and dignity; she can laugh at the days to come (Proverbs 31:25 NIV).

This verse is the heartbeat of what it means to me to be a kingdom leadHER. Leading doesn't always mean standing on a stage; it means standing firm in faith when the storm comes. It means showing up when it would be easier to quit. It means loving fiercely, forgiving freely, and walking humbly with God while encouraging others to do the same.

LeadHERship, for me, now looks like guiding others through faith and example, loving through action, listening without judgment, and reminding women that we don't have to have it all figured out to be used by God. He's not waiting for perfection; He's waiting for surrender.

> He gives strength to the weary and increases the power of the weak (Isaiah 40:29 NIV).

I often think about the women who are still sitting in their own "Christmas service" moment: tired, afraid, unsure how they'll make it through the week. If I could sit beside them, I would tell them this: *You are seen. You are chosen. You are not forgotten.*

God is not done writing your story. That five dollars of surrender may look different for you; it might be letting go of control, forgiving someone who hurt you, or finally believing that you are worthy of love. Whatever it is, release it. Because the moment you do, heaven moves.

My journey has taught me that faith isn't about having it all together; it's about trusting God when everything feels like it's falling apart. It's about showing up with an open heart and saying, "Lord, I don't understand, but I'll obey." That's where transformation begins.

> Being confident of this, that he who began a good work in you will carry it on to completion until the day of Christ Jesus (Philippians 1:6 NIV).

Now, when I look back at that December night, I see more than the pain; I see the beginning of purpose. God took my surrender and turned it into strategy; He turned my fear into faith and my emptiness into overflow. What once felt like the end was really the beginning of becoming who I was created to be.

So, to the woman who feels unseen or uncertain, know this: Your surrender is not your end, it's your beginning. Every "no" you've faced, every tear you've cried, every time you've felt overlooked, God has been quietly building a testimony that will one day help someone else rise. Don't despise the waiting. Don't underestimate small obedience. The same God who met me in that church service will meet you right where you are.

I am still walking this journey—still learning, still growing, still leading. But now, I do it all with peace. I no longer measure my worth by what I can provide, but by who I am in Christ. I am a woman who trusted God with five dollars and received a future beyond value.

And now, I pour that faith into others—into my daughter, into every mom I meet, into every woman who needs to be reminded that God sees her, too. Because this is what authentic leadHERship looks like, not leading from perfection, but leading from *presence.*

Let all that you do be done in love (1 Corinthians 16:14 ESV).

That verse carried me from the dark place I was in to who I am today. From a woman who gave out of desperation to a woman who leads out of abundance. From surviving to serving. From brokenness to boldness.

And by the grace of God, my best chapters are still being written.

Dawn Connelly

Dawn Connelly owns a document shredding and medical waste disposal company with her husband, Brian, and is a lawyer and a leadership and business coach. After her career as a trial attorney, Dawn began coaching top-level executives and businesses on breakthrough growth and strategic planning, integrating biblical principles with her strong faith.

A University of Florida and Chicago-Kent College of Law graduate, Dawn practiced commercial litigation at McDermott, Will & Emery, LLP for eight years, arguing before the U.S. Court of Appeals for the Seventh Circuit, drafting a writ of certiorari to the U.S. Supreme Court, and representing Fortune 500 companies in multimillion-dollar cases. She clerked for the Honorable Blanche M. Manning of the U.S. District Court for the Northern District of Illinois.

Dawn received an award for "Outstanding Achievement and Commitment to Pro Bono Service." Her most meaningful case was winning asylum for an Albanian woman sex-trafficked from Albania. A founding member of the John Maxwell Leadership Team, Dawn serves on the Hearts for Moms board. She and Brian have four children who live in South Florida.

Leading with Communion

By Dawn Connelly

We just sat down to dinner with our two youngest children when my husband's phone rang. The call was coming from our 17-year-old son's football coach. Austin was at football practice; receiving a call from his coach in the middle of practice immediately sounded an alarm bell in our minds.

"That's not good," my husband said.

"Answer it!" I exclaimed.

It was the call every parent dreads.

"Mr. Connelly. Austin took a hard hit in football practice today. He's not able to move his arms and legs. He is unresponsive on the field. A trauma helicopter has been called and is on the way. You should go meet him at the trauma hospital."

In that moment, Holy Spirit took over. I had recently finished Beni Johnson's book, *The Power of Communion*[1]. In that book, Beni wrote, "[e]very time you take communion, you remind the devil of his failure." My heart was racing, and I was fighting back fear and panic. I pulled out four cups, juice, and matzah. We took communion with our two youngest children, declaring Austin's healing and thanking Jesus for dying and making a way for Austin to be fully healed. Then, we got into the car and drove to the trauma hospital, continuing to declare Austin's healing and praying in the Spirit for the 40-minute drive.

> *Surely He has borne our griefs*
> *And carried our sorrows;*
> *Yet we esteemed Him stricken,*
> *Smitten by God, and afflicted.*
> *But He was wounded for our transgression,*
> *He was bruised for our iniquities;*
> *The chastisement for our peace was upon Him,*
> *And by His stripes we are healed.*
> (Isaiah 53:4-5 NKJV)

I didn't always know my spiritual authority. I was not raised in the church. My father is a "culturally Jewish" atheist, and no one in my family ever told me about Jesus. But, looking back, Jesus has been pursuing me all my life. And He has been pursuing you.

> The Lord is not slow about His promise, as some count slowness, but is patient toward you, not wishing for any to perish but for all to come to repentance (2 Peter 3:9 NASB).

I accepted Christ when I was in my 30s, and have since been on a surrendered journey to walk in the fullness of the power and authority Jesus died to give us. I have also been determined to raise our four children to know Jesus, not just as their Savior, but as their best friend and healer.

One week before our son was paralyzed on the football field, his spiritual mentor prophesied the voice of God over him at their weekly breakfast. "Austin, you are going to go through a trial, but God will be with you in the trial, and you'll come out of it stronger and better."

Austin came home from that breakfast shaken. I encouraged him, "God only prophesies through His children for their edification and good."

> But one who prophesies speaks to men for edification and exhortation and consolation (1 Corinthians 14:3 NASB).

As a result of that prophecy, our son memorized Deuteronomy 31:6 that week, right before his accident.

> Then Moses went out and spoke these words to all Israel... "Be strong and courageous. Do not be afraid or terrified because of them, for the Lord your God goes with you; he will never leave you or forsake you" (Deuteronomy 31:1,6 NIV).

We spent the next three days and nights in the trauma intensive care unit of a nearby hospital while my mom stayed with our younger children.

At the hospital, the doctors ran brain scans, including magnetic resonance imaging (MRI) and computed tomography scans (CT), and did blood work. Nothing revealed why our son could not move his arms and legs. He began having what appeared to be violent seizures, suddenly convulsing and contracting while his eyes rolled back in his head. Some of these episodes lasted as long as 45 minutes. We fought with the weapons the Lord gave us—playing worship music, praying in the Spirit, declaring the Word of God, and taking communion daily.

Knowing that the spiritual realm is far more real than the physical world, our declarations were in direct opposition to what we saw and heard from the doctors. It was difficult to hold onto God's truth in those dark moments, but we fought to do so, continuing to take communion every day while reminding ourselves that Jesus died for our sins and our sickness. When

Jesus went to the cross, He carried every evil thing the enemy tries to put on us—we applied that healing through communion. Communion, the body and blood of Jesus, unlocks miracles and healing power. Throughout Scripture, God often revealed Himself to Israel as the God who heals.

"I am the Lord who heals you" (Exodus 15:26 NKJV).

He sent His word and healed them (Psalm 107:20 NKJV).

On the third day, a group of five doctors came into Austin's hospital room, all stating negative diagnoses. They said it was likely Austin would need to be on anti-seizure medication for the rest of his life and that, although there was a slight chance that the feeling and use of his arms and legs would return, after 72 hours (we were at hour 70), improvement would be unlikely. As a last resort, they could surgically remove the part of his brain they believed was injured, but they were not sure he would ever be able to walk again.

At that point, from his hospital bed, Austin shouted to the team of doctors, "GET OUT! ... GET OUT!"

I watched in shock as all five doctors turned around and, in a single file, walked out of the room. I asked Austin what was going on. He said he wanted us to leave, too. He needed to be alone with God.

I learned later that in that moment, Austin cried out to God for healing. Our teenage son sent the doctors out because he understood the power of words and his own spiritual authority. His apparent teenage outrage was actually him claiming spiritual authority and rejecting the destructive sentence the doctors were speaking over him.

> *"No weapon formed against you shall prosper, and every tongue which rises against you in judgment you shall condemn. This is the heritage of the servants of the Lord...," Says the Lord* (Isaiah 54:17 NKJV).

My husband, Brian, and I also had to shut out voices—some of which belonged to our own family. There are many doctors and nurses in my family who only see with their physical eyes because they do not know Jesus. We knew we needed to see with our spiritual eyes and only allow in the voices who understood that God is a miracle-working God.

Whoever walks with the wise becomes wise, but the companion of fools will suffer harm (Proverbs 13:20 ESV).

Austin's seizures got worse and more frequent. My husband and I continued to take daily communion in the hospital room, declaring healing despite the situation before us. Communion is not for God; it's for us. It's a reminder of what He died for. John recounts that when Jesus was talking with the disciples, He said, *"I am the bread of life"* (John 6:35 NASB). And when Jesus broke the bread at the last supper, He said, *"This is My body"* (Mark 14:22 NJKV).

Jesus offers those who believe in Him the ability to align our bodies with His body, which was broken and resurrected for us. He is our *"bread of life"* (John 6:35 NIV)—our hope and our healing.

Our entire community was praying for Austin. His story quickly spread to believers and pastors in other states and countries. Text messages and videos came pouring in—Austin was blanketed by the power of prayer.

> *Is anyone among you suffering? Let him pray. Is anyone cheerful? Let him sing praise. Is anyone among you sick? Let him call for the elders of the church, and let them pray over him, anointing him with oil and in the name of the Lord. And the prayer of faith will save the one who is sick, and the Lord will raise him up* (James 5:13-15 ESV).

I felt a heavy darkness in that first hospital; the atmosphere almost felt demonic. I have learned to trust my gut in these situations—often that "gut feeling" or "intuition" is actually the voice of the Holy Spirit whispering to me. We made the decision to move Austin to Nicklaus Children's Hospital in Miami. In the middle of the night, our son, totally drugged out on anti-seizure medication, was loaded into another trauma helicopter to go to the pediatric trauma ICU in Miami, where they would rerun tests in an effort to explain why he was paralyzed and having seizures. My husband and I left that hospital for the first time since the night we got that devastating call, and, because we could not go in the helicopter, drove the long two and a half hours to the next hospital.

The atmosphere of the second hospital was entirely different—I could feel and sense light. My hope was renewed just by the way the room felt; however, Austin's condition did not improve. He still could not move his arms and legs, and the seizures continued.

For months before Austin's accident, my husband, who hardly ever dreams, started having recurring dreams about casting out demons. We didn't understand the dreams—until the second night in that Miami hospital. While Austin slept, my husband Brian informed me that he thought a demon was causing Austin's condition—this was new for both of us. We had read about deliverance in the Bible and learned about it at our church, but we had never seen it, let alone been the ones performing the deliverance. But God had been preparing Brian in his dreams.

That night, Austin's seizures continued. Wires and electrodes attached to his head monitored the seizure activity. His body would get rigid and stiff, and saliva or foam would form around his mouth. For three hours in the middle of the night in that pediatric trauma ICU room, my husband and I claimed our heavenly authority as we prayed in the Spirit and cast out multiple demons. We believe that whatever was on the player who took an illegal hit at his own teammate in practice got on Austin. The Bible speaks of this.

In Luke 13:10-12, we are told, *A woman was there who had been crippled by a spirit for eighteen years. She was bent over and could not straighten up at all. When Jesus saw her, he called her forward and said to her, "Woman, you are set free from your infirmity"* (NIV).

Mark writes of a man who brought his son, who was having seizures caused by an evil spirit, to Jesus, saying, *"Teacher, I brought you my son, who is possessed by a spirit that has robbed him of speech. Whenever it seizes him, it throws him to the ground. He foams at the mouth, gnashes his teeth and becomes rigid" ...[Jesus] rebuked the impure spirit. "You deaf and mute spirit... I command you, come out of him and never enter him again"* (Mark 9:17-18,25 NIV).

Jesus became human and died so that the Holy Spirit, who has the same power and authority to heal, could dwell in us. Jesus proclaimed that it was better that He go away so God's Spirit could live within us.

> *"Nevertheless I tell you the truth. It is to your advantage that I go away; for if I do not go away, the Helper will not come to you; but if I depart, I will send Him to you"* (John 16:7 NKJV).

In Acts, Jesus announced, *"But you will receive power when the Holy Spirit comes on you; and you will be my witnesses in Jerusalem, and in all Judea and Samaria, and to the ends of the earth"* (Acts 1:8 NIV).

Before the Holy Spirit was given to followers of Jesus, believers could hear from God only if they were in Jesus' physical presence; before Jesus was born as a human, hearing from God was quite a rare and highly exceptional event. I am so thankful that we get to live in a time when we have 24/7 access to the Holy Spirit. I'm so thankful that a lost girl like me, who was never taught about Jesus or the Holy Spirit, learned of my spiritual authority for such a time as this (Esther 4:14 ESV). God does not want us walking around powerless. He gave us His Holy Spirit so we could walk in full power and authority! Through Him, Jesus taught, we have the power to heal and to cast out demons! *"In My name they will cast out demons; they will speak with new tongues; they will take up serpents; and if they drink anything deadly, it will by no means hurt them; they will lay hands on the sick, and they will recover"* (Mark 16:17-19 NKJV).

The day after my husband and I spent three hours claiming spiritual authority over our son, Austin was able to get up and start walking. It was very slow and labored at first. The doctors sent us home that day and, within a week, Austin was working out and living normally. He's never had another "seizure," and he went back to earn the starting quarterback position for his senior year of high school, leading the team to an undefeated season. The doctors had no medical explanation! My atheist dad had no explanation. Some of the medical staff recognized it as a miracle. Others, like my dad, refuse to believe what science cannot prove and came up with a series of rationalizations for what medicine could not explain. My hope rests on the promises in God's Word,

For this reason also, God highly exalted Him, and bestowed on Him the name, which is above every name, so that at the name of Jesus EVERY KNEE WILL BOW, of those who are in heaven and on earth and under the earth, and that every tongue will confess that Jesus Christ is Lord, to the glory of God the Father (Philippians 2:9-11 NASB).

While in the hospital, Austin was unable to read the Bible as he couldn't use his hands to hold either the Bible or his phone. But the Lord had prepared him, using that prophetic word from his mentor to prompt him to memorize Deuteronomy 31:6, and Austin prayed that verse regularly. I just love how God is such a good Father that He used an obedient friend to equip Austin in advance with His Word. The prophecy that Austin would go through a dark trial but come out stronger and better was fully realized. When Austin returned to earn the starting quarterback position, he was indeed faster, stronger, and better than he was before the accident. God goes above and beyond what we can imagine.

*Now to Him who is able to do exceedingly abundantly above
all that we ask or think, according to the power that works in us,
to Him be glory in the church by Christ Jesus to all generations,
forever and ever. Amen* (Ephesians 3:20-21 NKJV).

But not only had Austin become a better athlete, he had also become better equipped to live out his purpose beyond football. What the enemy meant for harm, God used for good, giving Austin a powerful platform to share his testimony with the world. From a moving ESPN interview to podcasts that quickly went viral, his story inspired many, especially the youth. He created a YouTube video that reached thousands and even used TikTok affiliate marketing as a unique way to weave in his testimony. Every setback became a setup for God to show His glory through Austin's voice and victory.

Taking communion as a family before we even left the house—demonstrating our faith in what Jesus did on the cross—set the stage for Austin's healing. While in the Miami hospital, there were times we took communion with part of Austin's grilled cheese sandwich and Cuban coffee. God does not care what we use—He sees our hearts. We refused to accept anything less than full healing; that is what Jesus died for. In the face of what looked like defeat, we professed out loud the promises of God as a reminder to us and the devil that the victory was ours. Jesus said to His disciples, and He says to us, *"Behold, I give you the authority to trample on serpents and scorpions and over all the power of the enemy, and nothing shall by any means hurt you"* (Luke 10:19 NKJV).

We must think and act with the authority that has been given to us as co-heirs with Christ. We are not victims of our circumstances—we are victorious in Him. The same Spirit who raised Jesus from the dead lives in us, empowering us to pray bold prayers, believe for the impossible, and walk in healing, wholeness, and hope.

Even in suffering, confusion, or delay, we can trust that through God, all things work together for good to those who love God, to those who are the called according to His purpose (Romans 8:28 NKJV).

God's purposes never fail.

If God is for us, who can be against us? (Romans 8:31 NKJV).

No sickness, no accident, no diagnosis, and no setback can override the authority of Jesus. He does not heal only bodies—He heals hearts, minds, and destinies. Jesus restores what is broken and redeems what is lost. In Him, we are not just survivors—we are more than conquerors.

Jesus wins. And because we are in Him, we win too.

---

[1] Johnson, Beni, *"The Power of Communion" Accessing Miracles Through the Body & Blood of Jesus,* (Destiny Image Publishers, 2019).
[2] https://youtu.be/6EIVFiaTtul

Leading with Humility

By DeAnn Alaine

Many years ago, I was singing and playing keyboard on my church's praise and worship team, had written a curriculum for a women's Bible study which I was teaching, and was writing a blog that began to expand beyond our church. By ministry standards, I had the walk of a successful, professional servant using all my gifts and talents for the Lord.

However, if you had looked at the condition of my heart, you would have seen arrogance and pride. The real contents of my heart told me that I had earned a double doctorate in DeAnn Alaine and all things pertaining to her ego! I had MY ministry and MY career path tracked out.

Then the Lord asked me, "How many times have you sung that song, 'Have Thine Own Way, Lord'? Well, now I'm going to have my own way with you because you've given me permission all these years to do what I've wanted to do in you. Unfortunately, you became a professional at setting up your own life and ministry. Now, I'm going to free you of that."

Very shortly after getting married, everything about my life changed—my job, my family dynamics, and my ministry. In fact, every door of ministry was shut tight. So there we were, on the road going somewhere but not knowing where. Up to that point, my life had become so predictable. It took time to learn that I was in control of myself and my actions. For so many years, I thought I was living by faith, but came to find out that I was living by "me". For two and a half years, I was on the road of Humility Avenue.

With our ministry doors closed, my husband and I, professed and called evangelists, weren't invited to minister at churches. So I asked, "Lord, what do You want us to do?"

He told me that He hadn't changed His mind about our call to evangelism, but He wanted us to think outside the box.

So, I took the pink suit that I was married in and had it embroidered with, "My husband used to be a sinner, but Jesus set him free. 2 Cor. 5:17."

> *Therefore, if anyone is in Christ, the new creation has come; The old has gone, the new is here!* (2 Corinthians 5:17 NIV).

My beloved already had some of his clothes embroidered with the same message. Each Sunday, we would walk into a different church with our message of freedom, and when the pastor would invite people to meet and greet someone new, no one would come near us. It really hurt. I now understand that was by God's design, because I used to see "church" as my own personal fan club. What really hurt was my pride. God's love for me included a very valuable lesson in humility.

Minister Natalie B. Green, who has written a chapter in this book, said something to me I had never heard: "You become what you behold." Today, I am a new creation because the Lord invited me to hold on to Him when there was nothing else to hold on to, leading me to a place of leadHERship in humility.

Are you following the Lord's agenda or your own? Ask yourself, "Am I bound to a schedule?" as you pray for the Lord to reveal to you how you actually feel and think about things and yourself. He calls us to lead for Him, so we must lead with humility. *Humble yourselves [with an attitude of repentance and insignificance] in the presence of the Lord, and He will exalt you [He will lift you up, He will give you purpose]* (James 4:10 AMP).

As leadHERs called according to God's purpose, we must understand that His ultimate purpose for us is salvation. I know that we "know" that, but let me get to the nitty-gritty. God knows that we need to be saved from ourselves, so He calls us to reflect: When we speak on a platform, are we just so thrilled with ourselves because "we made it," or do we have an authentic desire to serve people? When we author another book, is it to become a best-selling author or so we can serve people? When we paint or write a song or set up a business or mastermind class, is it with our name in mind or His?

As we lead or step into our calling to lead, we must submit our actions *and* the motives of our hearts to God. If we are serving our ego instead of serving the Lord, we won't leave behind a legacy; we'll only leave a mess.

. . . .

Sandra Tuff-Galvin

Sandra Tuff-Galvin is a wife and mother of two adult children and one very loving, plump cat named Chocolate. Sandra was born in Germany and has lived in Texas, Georgia, and Florida.

Sandra has an associate's degree in accounting and is currently a real estate broker. Her path to becoming a real estate broker wasn't direct—it took many twists and turns over the years. Some were funny, such as being a men's hairpiece salesperson; others were soulful, such as being a licensed massage therapist; still others were serious, such as being a Christian school principal. No matter the job, she has always had a heart to help people.

Sandra came to know Jesus Christ as her personal Lord and Savior at the age of 21, and her life has never been the same! Now, her goal is to be like Jesus Christ everywhere she goes and in all that she's called to do. In her spare time, she loves to read *Pride and Prejudice* and cuddle with her beloved cat.

Following Your Calling

By Sandra Tuff-Galvin

I was a young Christian, and it was my second week working in the church office. I had attended church most of my life with my mother, but now I was pursuing the Lord for myself. After the birth of my daughter, the church invited me to work in the office full-time and allowed me to bring my baby with me whenever the sitter was unavailable.

One afternoon, the pastors were out of the office to prepare for a big summit that our church was hosting and had left me with a long list of duties to attend to in their absence. In the quiet office, one of the brothers in the church leaned his head around the doorframe and asked me a question: "Sister Sandy, what are you called to do?"

I swiveled around in my office chair with an inquisitive look on my face. I didn't understand his question; I repeated it back to him, "What am I called to do?"

A smile came over his round, joyful face. "Yes!"

Dumbfounded, I sat in the chair staring at the computer, wondering what the correct answer to such a deep question would be. I didn't realize that people were "called" to do anything. Until that very moment, I actually thought only pastors of churches were "called." Surely God wouldn't waste time calling on me to do anything. I wasn't qualified.

My brother from the church stood patiently in the doorway, waiting for my answer, as my stomach rumbled with hunger. (I felt "called" to go eat my lunch!)

Shrugging my shoulders, I turned back toward the door and answered, "I don't know."

Smiling, he replied, "Well, maybe you should find out." And with those words lingering in the air, he sauntered away, leaving me staring blankly at the computer screen.

I lifted my arms to God in surrender and prayed out loud, "God, what am I called to do?"

Eventually, I learned that I am called to obey the voice of God's Holy Spirit; all day, every day. But I'm getting ahead of myself.

As I continued seeking God's will for my life, my husband left me for another woman. I pushed forward, found a great job with excellent pay, and managed to put away some money. I had good credit, and I really wanted to buy a home for my daughter and myself. A woman at church was a mortgage broker; I was ecstatic because she was a sister in Christ and would be able to lead me down the pathway to getting my first home!

I scheduled an appointment with her, gathered all of my financial papers, and went to her office at the bank. After passing my paperwork to her, I sat nervously with my little girl on my lap, waiting to hear the woman's wisdom and guidance on how I could buy my first home.

Finally, the lady sighed deeply. Looking over the top of her thick glasses, she surveyed me and my daughter with a look of disdain. Then, she neatly stacked my papers together, placed them into the folder, slid the folder back across the desk toward me, and said, "I can't help you."

"What do you mean you can't help me?" My voice cracked as I struggled to hold back the tears that strained to get out behind my rapidly blinking eyelids.

"You need a man," she barked with surprising anger. "Come back and see me when you have a man."

Stammering to find the right words, I restated my case. "But I have great credit, and I make great money, and I have money saved up!"

Her facial expression became as cold and hard as stone. She silently turned her office chair to attend to another stack of papers and refused to speak another word to me.

Tears streaming down my cheeks, I could not understand what had just happened! Why did I need a man to buy a home? I was angry... even outraged!

After I fastened my daughter into her car seat, I prayed loud enough that everyone in that parking lot could hear me, "Lord, if you EVER allow me to get into real estate, I will NEVER treat another woman as I have been treated here today!"

I raced home and threw myself on my bed, where I wept for hours. I didn't realize it, but that was the beginning of my calling!

Sadly, I did not attempt homeownership again for 20 years. But, many years later, with my daughter in high school, I got my real estate license. And God reminded me of the promise I made to Him on that dark and terrible day.

I was working at a real estate firm for a dear Christian sister who was the broker-owner. She called me one afternoon and said that she had decided she would no longer be a broker, as teaching others how to sell real estate had become too time-consuming. She ended our conversation with, "I guess it's time to get your broker's license!"

I decided to go where I've always gone—to the Lord in prayer. "God, do you really want me to do this?" I felt a yes in my heart, but I was still uncertain. Besides, I didn't even have the money to attend the real estate broker's class!

Calling a precious prayer partner and friend, I asked her what she thought.

She said, "Yes, Sandy, do it! I'll give you the money!"

There I sat on my couch without an excuse. This was it; I was going to become a real estate broker. Dear God! I didn't have a clue what I was doing. I prayed earnestly on the couch that day: "Lord, if you really want me to do this, you'll have to help me and teach me every step of the way."

I don't know what I would have done without my precious friend at that time. She and God were the only two who believed in me.

One class at a time, I walked it out. Some days it felt like a walk on a tightrope; nevertheless, I made it through the classes, took the test, and got my broker's license! By nothing more than the fervent prayers of my friend and God's grace.

I would love to tell you that once I became a leadHER as a broker, things became easier, but that wouldn't be honest. The truth is that the road was difficult.

One woman desired to join the brokerage, and then others decided to come on board, and things started moving very fast—faster than I could keep up with. The demands of the women became too great for me to handle. They wanted and needed emotional support, family help, and immediate financial income. As badly as I wanted to provide those things, I was just starting out, so I lost all of my team to other, more lucrative opportunities.

For over a year, I beat myself up. I felt like a failure. Then, one day in prayer, it felt as though God asked me how much longer I was planning to drag that bag of rocks around with me! I began to laugh and laugh, and the depression went away immediately.

I learned through that experience that when things start to go at breakneck speed, I should slow down and sit at the feet of Jesus even more than usual.

Today, when people say they'd like to join the real estate brokerage, I pray, fast, and wait to hear from the Lord! It doesn't matter who they are or how much money they've made before. All that matters is my question before the Lord. "Lord, is THIS your will?"

I don't want to see a new person join the firm so that I can say I have a ton of people. Sometimes, God wants me to confirm to people who come my way that they should be pursuing another path and NOT join the brokerage.

I've learned that the foundation for leading is stewardship, and all I have to do is obey God; this significantly reduces stress and performance pressure. If I lead well, it's only because I've followed His instructions. I am no longer on my own; I have God at the forefront of every decision. He is my best friend, business partner, and the one I can tell all of my worries to through prayer.

My life has changed for the better. I'm no longer stressed out and short-tempered with my family all of the time. My prayer time is more fulfilling as I spend quality time with God, who is the head of the company, the head of my life, and my best friend!

As I've embraced this calling to obey the voice of the Holy Spirit, the joy of serving others has returned to my heart with fresh passion! It is no longer a depressing chore to get out of bed and work, but each day is filled with a desire to love, help, train, serve, and help others succeed, even if I just make their day a little better with a kind word of appreciation. Every day is an adventure with my heavenly Father leading the way.

The author, John Maxwell, wrote in one of his books many, many years ago, "It would be a shame to climb the ladder of success only to realize that your ladder is on the wrong wall."

Even though John Maxwell isn't the originator of that statement, it was the first time I had ever heard it! I could imagine myself climbing this gigantic ladder with sweat running down my face, streaking my corporate makeup, and blisters on my hands from grasping the rungs of the ladder too tightly. Then, I'd finally reach the pinnacle of my success at the very top, only to realize that the ladder was actually leaning against the wall of our local trash dump!

The Lord wasn't satisfied with me following my calling to lead others as a broker; He wanted me to follow a calling we all have: to let Him lead us in every step. That is HOW we succeed in our calling!

I read John 3:13, where Jesus washed the feet of His disciples. Wait, what? Jesus got on His knees and washed dirt off their feet? Have you ever had your child come home from a long, hot day at school and kick off their shoes? The stench is so powerful, you have to run from the room, gasping for air! But Jesus didn't flinch. NO, He humbly removed His outer clothing, grabbed a towel, wrapped it around His waist, and started washing! And then, He instructed His followers to do the same.

What on earth does foot washing have to do with my calling? EVERYTHING! Jesus goes on to explain in John 13:15-17, *"I have set you an example that you should do as I have done for you. Very truly I tell you, no servant is greater than his master, nor is a messenger greater than the one who sent him. Now that you know these things, you will be blessed if you do them"* (NIV).

You see, when we follow God's calling, no matter what that calling is, we are to care for others and lead as a worthy example in both our private and business lives. That's washing feet!

When I read that Scripture all those years ago, I realized that it isn't only *what* I do that matters to God, but *how* I do it. I could go the world's way and bark orders to those I lead to wash their co-workers' feet or face losing their jobs. Or, I could grab a towel and wash the feet of others myself, teaching and leading those whose feet I am washing as well as those who are watching.

It's not always easy to lead in a godly manner: with love, kindness, and humility, seeking God's wisdom about when to be firm or stern. Some people will think you're stupid, foolish, a kiss-up... you name it. But, putting the incorrect judgments of those people aside, being a kingdom leadHER is so rewarding!

At the end of each day, my heart is full of joy because I didn't try to get one over on someone or lie or manipulate to get ahead. I wake up for prayer in the morning, excited to discuss everything with my best friend and true CEO—what happened the day before, what He has for the day ahead, and what wisdom He has for me; and then I write it all down in my prayer journal.

Does God already know everything that happened yesterday and exactly what will happen tomorrow? Of course He does! But does that ever stop me from telling Him anyway? Absolutely NOT! He's my best friend, who knows the entire universe and beyond, so why not tell Him everything? He's the only one who can fix the problems I face and truly comfort my heart when I'm hurting. Others can be kind, empathetic, offer hugs or prayers, and those are wonderful, but He's the only one who can comfort me from the inside out.

What is *your* calling? I think the first question to ask is, whose voice are you listening to? Is it God or the devil? If it's God, following His call will be a blessing to others as well as yourself. (That doesn't mean it won't be hard work!) If it's the devil, you will find that you'll need to do a lot of lying, cheating, and manipulating to get where you think you should be.

When you follow God's calling, expect resistance from others. Michael Jordan's coach told him that he would never make it in basketball. Don't be surprised when family members or friends don't support what God has told you to do. Don't argue and try to persuade them. Forgive them and take their objections to God in prayer, asking Him to give you His wisdom on what to do and how to handle their objections.

One of the best ways to discover your calling is to ask yourself, *What am I passionate about?* (Chocolate and fries don't count.) *What is the thing you would do if you no longer needed money?* (Getting a better tan on a beach in Tahiti doesn't count as an answer.)

A few years ago, my niece was having a hard time trying to figure out what to do as a career. We come from a long line of college-loving professionals who run the gamut from registered nurses to teachers to crime investigators to human resource directors. In our family, it's frowned upon if you aren't the holder of at least a four-year college degree. (I only have a two-year associate's degree; the black sheep that I am.) However, after high school, four more years of studying and going to class didn't suit my niece. I asked her what she would do if money weren't an issue.

After quiet consideration, she stated that she would love to teach children with disabilities. We prayed and asked God to open a door of opportunity for her in that area. Shortly after, she got a job as a teacher's assistant, teaching children with disabilities. She became so popular with the parents and their children that she was asked to sign on for another year!

I think one of the greatest things we can do for ourselves is to pause and ask God the big questions in life. If we listen to Him, He will reveal our God-given mission and open doors of opportunity we never would have pursued if we hadn't asked the big questions.

Your calling doesn't automatically involve going to Africa to serve orphans. I have a friend who is a missionary; she is an amazing person who travels all over the world helping women and children, and I don't even have a passport! Does that make my calling less important than hers? Of course not! The Bible warns us not to compare ourselves with each other. That same friend has laughed heartily with me, stating jokingly that if she had to put up with the crazy things I deal with in real estate, she would snatch someone's hair right off their head!

Your calling is just as important as the next person's. God crafted your calling just for you. But it's not just *what* God has given you to do that is important—it's *how* you respond to what He has called you to! Are you pursuing the calling through God by seeking His heart on how He wants you to wash others' feet? Or are you out there on that old rickety ladder of success leaned against the wrong wall, like I was?

My dear friend, as you take each step with faith, just as He instructs, money will come, influence will come, opportunities will come. You won't have to chase them; they will simply open up to you at the right time. You won't have to step on others to achieve success, but you will be able to help others succeed while you succeed. This is what the foot washing concept is all about—serving and loving people along the journey to your destination.

Are you ready? Ask God to show you the next step to take, then trust Him as you grab your towel and get out there, loving and leading others.

You are about to begin one of the greatest journeys of your life!

I will leave you with this last nugget of wisdom. Following God's call as you intentionally serve others will make your life very full—of love, joy, peace, and lasting friendships. You'll be living on the edge and walking on the wild side of faith every single day! It won't always be easy, but it will be worth it!

So... what color is your towel?

Connie A. VanHorn

Connie A. VanHorn has a heart for encouraging others to find their God-given purpose. She serves on the Women World Leaders' Board of Directors and on the Leadership Team as an ambassador and administrative assistant to Kimberly Hobbs.

Connie, an International best-selling author who also writes for *Voice of Truth* magazine, resides in Winston-Salem, North Carolina, where she has participated in several discipleship classes and taught Sunday school to international students. She attended Bible classes at Vintage Bible College.

Being a mother is by far Connie's greatest accomplishment and her first, best ministry. She dreams of changing the world by sharing Jesus and raising world-changers who have a kingdom perspective. Besides spending time with her children and family, Connie enjoys making bracelets, journaling, and writing fiction.

Connie wants her readers to know that it's ok to be broken—it's in the broken places that we find God. Come as you are! See past messy, see past broken, and you might just see a miracle.

Contact Connie at: Connie@womenworldleaders.com

A Crown with Purpose

By Connie A. VanHorn

When I was a little girl, I was never called "Princess" and didn't even have one of those little plastic tiaras, but I loved to play princess through my imagination. I would pretend that I was in a castle, standing tall as royalty; that I was someone important and special.

In my backyard, we had a metal playset with monkey bars. I would climb to the top, imagine that I was at the top of a big castle, and make believe that I was the royal princess. And when my home turned to chaos and fighting, I would hide in closets, escaping into my daydreams and pretending I was hiding from dragons.

As I grew older, I would hop on my bike, ride to a park near my house, and fantasize that the entire park was my enchanted forest and the playground was my land. As I got older, I would wear my mother's costume jewelry and, in my imagination, summon a prince to join me.

I spent a lot of time alone, but I didn't hate that. My daydreams saved me and gave me a way to believe in my future and the impossible. They gave me hope and made me feel safe. And, along the way, God was kind to send a few angels!

One of those angels during those early years was my Aunt Rita. She lived somewhat close to us, and I remember being thrown into her car in the middle of the night on several occasions. She was kind and very warm to touch—I loved her hugs and sitting on her lap. I can still close my eyes and smell the sweat from her neck and oversized shirt. My brain refuses to allow her memory to fade. I treasured being wrapped in her arms, where I felt safe.

My Aunt Rita's home is now in what we would call "the projects," although I did not use that term as a child. To me, her house felt like a castle, and I was the princess. The walls and the floors were utilitarian brick cement—my feet would turn completely black from the dirty, impossible-to-clean floor. And I am quite sure the Florida house lacked central heat and air, as it was often very hot. I slept with a big fan blowing directly on me. Roaches covered every part of the kitchen; the little critters lived happily and seamlessly with the rest of the house. None of this bothered me, however. I loved being at her place, where I hid from my life, found rest, and felt loved.

Aunt Rita had two grandsons whom she adored. When they were toddlers, she often put those charming little boys in beauty pageants; her bedroom was filled with trophies, plaques, and ribbons from their countless contests. One weekend, she invited me to join them, so I went along without expecting anything for myself. I have a love for dresses; I always say, "A pretty dress can change the outlook of your entire day!" It wasn't unusual for me to wear a dress on any casual day, including to a park or a ball game, and that day with Aunt Rita was no different.

Upon our arrival at the pageant, while registering for the day's events, Aunt Rita noticed a girls' category that had just a few contestants; she was quick to ask if I could participate. I was very shy, but she encouraged me, insisting I was the prettiest girl and was sure to win. She was always boosting everyone's confidence, and I always felt special to her.

Surprisingly, there were only three girls in my age group, and I ended up winning! Wow! I couldn't believe it. I had not won much in my childhood, and I felt like the most beautiful girl in the world as I rode home, clasping my ribbon.

Unfortunately, that short-lived feeling of beauty and validation faded quickly. I returned to the brokenness, insecurity, and shame that anchored my identity. No matter how often I attempted to reclaim the delight I felt that day, complete emptiness always rushed back in to fill me.

My childhood was difficult and filled with trauma in every sense: abuse, addiction, constant fighting, and chaos. I grew up in an unsafe environment, and was shifted between my auntie's house, foster homes, and even different states. My siblings and I experienced the presence of police far too often.

This chaotic childhood shaped me into a person who buried her trauma as deeply as possible, even as I put on a dress and a smile... pretending to be happy in front of others. I became really good at pretending and hiding everything about myself, but unhealed trauma eventually finds a way to surface. We can only hide for so long. For me, it manifested as fear, causing me to run when things got hard and to yield to people-pleasing behaviors. I lived afraid of nearly everything, and ran straight into relationships that hurt more than they healed. Along the way, I made so many mistakes, chasing the wrong crowd and making terrible decisions.

As I grew into adulthood, being a leadHER or wearing any kind of crown or having any title became the furthest thing from my reality. I didn't have a true understanding or model of what leadHERship should look like; I went about life without purpose and continued to search for validation in all the wrong places, people, and things.

This became my story.

So you can understand that I doubted that God would choose me to be a kingdom leadHER. Why would He? I was messy, broken, and completely lost. I didn't come from a stable home, had no educational background, and did not have a supportive community or family surrounding me. I was struggling to lead in my own life and home, let alone in anything meaningful. But, even in my broken life, God had His eyes fixed on me.

> Blessed is the one who perseveres under trial because, having stood the test, that person will receive the crown of life that the Lord has promised to those who love him (James 1:12 NIV).

As you read this, I want you to know that God has His eyes set on you, too. You are the daughter of God! His choice is not based on your past or your perceived limitations but on His perfect love and purpose for you. God often chooses the unlikely vessels to fulfill His greater plans.

God finds us in the most unlikely places—He found me on the floor of a Quality Inn. I was running from someone, and I was running from God. Alone with my children, surrounded by bags filled with our belongings, I felt isolated and without a path or a future. I had nothing to offer anyone; I was the very definition of messy. But God is faithfully loving, always. He caught my tears and pursued me, even when I was running in the opposite direction. Even when I was alone. Even when I had nothing.

God finds a heart set on Him, calls it out, and claims it as His own. He doesn't look for perfect people; He seeks willing hearts. God invites all of His children to come as we are, and then He does the fixing within us—putting back together what the world has ripped apart.

I once read a quote that said, "I know what it's like to lose yourself so badly that you don't know if there's a you or ever was one." That is how I felt most of the time—lost, alone, and confused about my identity. I found that when we enter into a relationship with Jesus and walk hand in hand with our Creator, God comes in and fills the spaces that the world tries to fill with lies.

No matter where you are, know that your story, just like mine, can become a testimony of His grace and transformation. Your story can change lives and lead others to Him.

In the heart of every woman is a true leadHER, and a calling that shows God's purpose for our lives. LeadHERship in ministry is not just for those who have degrees or big qualifications; instead, leadHERship is developed by faith, love, encouragement, and community. We've all heard the saying, "God doesn't call the qualified; He qualifies the called." This has been absolutely true in my case.

My leadHERship journey blossomed when I became involved with Women World Leaders, where I was surrounded by the most amazing and kind women of God who saw not only my insecurities and imperfections, but also the promise of who I could become as a daughter of the King.

I entered this ministry feeling very unqualified, unsure of who I was, and weighed down by so much brokenness, constantly questioning what I could possibly offer and thinking, *I am unworthy.* Those words played in my mind through most days. But the incredible women who guided me poured love, kindness, and courage into my spirit. CONSTANTLY! They spoke life into my heart and helped me see myself through God's eyes. They showed me my worth and purpose and invited me to sit next to them. They straightened my crown.

A crown I couldn't see at the time.

They showed me how to truly live and to love others. They showed me how to lead.

I don't often share that throughout my life, I've had moments of not wanting to live. I never thought about suicide, but in one of my hardest seasons, I battled feelings of being unloved and that I would be better off not in this world. I was going through something that felt unbearable, living without purpose, and struggling in the environment around me. Spiritually, I felt alone, having completely isolated myself from my church community.

I was ashamed of how I was living and the unhealed wounds within me. No matter how hard I tried, I couldn't run from that "never good enough" feeling.

I'll never forget the first real breath that I took, when I felt God was pouring life back inside me.

The women in Women World Leaders, two in particular, taught me that as daughters of God, we are cherished and set apart for a greater purpose. It was through their constant love and support that I began to see myself through God's eyes and as a vessel, equipped to lead, encourage, and bring change to the world.

When I first met Kimberly Hobbs and Julie Jenkins, I was wearing so many weights around my waist. I was chained by who I used to be, and held captive by my choices and the hurt that others caused me. I was trapped in a prison of secrets and haunted by the actions of those who mistreated me—people who should have loved and cared for me.

I was living in a prison I had built around myself, and I was shackled by the weight of others' expectations of me. I somehow thought that I deserved it all. The burdens of pleasing the people around me left me trapped in a cycle of never feeling good enough. I didn't feel like a leadHER or anyone special because I wasn't seeing myself through God's eyes. I wasn't finding my identity in the one who created me. But the women in this ministry saw God in me and through me. They saw me as my Father created me, in His image.

> So God created mankind in his own image, in the image of God he created them; male and female he created them (Genesis 1:27 NIV).

These women, and the MANY others who wrapped their arms around me, believed in me and in my dream. I had a beautiful vision that God was going to use all the hard things I went through and my life to help others. I daydreamed about being a writer one day!

Jesus said just a little faith—the size of a mustard seed—can move mountains!

We all have hopes and dreams, and we all have hard things in our lives that we wish God would turn around. We ask God for possible things, but what if God wants to do something impossible—beyond what you can imagine?

In August 2014, I gave my heart to Jesus, which completely changed me and gave me a purpose. God saved me from my past and the pain that had chained me down for years. I finally got it. I finally got what Jesus did for me, so I could begin to live and lead with purpose, as the daughter of God!

After I got saved, I started journaling, documenting my journey with God. I wanted to remember everything that I was learning and the miracles I experienced along the way. I titled it "Chasing Butterflies" because I was chasing my new life and wanted to share the amazing love and kindness of Jesus with others!

It became my mission to share my testimony with as many people as I could.

I had a vision to write a book!

But how?

One morning, I opened Facebook and saw that my longtime friend, Candace, had posted about the launch of a book she contributed to. The book, titled *Courageous Steps of Faith*, had a beautiful pink cover that caught my eye. I love everything pink!

I messaged her right away to share my excitement and let her know I was going to order a copy. I told her that writing a book was a big dream of mine. At that moment, I really started daydreaming about the possibility of it happening for me, though I felt unqualified. She responded with excitement, offering to send me some resources to encourage me and suggesting that I consider sharing my own God story.

I remember thinking, *Wow, God, this feels like another miracle. How am I having this conversation with someone?* The next step was to talk to Kimberly and then write a summary of my testimony and send it to Kimberly and Julie.

I still remember the day I hit <send> and thought, *I'll never hear back.* I didn't feel good enough or worthy! I read my summary a hundred times, trying to fix any grammar mistakes and avoid feeling like a failure.

A few days later, I opened my computer to find an email from two of the sweetest women. They invited me to be part of their book and ministry! They encouraged me along the way and replaced the lies told to me about myself with truth! I couldn't believe it because I didn't believe in myself, but little by little, the doubts I had about myself began to be overshadowed by confidence and the love of Jesus! Little by little, my mustard-seed-sized faith turned into very courageous, big steps of faith!

This marked the beginning of my journey with Women World Leaders, and more importantly, the start of something new and beautiful with God. It was at that moment that I saw the crown that God placed upon me as He called me His precious daughter!

I have been changed not only by God, but also by all women, stories, and my participation in WWL. My life has been forever transformed; I now see myself as a kingdom leadHER and wear my crown with confidence.

True leadHERship comes from understanding who we are in Christ and recognizing that our value comes from God. Being a leadHER is not about a title or recognition; it's not about comparing ourselves to others. Being a leadHER is about serving others with humility and grace. Serving others with LOVE!

The encouragement and LOVE I received from these precious women allowed me to see my own qualities as a true leadHER, and now I want you to see yours. God equipped you to be a leadHER; spending time with Him and in Christian community can show you how to put your leadHERship into action!

Your story is not finished! You are God's daughter simply because of your faith in Jesus Christ, and He has a plan for your life!

In Christ Jesus, you are more than any pain you bear or past mistake you've made. You are more than what happened yesterday, and more than what you think today or tomorrow holds. You are more because God is working on you until you go home. You are more because of who God is and who God says you are.

You are the daughter of God; you belong to Him! No amount of accolades or achievements will ever offer you your full worth. You were born worthy because you are the daughter of God; He has placed a precious crown on your head meant to last for all eternity!

Worldly crowns are temporary; they won't last. However, the crown our heavenly Father places on your head will allow you to make an impact that will last for eternity. Knowing this, I now touch the lives of those around me by loving and leading them faithfully to Jesus. I now confidently wear my crown with purpose.

As you step into your role as a leadHER, whether in ministry or within your home, job, or community, remember that you are not alone. If you feel God's calling in your heart, know that we at Women World Leaders stand ready to support you in discovering the purpose God has for you. Wear your crown with courage, confidence, and purpose!

You are wearing a crown that will last!

As Ephesians 3:20 reminds us, God can do exceedingly abundantly above all we ask or think. Trust in His power and believe that you have an important role to play in advancing His kingdom.

Girl, remember who's daughter you are and fix that crown!

Leading with Generosity

By Stacy Jo Coffee-Thorne

Generosity is one of the clearest reflections of God's heart. It is not measured by the size of what we give but by the spirit in which we give it. True generosity flows from gratitude, not obligation. It recognizes that everything we have—our time, talents, influence, and finances—comes from God and belongs to Him. When we live with that understanding, giving becomes an act of worship rather than an act of sacrifice.

Jesus spoke often about generosity. Scripture records Him talking more about money, stewardship, and giving than almost any other subject. Jesus knew how easily our hearts can become attached to what we own. Matthew 6:21 records Jesus' teaching, *"For where your treasure is, there your heart will be also"* (NIV). He was not condemning wealth; He was teaching us to hold it correctly. Jesus understood that generosity keeps our hearts free. When we give, we declare that money is not our master, that our trust is in God as our source.

Financial generosity is an essential part of kingdom living. Giving back to God through tithes and offerings is not about losing what we have but about honoring Him with what He has entrusted to us. Our giving fuels ministry, meets needs, and advances the gospel. It reminds us that God can do more with ten percent surrendered to Him than we can do with one hundred percent held tightly in our own hands.

Generosity goes beyond money. We can also be generous with our time, encouragement, compassion, and wisdom. Some of the most meaningful acts of generosity come through a kind word, a listening ear, or a helping hand. Leading with generosity means living with open hands in every area of life. When we give freely, we create space for God to move through us.

A generous person will prosper; whoever refreshes others will be refreshed (Proverbs 11:25 NIV).

That verse captures the heart of kingdom leadHERship. When we pour into others, God pours back into us. The more freely we give, the more He can entrust to us. Generosity is not about depleting ourselves; it is about becoming a vessel for His blessing. Did you know that we can't outgive God? God's economy is never one of lack. When we lead generously, we live in the flow of His provision.

As leadHERs, our example matters. People watch how we handle what we have been given. LeadHERship is not about accumulation; it is about stewardship. A generous leadHER gives more than direction; she gives opportunity, encouragement, and hope. She gives without expecting anything in return and uses her position to serve rather than to be served. Generosity in leadHERship creates an atmosphere of trust that tells people they are valued. And when people feel valued, they give their best in return.

Remember this: Whoever sows sparingly will also reap sparingly, and whoever sows generously will also reap generously. Each of you should give what you have decided in your heart to give, not reluctantly or under compulsion, for God loves a cheerful giver (2 Corinthians 9:6-7 NIV).

God does not want us to be generous due to guilt or pressure. He wants us to share our resources willingly with hearts of joy. A joyful giver understands that every seed planted in generosity carries eternal purpose. Giving with joy is not about what we forfeit; it is about what God will do through our act of release.

When we lead with open hands, God uses us as vessels of His love and provision. Our words can build someone's confidence. Our encouragement can restore faith. Our financial generosity can change the course of someone's life. Every act of giving, whether spiritual, emotional, or material, carries kingdom impact.

At the end of the day, generosity is about trust. It is about believing that God is faithful to provide and that He will always supply what we need to continue blessing others. Nothing we give in His name ever goes unnoticed. When we live and lead generously, we reflect the heart of Jesus, and that kind of leadHERship changes the world.

· ·

Rozanne "Roxy" Brown

Roxy Brown knows loss. She knows grief. And she knows that love isn't a feeling—it's a choice made daily.

A child of God, daughter, sister, wife, mother, and grandmother affectionately called "Gigi," Roxy carries the weight of personal tragedy with grace that only deepens her compassion. In 2017, when most would have turned inward, she turned outward—founding CareBag Inc., a grassroots lifeline for those in need.

Today, four mobile shower units roll across six South Florida counties, restoring dignity one warm shower at a time. Her mobile hygiene pantry meets families at their breaking point, offering not just supplies, but hope.

As President of J&R Enterprise Transport Inc. and CEO of CareBag, Roxy doesn't just lead—she *serves*. Her heart fuels a mission born from pain and sustained by purpose.

Roxy doesn't see the homeless—she sees *people*. And in their eyes, she finds her calling.

Because access to dignity isn't a privilege; it's a right.

The Weight of Grace

By Rozanne "Roxy" Brown

I sat on the patio by the pool, drinking my third cup of coffee. My hands trembled slightly as I set the cup back on the table.

It had been 17 years of mounting losses; the grief still hit me in waves. Sometimes it came in gentle ripples, other times, it came as crushing tsunamis that left me gasping for air. But this time was different; the losses had come one after another over the last six months—five friends, four family members, and then Blu', our family dog, my constant companion for over 13 years through many difficult periods in my life.

Oh, my goodness, it hurt like needles piercing my side.

And then through it all, I also learned that friendships can die. I knew I had to walk away when compromising meant sacrificing my values. What seemed like loyalty was actually destruction, both theirs and possibly mine. Laughter masked deeper pain, and I chose to ignore it. I realized that friendship should never require abandoning the values that define who I am and who I am meant to be.

The hardest part was accepting that love and friendship sometimes mean letting go. Setting boundaries felt like betrayal, but staying would have been worse. I pray for their healing from afar, understanding that some relationships must also die for my soul to survive.

The Lord is close to the brokenhearted and saves those who are crushed in spirit (Psalm 34:18 NIV).

These were the words I had to learn; they became my anchor in the storm.

"Grandma, are you okay?" My five-year-old granddaughter's voice broke through my daydream. She stood in the doorway leading to the patio, backpack slung over one shoulder, concern stamped across her young face.

I forced a smile; the same one I'd perfected over these many years of loss. "Of course, sweetheart. Just thinking about the day ahead."

My granddaughter nodded, but her eyes held that knowing look children develop when they've witnessed too much adult pain. "Papa says you're helping lots of people today with your work."

"That's right," I replied, standing to adjust my granddaughter's backpack. "And you're helping too by being such a good princess."

As my granddaughter leaped toward the car where Papa waited, I whispered a prayer I'd repeated countless times over these six months: "Lord, give me strength for this day. Help me be who they need me to be. *I can do all this through him who gives me strength* (Philippians 4:13 NIV)."

We drove off in the car filled with the usual morning chatter, but my mind wandered to the board meeting scheduled for later that week.

CareBag ministry, a nonprofit, provides access to proper hygiene to the unhoused and families who are struggling. We carry the weight of hundreds of lives, all dependent on my decisions. This organization grew from church members packing fresh sandwiches and delivering them in the woods to individuals and families on Sundays. We worked out of our garage for years until we expanded. With the grace of God, we serve a large area in Florida, from the northern part of the Treasure Coast down into the Palm Beaches. God is amazing!

As we drove, I was keenly aware that every decision felt enormous, every choice was shadowed by the question, *With how I'm feeling, can I still do this?* Since losing so many dear ones over the previous six months, I felt like an anchor was pulling me down. I was the one everyone turned to when life got complicated; now I needed rescuing. I knew I had to share that I needed help. But when could I? I was being pulled from left to right.

Later, I logged on to my virtual office; my assistant greeted me with my schedule and a stack of urgent messages. "Good morning! Here's your schedule for today: you have the board meeting this week to prepare for, and then you need to set up dates with council members and commissioners for the upcoming meetings. Also, we need to start planning our fundraisers. And there is an urgent call from a mother who needs help."

I nodded, sorting each task. This was my gift and my burden: the ability to hold multiple responsibilities while still functioning, still leading, still caring for the over 460 families we serve monthly, even when my own heart felt shattered.

The urgent call was from a mother with three children, including a five-week-old baby. They were stranded. I could hear the infant crying in the background as she spoke, her voice breaking with exhaustion and desperation.

"I'm so sorry to bother you," she whispered, trying to speak over the baby's cries. "We haven't showered in over a week. My car ran out of gas, and I don't have the money to get to your location. My baby won't stop crying, and my other kids... they're asking why we can't go home."

I reached for my keys immediately. "Don't apologize. Give me your location,

I'm coming to you."

She responded softly, "I can't pay for gas, and I don't know when I can."

"You don't need to pay me for anything. That's not what this is about." The words came from a place deeper than my professional training; they emerged from my own journey through a valley of despair, where I struggled to wake up, take a breath, and figure out what to do. While I was battling feelings of hopelessness, she was yearning for hope.

> Even though I walk through the darkest valley, I will fear no evil, for you are with me; your rod and your staff, they comfort me (Psalm 23:4 NIV).

As I drove to meet the family, I felt the familiar tug of purpose that had sustained me through the darkest months. Grief is love with nowhere to go, but I had learned to channel that love outward into my family, our mission, and my friends.

I found the weary foursome in a parking lot behind a gas station—a young mother holding a crying baby while two other children, 6 and 8, sat quietly in the back seat. I pulled up beside them and got out.

"I'm from CareBag," I said gently. "Let's get you some gas first, and food, then you can follow us to our mobile unit."

The relief in the mother's eyes was immediate. As I filled her tank, she told me their story. First, their lights were cut off. Then, they were evicted three days ago. They had stayed in the car, the mother trying to find work while caring for her newborn.

The baby finally stopped crying and nestled against his mother's shoulder. "I don't know how to thank you," she said.

"You don't need to thank me. This is what we're here for: to restore dignity, one shower, one item at a time."

Carry each other's burdens, and in this way, you will fulfill the law of Christ (Galatians 6:2 NIV).

When I returned, I started on my executive report to the board, which tested every ounce of my composure. I didn't want to speak to anyone. Budget shortfalls, volunteer challenges, and the constant pressure to serve more families with fewer resources created a perfect storm for my stress.

The day of the board meeting arrived; I sat in front of my computer as the virtual meeting was called to order.

The words of one board member rang out: "You've been through so much." Silence followed. I felt the weight of the board members' collective gaze, the unspoken question I thought was hanging in the air: Could I, grieving, effectively lead an organization dedicated to helping others rebuild their lives?

I spoke slowly, my voice steady despite the storm on my chest. "Six months ago, I thought grief would break me. I thought losing my friends and my family members, all in one short time, meant losing my ability to lead, to mother, to serve. But I've learned something profound: grief doesn't disqualify us from service; it qualifies us for deeper compassion."

But he said to me, "My grace is sufficient for you, for my power is made perfect in weakness." Therefore, I will boast more gladly about my weaknesses, so that Christ's power may rest on me (2 Corinthians 12:9 NIV).

I looked at the faces on the screen, which had become family over the years. "Every family we serve is grieving something lost: homes, jobs, dignity, hope. When I sit with them and talk with them, I'm not just offering professional service. I'm offering the understanding that comes from walking through their own valley of shadows."

My answer to so many who asked me was, "Yes, I'm grieving. Yes, some days I can barely get out of bed. But those are the days when I remember that stewardship isn't about being perfect, it's about being faithful. It's about showing up even when showing up is the hardest thing I've had to do."

> Each of you should use whatever gift you have received to serve others, as faithful stewards of God's grace in its various forms (1 Peter 4:10 NIV).

The board members agreed with me and had one question: "What do you need from us?"

My answer was: "Patience when I'm not at my best, grace when I make mistakes, and trust that God can use broken vessels to pour out His love."

The leadership of the nonprofit offered me their unanimous support and a commitment to their continued support. As we finished our meeting, several members texted and called, giving me words of encouragement. When I saw some of them in the coming days, I received embraces with squeezes and hugs, which felt good.

Sometimes, when I feel like I'm barely keeping my head above water with just my own responsibilities, I look around and see what so many people are going through. We all have our own grief, and we carry it in different ways. Despite that, we are all doing more than we know. Being a good person is not about having the answers; it's about showing up with love even when you're tired, even when you're scared.

I learned from my father, who passed away 13 years ago. He always shared profound insights that I hold dear. He taught me that love isn't a feeling. It's a choice. Every day we choose to love by our actions.

When I go to help families, I'm choosing love.

When I come home and I'm tired, but I still help with homework, I choose love.

When you're kind to your brother, sister, husband, or wife, you're choosing love.

Love matters the most.

I receive calls at all different times of the day; people don't know where to go or what to do. That familiar sense of purpose carries me through. This is my calling, not despite my grief, but because of it. My own experience with loss has created space in my heart for others' pain.

> Praise be to the God and Father of our Lord Jesus Christ, the Father of compassion and the God of all comfort, who comforts us in all our troubles, so that we can comfort those in any trouble with the comfort we ourselves receive from God (2 Corinthians 1:3-4 NIV).

I heard my pastor give a sermon in which he spoke about the parable of the talents, about faithful stewardship in the face of uncertainty. "God doesn't call the equipped," he said. "He equips the called." I had felt unequipped for months; unequipped to lead through my grief—to parent, to be a good wife and a good friend, to face the future—without the presence of so many people who were so important to me. But each day brought small confirmations that being properly equipped isn't essential; being faithful is.

Every day continues to bring new challenges—a funding crisis, a volunteer conflict, or a mother with three kids who has been evicted. I move through each situation that greets me with a steady grace I've developed, not because I feel strong, but because I'm willing to go on, trusting God's strength.

I'm learning that grief and purpose can coexist. I miss my family and friends terribly; however, I still show up for the people who need me. That's what my father would have told me to do; he always believed that pain could become our ministry if we let it.

> *And we know that in all things God works for the good of those who love him, who have been called according to his purpose* (Romans 8:28 NIV).

One of my team members presented me with a beautiful orchid that looked so fragile. The first thing I said as I touched the delicate flower was, "I don't want this plant to die." We chuckled.

Then, she said, "Give it one ice cube every Friday."

This was another reminder that growth is possible, even in difficult soil, and that beauty can emerge from struggles.

In the weeks that followed, I started to get back into the rhythm of challenges and grace. I learned to navigate board meetings with confidence born from vulnerability, and to parent my grandchild through the loss with the fierce tenderness of someone who understood how precious and fragile life could be.

One evening, as I tucked our grandbaby into bed, she asked, "Gigi, do you think Blu' still remembers me?" Blu'—our beloved dog who had passed. I considered her question carefully, and before I could reply, she continued, "Gigi, when God and Jesus come, we will see Blu' again." Then, she started remembering the names of some of our friends and family that we'd lost. As she did, she held my hands and prayed for each one.

Start children off on the way they should go, and even when they are old they will not turn from it (Proverbs 22:6 NIV).

I had a presentation to do. My voice was steady, my presentation thorough, my passion evident. The grief was still there. It would always be there, but it had become integrated into my purpose rather than separate me from it. I was told, "Your organization has shown remarkable growth and impact over the past couple of years. What drives your commitment to this work?"

I paused. I started thinking of all my family and friends and the hundreds of families I've served. About the plant sitting in the corner of my windowsill in my kitchen that had started to grow and transform from different circumstances.

"I've learned that stewardship isn't about managing resources when life is easy," I said. "It's about faithfully tending what you've been given, especially when tending feels impossible. Every person we serve is someone's child, someone's parent, someone's hope for the future. When we care about them, we're caring for a part of ourselves that knows what it means to need grace."

As I went home that evening, I sat down on my patio looking out at the pool and thought about my life, which had been torn but was being rewoven. I thought about the journey I'd been on since that morning six months ago, when I could barely hold my coffee cup steady, to this evening, when I felt anchored in my purpose despite the ongoing aches of loss.

My grief hadn't vanished. It had been altered into a greater ability for empathy, a stronger commitment to minister, and a more calculated approach to love. As the stars began to shine, I whispered a prayer of gratitude for the strength I'd been given to continue, the family who surrounded me, the work that gave me purpose, the team God blessed me with, and the understanding that, even in my brokenness, I can be a tool of healing for others.

Weeping may stay for a night, but rejoicing comes in the morning (Psalm 30:5 NIV).

The weight of grief will always be part of my story, but so will the weight of grace that empowered me to carry the grief while caring for others. In learning how to press on, I realized that the ultimate stewardship was not managing what I was doing easily but undertaking challenges with grace. Through God's strength, I attained a transformation, rather than just merely existing. Now, the weight is lighter.

Jocelynne Isaacs

Jocelynne Isaacs is the Director of Operations & Bookkeeping at Freedom Support Solutions, where she combines strategic structure with a heart for service to help businesses and ministries thrive. With years of experience in customer service, office management, and financial operations, Jocelynne brings precision and purpose to every client relationship.

Jocelynne is a QuickBooks ProAdvisor, a member of the American Association of Daily Money Managers (AADMM), and a Certified Director of Operations through The Ops Authority. Additionally, she is a Certified Diamontologist through the Diamond Council of America—a fun fact that perfectly mirrors her belief that true leadership, much like a diamond, is refined under pressure and meant to shine for God's glory.

Originally from Ohio, Jocelynne resides in Stuart, Florida. A trained vocalist and worship leader with Message Parlor, she leads worship at various recovery events and rehabilitation centers.

Jocelynne is passionate about equipping women to lead with confidence, clarity, and Christ-centered conviction. She believes kingdom leadHERship begins within—where God polishes purpose, shapes character, and prepares His daughters to lead with grace and grit.

The Root of LeadHERship Identity

By Jocelynne Isaacs

I was born into leadership—not by title but by birth order. As the oldest child, my role was unofficial but understood: protector, example-setter, fixer, and sometimes even third parent. I didn't have to be told to lead; it was expected of me, silently and consistently. And I wore it like armor. What I didn't realize, though, was that although I was leading, I was doing it to meet others' expectations of me. So it isn't surprising that somewhere along the way, I began to equate leadership with performance. If I led well, I thought I was worthy. If I failed, I felt as if I wasn't enough. It wasn't long before "what I do" became louder than "who I am."

On top of being the oldest and natural leader of four, when I was 9, I witnessed my parents go through, in my eyes, a very messy divorce. This made me feel responsible to step up even more than I had before, as if I needed to be the one to look after my siblings and myself. I had to decide if I would continue being a kid or step up and be the leader that my siblings needed. I chose the latter. I knew that because my parents were no longer together, my role as the oldest had changed. I went from being a kid to being the "mini adult," the "ultimate oldest." I saw my mom cry, and I worked hard so she wouldn't have to worry after a busy day at her job, ensuring my siblings had dinner, my middle sister had her homework done, and everyone was taken care of. I was the new leader, which often led to putting myself last.

There's a unique kind of pressure that comes with being the firstborn. We are often praised for being mature, responsible, capable—yet admonished as the ones who "should know better." Behind the praise can be a subtle lie that says: *Your value is in what you do for others.* It didn't take long for me to confuse leadership with identity. If I was helping, fixing, or guiding, then I was valuable. But the moment I didn't know what to do or couldn't hold it all together, shame would creep in. I wasn't just failing at something—I was failing as someone. I wasn't leading from identity. I was leading to gain my identity.

Growing up in this way led me to live what I now call a "Martha life." In Luke 10 is a story that feels all too familiar to me. Two sisters, Mary and Martha, have vastly different experiences when it comes to spending time with Jesus. Mary spends her time with Jesus while Martha does all the work around them, which leads to Martha being frustrated (as I often was). So Martha asks Jesus to tell Mary to help her. But He simply replies: *"Martha, Martha,... you are worried and upset about many things, but few things are needed—or indeed only one. Mary has chosen what is better"* (Luke 10:41-42 NIV).

Martha was leading by organizing, serving, and managing. But she was leading disconnected from her identity. Mary, on the other hand, found her identity at the feet of Jesus. Mary knew that intimacy had to come before impact. That's the shift. When we lead from identity, we're not chasing affirmation; we're rooted in it.

One of the most powerful Scriptures about identity comes from Jeremiah. Before Jeremiah ever spoke a prophetic word, before he led anyone, God had already appointed him. That means God's calling was based on who

Jeremiah was, not what he did; on being, not doing.

"Before I formed you in the womb I knew you, before you were born I set you apart" (Jeremiah 1:15 NIV).

This is where so many of us get stuck, especially as firstborns: We try to become worthy of the call, but in Christ, worthiness is the starting point, not the reward. We don't lead for acceptance. We lead from it.

The search for my identity often took me down dark and winding paths. I became a rebellious pre-teen (although I don't think my mom would describe me like that) and started trying to fit in. I had my "church friends" and my "life friends." My life friends were school friends I spent weekends with. We were a bit edgy—wearing a lot of black clothing, dark eye makeup, and some of us had piercings. All the pressure of being a leader had resulted in me no longer wanting to be a leader. I wanted to be a follower—to do what my friends were doing, to let them lead me. This new attitude, however, didn't dispel my feelings of failing as a person. Instead, I felt like I was failing every single day, which led me into a deep depression.

My depression wasn't what you would typically expect from a teenager in the early to late 2000s. It took my whole life with it. I defined myself as depressed and often thought to myself, *I am not a leader. How am I a leader when I can't even control my emotions?* But every single day, I would go home and pretend to be a normal, functioning teenager. If people could see me as a leader, then I was a leader. And if I was a leader, I wasn't failing as a person; I was doing fine. In their eyes, I was still a leader because I wasn't failing them. But I was searching for a new identity, and every once in a while, I would find it. Every youth conference got me closer to finding my identity in Christ, but when I went home—and returned to school—my insecurities and lack of identity came rushing back.

By my senior year of high school, I was sure that I knew who I was. I was no longer as depressed, but I was just existing. I was leading at church on the worship team and as a Sunday School teacher, and at school as the Vice President of Pep Club, President of Warriors 4 Christ, and in my choir and theatre department. But I was still only leading to be seen, get scholarships, and receive recognition. I was leading for selfish reasons, including so that people would like me. Eventually, I began finding my identity in a relationship; I didn't need to be a leader anymore because I considered that the man I was dating was the leader. That's at least what I'd learned. So why would I lead if this man was leading me? And lead me, he did. He led me to a place of self-hatred, addiction, and surviving purely out of spite. I recognize today that he was not completely to blame; he led, but I chose to follow. And I take full responsibility for my part in that.

After a very messy breakup my sophomore year of college, I started to spiral. I dropped out of school and began partying, partaking in various drugs. That became my identity. Alcohol and drugs seemed to quiet the voice in my head that told me I was failing; they made me feel invincible. After all, I was still able to keep a job and be a productive member of society—just not between the hours of 10 pm and 4 am Friday through Sunday.

As many times as I've failed, I have been saved. On a very snowy and cold morning in February 2014, I knew that if something didn't change, I would die. That meant I would be the worst leader, because you can't lead when you're dead. The night before, I had gone a little off the rails. The night ended with one of my best friends breaking down a bathroom door at a party to carry me out. When I woke up the next day, I knew exactly what I needed to do. I needed to make a new start. Not only did I need to leave, but I needed to be with my mom and my siblings. The next day, I called my mom and told her I wanted to move to Florida the following month.

As of today, I am over 11 years clean of any drugs. Getting clean led me to my true identity: my identity in Christ.

I didn't understand my full identity in Christ until 2022, when I attended a new church. The day I walked into Anchor Church, I felt completely transformed. I felt an overwhelming sense of identity, something I hadn't experienced in years. This didn't come because I was leaning into leading; it came because, for the first time ever, the Holy Spirit became alive and active in me.

Sitting in one of the top rows of the sanctuary, a rush of sensations overcame me. I looked around, wondering what was happening. After the service was over, my emotions flooded my body. I had known Pastor Shaun and Pastor Teresa Blakeney for years, but seeing them that time felt different. They both wrapped me in a hug, and all the feelings I had been holding in came out in a rush of tears. I knew that I needed to be there, and I knew from that moment, my life would be transformed—I just didn't know how.

About two weeks into attending Anchor Church, Pastor Teresa approached me, "I know you sing. We're having worship team auditions in a few weeks. Pray about it." It was like she saw something in me that I had been pushing away for years. She saw a calling in me that I didn't even want to think about anymore. A calling that I thought I had thrown away.

I walked out of church that Sunday and called my mom, "I think I'm auditioning for the worship team." A few days later, I did. After only a few weeks of being there, I was leading again. But this time, something was completely different. I wasn't leading to be seen or gain recognition; I was leading because I felt a calling on my life.

My call didn't come from being thrown into leadership or feeling obligated to lead. Instead, it was as if a switch flipped and a light bulb ignited in my soul. I understood that all the failure I had felt was not a failure in God's eyes. I had not failed at leadHERship ordained by God; I had failed at performance-based leadership, which was what I lived for—it was the air I breathed. Leaning into my identity as a Christ-centered leadHER was something I had never experienced. Reprogramming my way of living and thinking was one of the most herculean tasks I've ever done, but I learned that past failures do not define leadHERship; God does!

I still catch myself slipping into performance-based leadership more often than I'd like to admit. When I'm trying to meet deadlines at work, feeling responsible for the outcomes of the social media team at church, or even just showing up for the people in my life day to day, sometimes there's still this whisper: "You have to hold it all together. If you don't do it, no one will. If you mess this up, it says something about you." That's the mindset of performance-based leadership. And it's sneaky—because from the outside, it looks like excellence, commitment, and responsibility. But internally, it can be driven by fear, insecurity, or the need to prove my worth.

So now, when I am feeling that tension—the urge to prove or produce to feel valuable, I pause. I ask myself the questions that recalibrate my heart:

- *Am I doing this to be loved, or because I already am loved?*
- *Am I leading to be seen, or because I've already been known?*
- *Am I driven by expectation, or led by identity?*

These are not just nice questions for me to reflect on—they're lifelines in the moments when I'm tempted to make performance instead of Christ my foundation.

When I'm working and everything feels urgent, I remind myself that I am not defined by the number of tasks I complete.

When I'm leading a church team and the outcomes aren't meeting my expectations, I remember I am a steward, not a savior.

When I'm with friends or family and I feel like I need to "be strong" or "keep it together," I remind myself that vulnerability is not weakness; it's often the truest form of leadHERship.

LeadHERship isn't about having all the answers. It's about being anchored in the One who is the answer. Because if I lead disconnected from who I am in Christ, I'll always lead from a place of depletion. I'll overextend. I'll overperform. I'll overcompensate. But when I lead from my identity—knowing I am loved, chosen, and already approved, I lead with peace, clarity, and joy. So, no matter the setting—office, sanctuary, living room, or even the quiet places no one sees, the goal isn't to impress people. It's to be present with God. Because leadHERship that lasts must be rooted in love that doesn't shift when the outcomes do.

For so much of my life, I saw being the oldest as a weight. It came with unspoken responsibilities, invisible expectations, and a constant need to be "on." I wasn't just the oldest sibling—I was the example, the fixer, the helper, the one everyone looked to and leaned on. Whether anyone ever said it out loud or not, I felt it in my bones: *You don't get to fall apart. You're the strong one.* And for a while, I wore that identity. It kept me moving. It made me useful. But eventually, it also made me tired. Resentful, even. I didn't just feel responsible for people—I felt responsible for their outcomes. If someone I led struggled, I took it personally. If something went wrong, I wondered what I could have done differently. The blessing of leadership began to feel like a burden I never asked for. But here's what God began to teach me—gently and consistently: *Being the oldest wasn't an accident. But it also wasn't my identity.*

Yes, I was born first in my family. But more importantly, I was born again in Christ. That means I no longer have to carry the false weight of being everyone's answer. I'm not the rescuer. I'm not the solution. I'm not the glue that holds everything together. That's Jesus. He doesn't ask me to carry others—He invited me to carry His presence. He doesn't expect me to figure it all out—He reminds me He already has. He's not impressed by my ability to lead under pressure, but He's drawn to my willingness to lead in surrender. And maybe that's the redemption of firstborn leadership: learning that I don't have to prove I was born to lead, but coming to trust that I was born again in His love.

There's a shift that happens when you surrender your firstborn mindset at the feet of Jesus. You realize that leadHERship is not a title to uphold; leadHERship is a calling to embody. And the calling doesn't begin with striving; it begins with belonging. I don't lead to become something anymore. I lead because I already am:

- A daughter of God
- A vessel of His Spirit
- A reflection of His love
- A leadHER—not because I earned it, but because He entrusted it

The blessing of being the oldest wasn't just in what I was born into—it's in what I was born for. And when I surrendered that blessing to Jesus, it became a holy responsibility, not a crushing weight. It became a joy, not a job. It became a ministry, not a mask.

LeadHERship is a daily part of my life, but now I carry it differently. I no longer lead because I'm the oldest, or because people expect me to have it all together. I lead because I know who I am in Christ. My worth isn't tied to my productivity, position, or performance—it is rooted in my identity as a daughter of God.

> Trust in the Lord with all your heart; do not depend on your own understanding. Seek his will in all you do, and he will show you which path to take (Proverbs 3:5-6 NLT).

That truth reminds me that I don't have to earn influence; I am simply to carry His presence. Now, whether I'm organizing a project, leading worship, or running a team, I show up not to prove myself, but to reflect Him.

I no longer lead to be seen, validated, or accepted. I lead because I've already been chosen. Already been called. Already been loved.

I now lead *from* identity, not *for* identity. That's the greatest gift of all. That is godly leadHERship!

Leading with Hope

By DeAnn Alaine

About one year into our marriage, on the Sundays that my husband and I didn't have a congregation to minister to as evangelists, we would attend the church that the Lord called us to visit. We didn't have a regular income, and pretty much every week, I would think, "Oh my gosh, I *hope* the Lord will move on someone's heart to invite us out to dinner after church so we can eat at a buffet and fill our bellies and be completely satisfied."

During those days, I continuously used the word "hope" flippantly as a circumstantial moment to keep me from going crazy! I can't even begin to guess the number of times I used the phrase, "I hope so," as a convenient reply to someone!

Hope in the Bible is not wishful thinking; it is the confident expectation that, as we abide in Jesus, He will fulfill His promises.

Now, looking back to that season of our lives, I realize how abusive I was to the word hope. While I was hoping for something good, as a Christian, I was neglecting to glory in the hope of the Lord Himself. In the Bible, when the Lord talks about hope, it goes far beyond our circumstances, centering on our hope in Him that stems from a right and pure intent of the heart. As leadHERs, we must provide hope for those around us that is far greater than what our service can offer. As God's commissioned people, we are to lead others to a proper hope in the Lord. The true hope of why we do what we do isn't for earthly gain, it's for the sake of salvation.

I needed to make a major shift in the object of my hope. I had to repent before the Lord for using Christian terminology simply as a means to keep me from going crazy, applying it improperly in my life, and not seeing the full extent of the magnificent hope Jesus offers us.

Here's what the Bible says about hope. *We have also obtained access through him by faith into this grace in which we stand, and we boast in the hope of the glory of God. And not only that, but we also boast in our afflictions because we know that affliction produces endurance; endurance produces proven character, and proven character produces hope. This hope will not disappoint us, because God's love has been poured out in our hearts through the Holy Spirit who was given to us* (Romans 5:2-5 CSB).

Oh my goodness, I was making hope only about what was happening in my life! Ugg. I needed to actualize a fundamental shift in my head and heart! Okay, what does it mean to be in one accord with what the Word says God's hope is, and what can I have hope in? Here we gooooo!!!

> I pray that the eyes of your heart may be enlightened so that you may know what is the hope of his calling, what is the wealth of his glorious inheritance in the saints, and what is the immeasurable greatness of his power toward us who believe, according to the mighty working of his strength (Ephesians 1:18-19 CSB).

What is the hope of His calling? Jesus' call to be born fully man on Earth was so that He could gain salvation for us! We have the hope of salvation because Jesus provided it on the cross.

We also have hope in the promises of God's Word! It's commonly stated that God made over 3000 promises to His people in the Bible. That's a lot of hope! And we know God will never go against His Word, so our hope is secure.

God wanted to make known among the Gentiles the glorious wealth of this mystery, which is Christ in you, the hope of glory (Colossians 1:27 CSB). Y'all, this means that believers have the confident expectation of experiencing

God's glory today, tomorrow, and into eternity!

The most glorious application of our hope as Christians is our anticipation of God's promise of our eternity in heaven. My hope must be in Jesus because of His finished work on the cross. His sacrifice and resurrection power give us hope more glorious than any buffet.

So if we're going to lead others to hope, let's lead them to the promises God has given us for today, and to the hope of glory! .

. . . .

Sybill Reardon

Sybill Reardon was born in the town of Salem, Ohio, and raised in a Quaker church, committing her life to Christ at a young age. She moved with her mother and siblings to Florida when she was 15, where she attended and graduated from G-Star School of the Arts. At 20, Sybill left home and moved back to Ohio to stay with her father. There, she struggled with losing her faith, drug and alcohol dependency, and homelessness after a miscarriage. After two years, she moved back with her mother in Florida. Though she was still struggling with drug addiction, she decided it was time to get her life back together. She asked for help from her mother and stepfather, who held her accountable, and she returned to church.

Sybill works in downtown Charleston at the Housing Authority. She also works part-time as a Social Media Manager at Freedom Support Solutions. She resides with her husband and her beloved animals and loves to spend her free time reading, watching movies, and being with her family and her husband.

Stepping Out of Delay and Into Destiny

By Sybill Reardon

> *"It shall not be so among you. But whoever would be great among you must be your servant, and whoever would be first among you must be your slave, even as the Son of Man came not to be served but to serve, and to give his life as a ransom for many"* (Matthew 20:26-28 ESV).

"Why is God letting me suffer like this? Doesn't He see or hear me?" I asked myself these questions countless times in my life.

I grew up in the church, was baptized as a baby, went to church with my family every Sunday, said the prayers, asked God to be my Lord and Savior, ate the stale cracker, and drank the grape juice. I did everything I needed to do to be a good Christian, so I thought. Yet, I still felt stuck in a place with no way out.

My parents divorced while I was young, and my father left my mom to raise four children on her own. My mom remarried soon after, and my life became filled with emotional abuse at the hands of my stepfather. I struggled through my days, which included constant broken promises from my biological father, rumors about me that circulated in school, and bullying. I didn't know who to turn to. I needed saving from an early age, but I didn't trust anyone enough to tell them. So the questions continued in my mind: *Am I damaged? Doesn't God love me?*

I was 15 when I first tried to take my own life. My mom had divorced her second husband and moved us from Ohio to Florida, leaving all my friends in Ohio. She decided to marry Allen. Allen and I were always bumping heads. In my mind, I was right, and he was wrong. He didn't know me; he wasn't my dad. *Who is this guy to think he can tell me what to do, who I can talk to, and who I can hang out with?*

I didn't make friends very fast, which left me to eat alone a lot of days at the beginning of my first year of high school. Even when I did finally make friends, I didn't want to share with them what I was going through because I didn't want to burden them. The devil would sit in my ear, whispering, "Why would they care about your problems?" So, I just suffered alone. Or so I thought.

When I was 21, I moved back to Ohio to be with my biological father. During that year and a half, I became homeless and addicted to drugs. I was drinking and partying almost every night, sleeping on friends' couches or in my car. I constantly worried about where my next meal would come from, where I would sleep that night, and if I would be warm enough in the harsh Ohio winters. I stole from stores when I didn't have the money to buy food.

I constantly lied to my mom on our weekly phone calls. Before I moved back to Ohio, she had warned me that it was not in God's plan for my life, so I would tell her that my life was great. Never once did I mention my drug use, homelessness, or hunger; I didn't want to worry her or hear the phrase, "I told you so." Even though I was at my lowest, I made it seem like I was looking forward to a great life ahead of me. I wanted to prove to everyone that I could make it on my own. I was a follower, and I knew it.

In the midst of my drug addiction, I suffered a miscarriage, which made me feel even more alone. I thought there was no way anyone on this earth could understand what I was going through. The pain I suffered mentally and physically was like pure torture. I felt like less of a person, like a part of me had died when I lost the baby. I allowed that pain and hurt to eat at me.

Only a few people knew about the miscarriage, including my father. When I told him, he said, "It just wasn't in God's plan for you." And although it wasn't, in the midst of going through what felt like torture, I didn't want to hear that.

My drinking and drug use became heavier as I tried literally anything to numb the hurt I felt inside. I didn't want to feel anymore. I couldn't face what had happened to me, what I had done to myself. I couldn't tell people that I failed as a woman, a mom, and a daughter. The devil sat on my shoulder and whispered degrading and harmful words in my ear, and I believed them. I believed him.

I traveled with a friend of mine to Pennsylvania; while there in the hotel, I decided it was time to call my mom. I didn't want to live that way anymore. I was tired of the drugs and sick of the pain. Drowning my sorrows in drugs and alcohol was not helping me numb anymore. I was exhausted mentally and physically.

With tears in my eyes, I took my phone and stepped into the hall of the hotel, out of earshot from my friends. I didn't want them to know yet what I had decided. My mom, step-dad, and siblings were in line at Disney, just about to get on a ride. My mom answered, and all I said was, "I want to come home." She was definitely happy to hear it.

My mom told my step-dad what I said, and he was on a plane literally the next day, coming to bring me home. He flew into the airport, I picked him up with my car packed with the few things I had left to my name, and we drove the 17+ hours back to Florida. He never hesitated. He never second-guessed my decision. He acted on God's words. Proverbs 3:27 says, *Do not withhold from those to whom it is due, when it is in your power to do it* (ESV). I thank God every day that my mom and dad had it in their hearts to act. To help me escape the mess I had made for myself, the mess I made of myself.

I made more mistakes after my return to Florida—I neglected to deal with the pain of losing my child, and addiction continued its grip on me. I also still hid my hurt because of embarrassment. I attended church with my family, was re-baptized, and did all the things a "good Christian" should do, but those things never relieved me of my pain. I would sit in service and listen to the preacher talk about God and how He is always there, but I never felt like those messages really applied to me. Surely, God hadn't been with me as I was going through my trauma. A young child forced to deal with a broken home, a woman, racked with guilt, pain, drugs, and a miscarriage. Surely, God had just closed His eyes to my pain, turned His head when I needed Him most. Why couldn't He see me then?

I sat in church, asking God, "Why would you let me suffer like that? Why didn't you do something?"

In Isaiah 41:10, God says, *"Don't be afraid, for I am with you. Don't be discouraged, for I am your God. I will strengthen you and help you. I will hold you up with my victorious right hand."* (NLT), but I couldn't see that. I didn't understand that He was always walking beside me, protecting and looking out for me. I didn't realize that He was waiting for me to recognize that He put people in my life who would help lift me back up. I needed to open my eyes to Him and His plan. I needed to extend my hand.

Remembering where I was back then and knowing where I am now, I am so grateful that God let me go through some of the things I experienced because they helped me grow into the woman I am today. As I look back on my past, I am just amazed at how much God was there with me through all of it. Not only did He get me through, but He used what I went through to put me on a path to help others with my testimony. I now have the privilege of assisting families in low-income situations with housing, which I do with compassion as I know the pain and loneliness of being homeless firsthand.

Although I certainly wasn't a leader for a long part of my story, God had a plan and was using all I went through to make me into the leadHER He made me to be.

When you look up the word "leader," the definition states that a leader is someone who guides, inspires, and motivates others towards a common goal. So what does God say about being a leadHER? The Bible defines leadership as someone who serves others, guided by God's principles and example, with a focus on spiritual growth and well-being.

So, what does it mean to be a leadHER for God? A leadHER is a person who serves others in a godly, purposeful, humble, empathetic, wise, and faithful way.

The Bible tells of Jesus washing His disciples' feet. I had read that story many times since I was a child. I actually memorized it. But it wasn't until I became an adult that I truly understood what it meant. In Matthew 20:26, Jesus told His disciples, *"Whoever desires to become great among you, let him be your servant"* (NKJV). Godly leadHERship is rooted in serving others, not in seeking to be served. Let's look at the bigger picture: If Jesus could stop to serve, so can we. When we serve His people, He equips us with the tools needed to be a leadHER.

I serve others through my job. Working in housing can be a thankless job sometimes—it is difficult work dealing with people day in and out. But being surrounded by coworkers who build you up and don't tear you down is a blessing. I thank God that He has provided me with my coworkers, who are godly, loving, and caring women. Each woman in my office is a blessing to me as she looks out for me, gives advice when I need it, and is a listening ear when I need to vent. I'm grateful that God's path for me included caring people in my life who lift me up.

Another difficult lesson I've learned is that a leadHER must be humble. Gaining humility was difficult for me. I wanted recognition—a pat on the back telling me I did a good job. I wanted the "attagirl"; after all, I pulled myself up from the mess I had put myself in. But honestly, I didn't pull myself up; all the glory goes to God. He was the driving force in my life. He pushed me to become a better person; to become the person I needed to be for my future self. Humility is something I still struggle with. When something goes the way I need and want it to, I tend to pat myself on the back and say, "Good job, me," then I realize it was never about me. It always comes back to His work.

The hard truth is, I am not the boss. I am not the one in control. God is the source of it all for me. He is the reason I am where I am today. Humility is not a form of self-depreciation. Instead, it is the realization of how great our God is and how much we depend on Him. I had to give up control of my own life to God to be able to walk with His purpose for me. As a control freak, that was definitely hard for me to do. However, taking a step back from my own problems and issues has shown me how little I really have to do in the process of my life. Yes, God gives us all free will, but when we relinquish that control to Him, He will do things in your life you never thought possible.

> Blessed is the one who finds wisdom, and the one who gets understanding (Proverbs 3:13 ESV).

Wisdom is a key factor of being a leadHER. Looking back through my life, I realize that God is now using my knowledge and wisdom to keep me on the straight and narrow. While I was abusing drugs, homeless, and grieving my unborn child, I couldn't see how God could possibly use me or my story to uplift people. How could my story help others? I am a nobody. Now, however, I can see that God was molding me and giving me wisdom and insight. I now use my personal experiences and stories to provide comfort and wisdom to other people who are in similar circumstances. I can tell my story to people, sharing that I understand and know where they are on their journey in life—because I have been there. And I've gotten through it by the grace of God.

Empathy is something I lacked for a long time. When I was going through my trials and tribulations, it was only about me, myself, and I. That's all that mattered to me. I did not care about other people's emotions or what they thought. All that mattered to me was how I felt; how I was suffering. Now, I can not only see how my actions affect others, but I've also learned to understand and share others' feelings—to empathize.

Empathy plays a huge role in leadHERship. It can be easy to get wrapped up in our own lives and our own work. When we focus on only ourselves—even on something as noble as work and accomplishing goals—we often fail to acknowledge what others are experiencing. It can be easy to see people only as problems that need to be solved, rather than as human beings who require love and attention. We all need someone to listen to and not judge us. A leadHER can be that person.

A word of warning: It can be easy to get lost filling other people's cups. Being a go-to person for a lot of people is difficult. Early on, I filled other people's cups without filling my own, and my emotional cup started running dry. I became burnt out, trying to help a lot of people at once because I didn't have someone I could trust. Or so I thought. I finally recognized that God put people in my life to talk to and lean on when I needed it most—like my husband. Deon became my God-given rock when I didn't even know I needed one.

Being accountable is essential to being a leadHER. The Bible emphasizes that leaders are accountable to God and the people they lead. I learned that even being under the influence of drugs did not dismiss me from being responsible for my actions. Being held accountable and being judged are two vastly different things. God didn't give me a pass because I was going through something difficult—I neglected to do what God called me to do as a Christian. Scripture says that a wise person accepts correction gladly because it helps them. Personally, I didn't know how to accept correction—that's something that I still struggle with today. God doesn't offer corrections to bring us down, but to move us to the right path. As you grow in Christ, be certain to surround yourself with godly individuals who will offer correction to help you grow, not in an effort to cut you down. And when God spurs you to offer correction to others as a leadHER, be certain you are guiding them with the correct heart—one that is leading them to God and His will.

My life now is far different than it once was; I have only God to thank for that. I have two stable jobs—leading people in need of housing and working as a social media manager. I have a roof over my head, food in my stomach, and people in my life who help guide me to be the woman God is calling me to be.

I am grateful that God has put me in a position where I can love others the way He loves me. I just had to stop trying to tell God what I wanted and listen to Him telling me where to go and who to trust. Because I listened, He has also given me a loving and caring husband and two beautiful bonus boys, who I get to learn from every day about what it means to be living in His light.

God calls us all to be leadHERs for His kingdom. Stop procrastinating and start today! You don't need to wait on God—He is already there, listening and walking beside you.

In fact, God may be waiting on *you*—to acknowledge Him, trust Him, and follow Him. I know He was waiting on me. I finally said yes. I stepped out of my delay into my destiny. I pray you will, too.

Natalie B. Green

Natalie B. Green is a passionate speaker, author, certified life coach, and entrepreneur who empowers people to boldly walk in their God-given purpose. Based in Miami, Florida, she is the visionary behind two powerful women's movements: Unbroken Women's Encounter and the Women of Purpose Fellowship and Conference, where she creates spirit-filled spaces for women to heal, grow, and lead.

With a heart to serve God and His people, Natalie does so with grace and unwavering faith at Heart of God Ministries Church, alongside her husband, James A. Green. She also leads several thriving businesses: Natalie B. Green International, Shift Masters, LLC staffing agency, and NBTT Event Management, all built on Kingdom values. She serves on the Advisory Council for the Association of Christian Businesswomen and the Board of Directors for Elect Ladies Kingdom Network.

Natalie's books, including *Get Out of that Box: Unleash the Giant in You* and *10 Superpowers of Effective Leaders: Neutralizing Toxicity in Team Culture,* reflect her heart for transformation, leadership, and kingdom excellence.

To learn more or book Natalie, visit www.nataliebgreen.com or email natalie@nataliebgreen.com.

I Belong Here

By Natalie B. Green

God called me into ministry at what I thought was the worst possible time in my life, and I can't say I stepped joyfully into becoming a pastor's wife and speaker. Though I didn't run, I thought God had His timing wrong; I was in the beginning stages of some of the most tumultuous times in my life. However, that didn't seem to matter to God. And I had no idea what was about to take place in the days, months, and years that followed.

> For our light affliction, which is but for a moment, is working for us a far more exceeding and eternal weight of glory (2 Corinthians 4:17 NKJV).

As the fifth of seven children born to a single mother, I had a very challenging childhood. We had very little and suffered much at the hands of unkind humans. At the age of 14, I became a follower of Jesus and, for many years, I served Him faithfully. He rescued me from much, so I had a sense that somehow God owed me, and would not allow terrible things to happen to me. After all, I was the good child, despite my environment, and I had already been through enough, or so I thought. I can say that in jest now, but with that attitude, I was in for a rude awakening.

I would come to know that all my righteous acts were as filthy rags (Isaiah 64:6) and that the depth of adversity I endured was allowed by the Father as a means of equipping me with the grace and glory I would need to carry out my kingdom assignment. If God had asked, I'm sure I could have offered a better plan to achieve His goal of refining me without all the gory parts, but He didn't.

My call to ministry began when my husband and I left the comfort of a ministry where he had been employed for about thirteen years to start a church in the inner city with a handful of people and no promise of support. Shortly thereafter, I began to receive invitations to speak at conferences and events; I could not understand how God was moving me forward despite the storms in my life. In hindsight, I recognize that my survival at the time literally depended on my pressing into God, so I was fully tuned into Him. The words written in James 4:8 became life to me: *Draw near to God, and he will draw near to you* (ESV).

There were times I was too overwhelmed with sorrow to formulate what I considered to be effective prayers. When I was overtaken with concern about how our family would survive this decision to answer the call to ministry with no source of sustainable income for our home and the ministry, I learned to offer sacrificial praise—to gather my strength and worship my heavenly Father, hoping He would read between the lines and meet me at the point of my need. I knew that God had a plan for me and that He uses everything—the good, bad, or indifferent. I also knew that eventually morning would break through the darkness of the night season I was in.

> His anger is but for a moment, His favor is for life; Weeping may endure for a night, But joy comes in the morning (Psalm 30:5 NKJV).

One of the greatest Bible stories that depicts someone embracing the fullness of a divine process to position themselves in a place of purpose, even when everything he encountered along the way appeared to be leading in the opposite direction, is that of Joseph. Joseph, the dreamer, turned into Joseph, the savior of a nation. In Genesis chapter 37, we find the beginning of the dramatic, big-screen worthy account. Joseph underwent a variety of adverse circumstances on the way to what we now know as his place of belonging.

Reflecting on the story of Joseph stirs up vivid memories of the turmoil I faced at the start of ministry, when, along with financial challenges, our teenage daughter began to struggle with behavioral issues. These circumstances led to many sleepless nights. Phone calls from the school, explosive arguments at home, and pushing of the proverbial envelope made for an extremely disturbing reality. As if that were not enough, the results of my husband's previously high-stress work environment began to show up in a way that felt like we were in the middle of a war zone. Everything seemed to be falling apart all at once, and I had no power to fix it.

I experienced so much shame in those days. I felt inadequate, disqualified, and displaced, but something inside of me kept telling me I was right where I belonged. From where I stood, ministry was to blame. I believed that being in ministry put us under a microscope that enabled adversity to hit us where it hurt the most. I probably quit a thousand times in my mind, hoping that if I walked away, the storm would pass. Then there was the moment when I knew. I knew that there was something inside of me that empowered me to endure beyond my own natural ability.

Joseph did not get a newer version of his previous dream. In the same way, I didn't get a new word from God about ministry—things just began to unfold before me. I recall being invited to speak at an event, and when it was over, I received a great number of comments from attendees about how powerful and life-changing the word was. This began to happen every time

I went somewhere to speak. One night, I told my husband I was surprised God was moving in such a way. Immediately, I heard a voice from within me say, "Don't ever say that again. You should expect me to move." Then Zechariah 4:6 dropped into my mind, *"Not by might nor by power, but by My Spirit," Says the Lord of hosts* (NKJV).

That was a turning point in my life. I knew then God had anointed and called me to do what I was doing. I learned that my circumstances did not disqualify me, but they prepared me for the place where I belonged. I must admit, the problems did not go away overnight. There was still a very long road ahead before a substantial change in our family dynamic would take place. The greatest change I experienced was not in the chaos outside of me. Instead, God dealt with the chaos swarming within me, and through the power and might of the Spirit of God, a mindset shift began. God gave me a different perspective on His processes, enabling me to observe my life and calling through a different lens. I call that surrender.

I realized that wherever I found myself, if I was on the pathway to fulfilling my destiny, I was never without the all-seeing eye of the Father who crafted me for a particular work. Wherever I was, if I surrendered to the call of God, I belonged there. Right in the middle of what I thought were the worst of times, an I-belong-here heart posture began to take shape within me.

In retrospect, God used that season to refine me and prepare me to be a pastor, speaker, and entrepreneur. This refining uncovered something about me that I could not see. The truth is, after all the years I had walked with God, there was a great need for sanctification in my life. Fear, impatience, pride, and self-reliance were exposed and uprooted out of my heart, assuring me that I desperately needed to walk out my calling. It's one thing to receive a calling, and another thing to recognize God's equipping to stand up under the weight of that calling.

My brethren, count it all joy when you fall into various trials, knowing that the testing of your faith produces patience. But let patience have its perfect work, that you may be perfect and complete, lacking nothing (James 1:2-4 NKJV).

To stand confidently in the place I belong, I had to stand faithfully through being a pastor's wife with a child who was being enticed into a reckless lifestyle that included addiction and idol worship. There was so much conflict in our home that it felt like a prison. We were being gripped by the darkness of poverty of soul, yet we were called. Our work of ministry continued, as did the process that produced a weight of glory that, to this day, elicits an awe that brings me to tears.

I belong here—in every place God grants me access, whether in ministry or business—not because I am special, but because I surrendered. Amid the adversary's attempts to take me out, I reached for the Savior. I continued to offer Him the sacrifice of praise.

At times, my own thoughts became my enemy. I told myself I was not one of God's favorites and I was not worthy to be used because my life was so imperfect. What I saw in others, I didn't see in myself, so I thought I was unqualified. I literally had to hang on to passages like James 1:2-4 like a life preserver, so I didn't drown in a sea of turmoil.

I lived and breathed the Bible accounts of Joseph, who thrived and rose to power with a grace and a conviction that what the enemy meant for evil, God uses for His own will and purposes. I held ever so tightly to Acts 27, where it is written that the Apostle Paul was caught up in a deadly storm but received a word from the Lord that if he remained on the ship (which I liken to remaining faithful to the call), he and all those with him would be saved.

> *For I consider that the sufferings of this present time are not worthy to be compared with the glory which shall be revealed in us* (Romans 8:18 NKJV).

Everyone's journey to where they belong is unique. We must each seek God, asking Him to reveal His glory in our lives. His sufficient grace is conferred upon each of us as the Spirit of God desires, based on the calling He has assigned. I came to understand that my journey was unique because my calling was unique.

I did not get a pass on God's calling because I was being processed. It was the process that gave power and authority to the calling. God's glory was on me. Many times, I felt I was ill-equipped, but I showed up anyway, accepting invitations to speak. I learned that if I gave God what I had, He would make up the difference through the power of Holy Spirit, who was ever with me. There was joy in the faces of the people, because God's glory was on me in the place where I belonged.

> *They that sow in tears shall reap in joy. He that goeth forth and weepeth, bearing precious seed, shall doubtless come again with rejoicing, bringing his sheaves with him* (Psalm 126:5-6 KJV).

A trail of tears—flowing both from my difficult circumstances and the wonder of God's presence—led me like breadcrumbs down the path to becoming a minister, where I belong. I became acutely aware that my tears are not spare parts; they are given as a gift by my Creator as a means of enabling me to release the pressure of both physical and soul pain. Instead of holding them back, I let them flow freely in painful moments, to wash me and serve as an offering of praise as I behold the wonder of His glory and power.

Many of us have been taught from our youth that "big girls don't cry," but I beg to differ. Psalm 56:8 (NLT) tells us, *You keep track of all my sorrows. You have collected all my tears in your bottle. You have recorded each one in your book.* I often say to the Lord, "My tears don't mean I don't trust You; they just mean it hurts." God gets it. He is not intimidated by our tears.

I sowed in tears of sorrow, but there came a day when my tears turned to joy because the harvest time had come. After years of great struggle throughout her teen years and leaving home before she was 18, my daughter returned to us and to the Lord. She is now a powerfully anointed worship leader with the heart of an evangelist.

I answered God's call to ministry while in the middle of much trouble. To this day, I find myself crying as I minister the Word of God. My tears are not for effect, but an expression of passion for the place of ministry where I belong. I pour my life out through tear-stained eyes. The I-belong-here paradigm causes me to believe that if I serve God's people, even through teary eyes, then God would send someone to minister to me and my family. Yes, He does!

I could not pray my way out of my process; I had to pray my way through it. Partnering with the Holy Spirit was an absolute must. There were days when, in my flesh, all I wanted to do was sleep all day and all night in hopes that something would have broken by the time I awakened. But in my spirit, I knew I had to get up and continue my journey, trusting God that my someday would turn into today. So, I got up! I would not allow my bed to become a prison. I held on to the promise and hope for a breakthrough. I literally spoke to myself, saying, "I am a prisoner of hope."

Holy Spirit reminds me time and again through Psalm 23 that the same Shepherd who provides for my needs and leads me to green pastures and beside still waters does not become missing in action when I encounter the valley and the shadows of death. He assures me that He is ever present, in the best of times and in the worst of times, I can count on Him to lead me through to the place where I belong.

The Bible tells us, *The gifts and callings of God are without repentance* (Romans 11:29 KJV); it does not tell us they are without trouble. The value of this understanding enables me to step joyfully into God's calling because I know the source of the call and the One who empowers me to complete the assignment.

But whatever I am now, it is all because God poured out his special favor on me—and not without results... yet it was not I but God who was working through me by his grace (1 Corinthians 15:10 NLT).

My journey through Scripture led me to pray prayers that challenged what I believed about myself. I had previously believed I didn't have what it took to be a pastor's wife, speaker, and businesswoman. I constructed and embraced an identity based on traumatic times in my life that produced an underlying fear, which remained hidden until a time when my calling required me to be fearless. I am so grateful for the season when the Father made me aware of this stronghold and stumbling block of fear, and graced me with the courage to confront and conquer it.

Arise, shine; For your light has come! And the glory of the Lord is risen upon you. For behold, the darkness shall cover the earth, And deep darkness the people; But the Lord will arise over you, And His glory will be seen upon you (Isaiah 60:1-2 NKJV).

The pivotal moment that changed everything! When I struggled to believe that I was where I belonged, God embraced me and reminded me that everything I had endured up to that moment had prepared me for what was unfolding before me, if I would only take the step forward and show up, shaking in my boots or not. I finally got the opportunity to speak to a group of people from various walks of life, which was something I had prayed for, but couldn't believe would really happen.

Wow! That moment in my life seemed so unreal to me. My life was about to take a turn in the direction of my prayers and dreams. There I was about to do what I had only imagined was possible. Yet, I held so tightly to the image

I had constructed about myself that it served as a gatekeeper of my destiny. Therefore, when the time to walk into the next season of God's intention for me had come, fear gripped me, and my heart was racing.

While waves of emotion rushed over me, I knew beyond any doubt that I was exactly where I belonged. I was confident that everything I had encountered up to that point in my life had prepared me for that moment. Yet I stood there, overcome with anxiety. This pivot would demand my boldness to ignore the deafening sound of dispiriting thoughts and take a life-defining leap of faith, and I took it! That was the moment I realized that faith is not required only for the prayers we pray and the dreams we dream, but also when we receive the answer.

Dear one, the point of this writing is to share with you how I stepped joyfully into God's calling as a kingdom leadHER. There is a moment in every season when the steps become joyful and exciting. However, my prayer for you is that this snapshot of my journey will encourage you and remind you that the Word of God is true! *Many plans are in a man's mind, But it is the Lord's purpose for him that will stand (be carried out)* (Proverbs 19:21 AMP).

I pray that you remain hopeful, no matter where you are in your own process. God's grace *is* sufficient. He will strengthen you as you travel along your own path to stepping joyfully into the calling He has placed on your life.

Leading with Prayer

By Stacy Jo Coffee-Thorne

If there's one thing I've learned about leadHERship, it's this: you can have the best plan, the most gifted team, and all the right resources, but if you haven't prayed, you're building on sand. Prayer isn't an optional extra to sprinkle on top of our leadHERship; it's the foundation on which everything else must rest. Without prayer, our efforts might look strong initially, but they won't last.

When we lead with prayer, we declare, "This isn't mine, Lord; it's Yours." We align our hearts with His before we send the first email, make the first call, or add anything to the calendar. Proverbs 16:3 (NIV) reminds us, *Commit to the Lord whatever you do, and He will establish your plans.* The word *commit* means to roll everything onto Him—your ideas, deadlines, obstacles, and hopes—and then trust Him to carry it all.

I've learned this lesson the hard way. When I've rushed ahead of God, even though things might have looked successful, I didn't have peace. But when I've paused to pray first, even if the outcome didn't change, I did. Prayer brings clarity that saves time, redirects our steps when needed, and settles our hearts with the reminder that God is already in control of the details.

Prayer transforms leadHERship, especially when we shift our focus from asking God to bless our actions to requesting that He allow us to join Him where He is already working. After all, leadHERship isn't about our control; it's about partnering with the Holy Spirit.

When we lead with prayer, we learn to ask deeper questions, such as: "Lord, what's on Your heart for this?" "Who do You want to bless through this?" "What do I need to let go of so I can receive Your plan instead?"

Those aren't just leadership questions; they're kingdom questions. If we are going to be kingdom leadHERs, we must keep prayer the center of everything we do.

LeadHERship can be heavy, and prayer strengthens us for that weight. People depend on us, expectations pile up, and sometimes we wonder if we're really called to lead. I'm certain I'm not alone in that. Prayer reminds us that God never meant for us to carry it all. It keeps us humble and dependent on Him, and brings us back to the truth that we were not created to lead in our own strength but under and in His authority.

Leading with prayer means beginning everything with Him in mind. Pray before you plan, before you meet, and before you speak; and maintain a posture of prayer throughout the day. Talk to Him as you go. Don't clock out of prayer once the meeting starts or once the plan is set. Listen for His gentle nudges in real time.

Surround yourself with prayer, too. Invite trusted friends and intercessors to cover you, your mission, and your team. There is strength and safety in a prayerful community. At Freedom Support Solutions, we open every staff meeting with prayer, and we have an Association of Christian Business Women prayer call every Friday morning, where women from all over come together, give praise, and lift prayer requests. Through these practices, we have seen God do incredible things—in real time!

Finally, be sure to end everything with prayer. When the work is finished or the event is complete, stop to thank God. Even if things didn't unfold as expected, prayer realigns your heart with His faithfulness. It's not about getting everything perfect; it's about keeping your relationship with Him first and giving Him the glory—always.

Prayer is powerful! It's how we partner with heaven and move from good ideas to "God ideas." LeadHERship without prayer is like setting sail without a compass: you might move, but you'll drift. When you lead with prayer, you're not just asking God to bless your plans; you're inviting Him to steer the ship.

Before you rush into your next meeting or jump into a strategy session, pause and ask the Lord to fill you with the Holy Spirit and lead through you. When prayer becomes your first response instead of your last resort, His presence becomes your strategy. And that kind of leadHERship leaves a lasting kingdom impact.

. . . .

Brenda Smith

Brenda Smith is a lifelong learner with an unwavering commitment to honor who God created each of us to be. Her enthusiasm and vision are nothing short of contagious and are a testament that each of us is designed to walk with perseverance and purpose. Her story is a beacon of hope, inspiring countless individuals to take action and receive God's grace and fullness in their lives. As a mentor and advocate for experiencing God's healing redemption from life's deepest hurts, Brenda brings hope and a vibrant light to even the darkest areas.

Brenda is married, and her most cherished gift on earth is family. Her heart continues to be captivated by the priceless moments spent with them. She enjoys discovering hidden wonders through travel, experimenting with new recipes, and mentoring those around her. She lives in a small town in the Georgia mountains and finds inspiration from all of nature. Brenda's creativity has evolved into a unique fusion of wood and resin, expressed through her prophetic art. Her passion for restoring life and beauty is gently balanced by quiet moments spent reflecting on God's goodness in her life.

Relentlessly Pursued

By Brenda Smith

What a marvelous God we serve! I never grow tired of His relational skills as He has relentlessly pursued my heart and subsequently my mind all of these years. My journey of sanctification and learning to trust Him has been nothing short of "thrills, romance, and adventure."

On March 13, 2013, I was in Pennsylvania at our family's farm. God woke me up at 3 am, as usual, to meet with Him. The windows were cracked open, letting in the crisp, fresh air, as we rested under multiple quilts to combat the chill surrounding us. I opened one eye and asked God if we could, instead, meet on the wrap-around porch after breakfast. But He responded that He wanted to meet me right then.

I rolled over and snuggled a little deeper into the covers, when out of nowhere the song "Creepin' In" by Norah Jones randomly started playing on our radio. Well, since I knew God wasn't about to take no for an answer, I decided to gather my Bible, journal, and devotions. Our relationship that morning was intense and flowed effortlessly. As the cadence intensified, I thought God was giving me a download for my mission statement, but He quickly corrected me, telling me that He was giving me my commission. I sat stunned, my mind whirling, taken off guard.

Within two weeks, I sat down for a Sunday morning service and had a vision that God was calling me to be an aqueduct. He shared with me that the water represented the Spirit flowing through me to the homes of others, bringing refreshing life. I pondered this vision the whole service. As my husband and I walked out of church, a pastor stopped us and told us about a marriage ministry he wanted to introduce to our church family, and he asked if we would pray about going to Dallas to start the implementation process. We had been facilitating small groups for marriages for years and desired to see couples fully restored to God's purpose and plan. I revealed what God had just shown me, and within three weeks, we were on the plane to Texas. My heart was full of joy.

Within a year, we were removed from the helm of that ministry due to a lie believed by an outside force. I knew God had placed us in the ministry, so we humbly prayed in the shadows for months. I asked God if He saw what was happening, to which He replied, "You're in good company." This made me giggle and assured me that He knew what troubled my heart and mind. He is well acquainted with being falsely accused, rejected, and scorned.

I went through a process of forgiveness and restoration that took some time and a lot of energy. God met me each step of the way through a series of dreams. When I got stuck, he would faithfully give the dream more than once. Each vision gave a new resolve and tenacity that sustained me in strength and dignity that only the Lord could have accomplished. I knew I was on the final legs of this process when I saw myself through the breakwaters of a turbulent sea. While there was still a storm tossing the waters into peaks and valleys, the pounding waves were no longer threatening to pull me down into the undertow.

> *Suffer hardship with me, as a good soldier of Christ Jesus. No soldier in active service entangles himself in the affairs of everyday life, so that he may please the one who enlisted him as a soldier* (2 Timothy 2:3-4 NASB1995).

The "suffering of the saints" is a real deal. The verses following, 2 Timothy 2:5-6, talk about winning the prize for following the rules, as well as being the first to enjoy the fruit of their labor. These are some great promises to plant in our hearts.

There is no substitute for an experiential meeting with our Lord. He tells us in Hebrews 12:2 (NASB 1995) that He is t*he author and perfecter of our faith.* I had a front row seat and saw Christ faithfully meeting me, carrying me, and bringing me through each of the steps to a deep freedom. He gave me an insatiable hunger for His Word, which transformed my worldview, erasing any separation or scarcity mindset, and grounding me in the truth that GOD IS ENOUGH!

My identity in Christ grew deeper as I sought the true meaning of His purpose and plan for me. Around each corner was another mind-blowing adventure or insight as we watched people get healed and delivered from heartbreaking circumstances. God restored my joy, and His authority became more profound than ever before in our lives.

As God relentlessly guided me into my calling, I began to name the steps He brought me through: explorer, pioneer, game-changer, warrior, and, finally, champion. Problems became possibilities as God taught me to respond with the Spirit's heart in all circumstances rather than reacting negatively.

> But the fruits of the Spirit is love, joy, peace, patience, kindness, goodness, faithfulness, gentleness, and self-control; [I love the last part...] against such things there is no law (Galatians 5:22-23 NASB1995).

Nothing can break the power of the fruit of the Spirit or overtake my countenance when I operate in and through Christ. That is the mind of a champion! I've always likened myself to a warrior chick, but my battle plan disputes all negative responses when I chose to lay them at God's feet. He is forming my heart to look like a modern-day Joan of Arc. I chose to take back the kingdom and glorify God with my battle cry! Let us lean into His sure victory!

When I woke up one evening in 2016, God told me to go see Heidi Baker, a Christian missionary and speaker. I didn't even know if she came to the United States to preach at that time. Well, as you can imagine, she was scheduled to be in a nearby town in nearly a month. I phoned a friend, and we booked the tickets to take an adventure to see Heidi. My anticipation and expectancy were off the charts. You could just sense the palpable presence of the Lord all over the conference. Something new was coming, and it was evident that my faithful Father was encompassing my heart and mind. I can just sit here and cry over the lavish love that He was pouring into me.

During the morning session on Thursday, August 11, 2016—this date will forever be in my memory—my husband and I both had our phones off. My brother-in-law tried to call me, then he called my husband. Usually, his wife, my sister, would contact us for events or plans. When my husband saw the missed call as we sat down for lunch, he immediately returned the call. As soon as the line was picked up, a darkness and dread came over my spirit. My husband asked me to hold his hand, and I refused multiple times. I just kept saying, "NO, I do not accept this!! I do not accept this!!"

No one at the table knew what was happening, but my spirit knew that my sister had mysteriously passed away at 56 years old. My sis, maid of honor, confidant, crafting buddy, and close friend all wrapped up in one, had suddenly been taken away.

The conference we were attending was in the same town where my sister and her husband lived. I knew God was giving me an opportunity to say goodbye. We arrived at their home before the police or coroner. As I journeyed through the depths of sorrow and loss, I was so thankful to be in her town for the first time ever on a Thursday afternoon. Despite how difficult that time was, I don't think I could've processed the loss without being there. After my brother-in-law's close friends arrived to walk with him through the next few nights and days, he felt I should return to the conference to finish what had already begun. I'm guessing it isn't a shock that Heidi Baker was speaking that evening.

As the service started that evening with the anointed and powerful praise and worship of Bethel Music, I couldn't resist the need to be alone with my friend, the Holy Spirit. His comfort and holy bubble wrapping around my heart and mind was overwhelming. So I put headphones on and listened to Stephanie Gretzinger sing "King of My Heart" over and over. I stayed in the back of the auditorium, being washed by the blood of Jesus through my tears. I have seen people worshipping in the Spirit with flags before, but I had never thought about getting up and trying it—until that night. It was my only reasonable response to the depth of gratitude and overflowing love washing away my grief.

> *"Blessed are those who mourn, for they shall be comforted"*
> (Matthew 5:4 NASB1995).

The comfort and grace I received could not have been administered to me by any human source. Jesus was healing the brokenhearted and binding up my wounds (Psalm 147:3) because of His great love for me. I know that what God allowed in His wisdom, He could easily prevent in His manifest power—but we must submit to the process. I have found that He never gives me a challenge in the natural that I'm not prepared for spiritually. What Satan meant for harm, God changed for good. Isn't this God's redemptive story for you and me?

By the end of the weekend, we found out that the Global School of Supernatural Ministry would hold its first satellite session twenty minutes from our home. We knew that we were to be a part of this impactful growth opportunity. We signed up to attend four hours a night, five times a week.

What a commitment! This, added on top of our already busy schedule, made us lean hard into God's provision and grace. I wouldn't exchange those nine months at GSSM for anything. Nothing would ever be the same after meeting the Lord there minute after minute. Having a surrendered posture at one of the lowest points in my life accelerated my growth. SURRENDER PRODUCES FAITH. I had learned to truly trust in the FINISHED work of the cross in my life, which fostered an environment where my true identity in Christ could stand out. His light is what reflects to others, and my only reasonable response is to shine for His glory!

I would have to label this next chapter of my life SUBLIME AUDACITY. God has continued giving upgrades so we can explore His love, grace, and favor. He continues to reveal the heights that He wants to engage in with us as we wait and find our rest in Him. As we give full access and gently breathe in His Spirit, God continues to do great works in and through us (John 14:12). Our limit is set by our own spiritual development.

"Purpose" seems to be a catch phrase thrown around in the Christian environment. Acts 20:24b pulls back the pages of the living Word to reveal that one of our purposes is to testify to the good news of God's grace. *My only aim is to finish the race and complete the task the Lord Jesus has given me— the task of testifying to the good news of God's grace* (NIV).

When he saw the crowds, he [Jesus] had compassion for them, because they were harassed and helpless, like sheep without a shepherd (Matthew 9:36 ESV). Sharing our experience, strength, and hope is a sure way to combat worldly disillusionment and meet this world right where they are. No gift will tear down walls like love and being present with those God brings into our lives. Thankfully, God always meets us in our failures or shortcomings. As we share our hope, knowing confidence gives wings for others to humbly come to God. Asking what God wants us to say to others about their current situation opens their hearts up to experience our faithful God. This is how hearts receive life-giving transformation. This activation is sacred and must be treated with the utmost respect and dignity.

As leadHERs, we will continually be called to persevere through challenges and hardships. God is too gracious to give us more than we can trust and believe for. Our worldview about ourselves, God, or others is key to how we navigate our decisions. Understanding our true identity comes from asking God what is most true about ourselves. The greatest gift I can give anyone is my identity, because Christ is flowing through me there. Red flags arise in areas stuck in poverty, scarcity, self-protection, perfection, self-interest, or fear. Being honest and confessing these to God is the key to releasing them. We must learn to rest and trust by letting go of these false views. Jesus paid the very high price to die for these lies, and as Graham Cooke says, Jesus is telling us to "give back His stuff! He died to take it away, and it doesn't belong to us."

Being a "game changer" and loving people to life is part of our commission from Christ. In Matthew 28:19-20, He commanded us to *"go and make disciples... teaching them to obey everything I have commanded you"* (NIV). The easiest way for us to reach others is for us to see them as Christ does. By doing this, we create a bridge that opens wounded hearts and blind eyes to the beauty of His love for them.

Seeing people through God's lens has never grown old for me. How precious it is to watch the Holy Spirit lead and guide people to fruition. While we are to sow seeds, it's imperative to remember that the outcome is not our responsibility. I definitely have learned that the hard way multiple times. Reflecting on my response in difficult situations allows me to be honest with myself and, therefore, with God when I have not given God all of the pieces. It's a great test to see if I'm self-promoting or seeking someone else to fill the void reserved for God.

Trusting God's sovereignty and love leads to a deeper connection with Him and others and allows us to know that we are enough in Christ. We will never know all of the answers, but the closer we get to God, the more we will recognize that knowing all the answers is not necessary or even our place. Trusting God gives us rest. *This is what the Sovereign LORD, the Holy One of Israel says, "In repentance and rest is your salvation, in quietness and trust is your strength"* (Isaiah 30:15 NIV).

Godly confidence looks fabulous on each of us. I've heard it called GODfidence. We can proclaim: "He holds me in the palm of His hand, and He is committed to helping me experience His fullness." God's relentless pursuit of our hearts is nothing short of miraculous. As I grow in Him, He continues to replace all my old ways of thinking with my TRUE IDENTITY, not for a performance or for me to DO something, but so I can continue learning how to BE in Christ. His glorious pursuit always leads us to life in abundance. Learning to hear His voice and acting upon it brings peace that surpasses all of our earthly understanding.

As I reflect Christ in this world, I must allow His power and authority to reign in me by being surrendered to the Holy Spirit's work in and through me. As we know, Our struggle is not against flesh and blood, but against the rulers, against the powers, against the world forces of this darkness, against the spiritual forces of wickedness in the heavenly places (Ephesians 6:12 NASB 1995). Christ has never left us defenseless! He instructs us, *Therefore, take up the full armor of God, so that you will be able to resist the evil day, and having done everything, to stand firm* (Ephesians 6:13 NASB1995).

I am so grateful for the army of mighty men and women God has strategically compiled around me. We all have had the opportunity to stand firm for God after we have done all that we know to do in and through Christ, and there is no better gift than knowing someone has your back when wave after wave of adversity buffets your heart and mind. Christ always goes before us, and the beauty is that when we ourselves are not shackled with a faulty worldview, we can be His army, supporting others to stand.

> *"No eye has seen, nor ear heard, nor the heart of man imagined, what God has prepared for those who love Him"* (1 Corinthians 2:9 ESV).

Know that God has His eyes on you. The calling you feel to be a leadHER? Trust that it is from Him; He has something miraculous prepared for you. God is pursuing you just like He pursued me. He has designed a unique role for you which you can step into by continually opening your eyes to His will and His ways.

Will you join me in surrendering to His pursuit? Will you rise to meet Him when He calls, even if the air is cold and the quilt is cozy? Will you submit your pain and trials to Him, knowing He has gone before you? Will you say yes when He calls you to embark on a new plan, new project, or new ministry, trusting His provision?

God *is* pursuing you. And His plan is good and fruitful.

He alone can lead you to a life of true joy.

Allison Pope Bramlett

Pastor Allison Pope Bramlett is a dynamic communicator, author, and podcast host with a passion for helping people live and lead with love. As Executive Pastor of Covenant Church in Douglas, Georgia, she teaches practical faith and leadership principles that empower others to walk in purpose, build strong families, and lead with integrity.

Through her podcast and her book, *Don't Take It Personally,* Allison encourages others to find freedom, grow in spiritual maturity, and lead from a place of authenticity and grace. Married to her husband, Jeff Bramlett, for over 30 years, Allison treasures her family and the legacy of faith they are building together. Her life and message remind us that no matter the season, love never fails.

Loving Deeply Without Losing Yourself

By Allison Pope Bramlett

As a young woman, I gave Jesus my "yes," and that one decision defined the entire course of my life. My heart's desire has always been to live a life that brings heaven to earth. Saying yes to Jesus meant surrendering not just my sins, but my future, my relationships, and my dreams. I look back now and see that every yes since then has been built on that first one.

I am deeply in love with Jesus, my husband Jeff, my children, and my beautiful grandchildren. After over 30 years of marriage, I can confidently say that our marriage is a miracle—a story of love, joy, forgiveness, and grace. It has not always been easy, but it has always been worth it. Early on, I made a decision to fight for my family, not with them. I'm a blessed mother, a Gigi, and a pastor to an incredible faith family; and yet, with all of these blessings, I have faced the very real struggle of leadHERship: leading with love, while guarding my heart and my home. To lead well, we must keep our love strong, our hearts soft, and our lives balanced, especially when the weight of leadHERship pulls us in every direction.

Over the years, I have given pastoral care to and prayed, laughed, and wept with people who knew exactly what the Bible said, but still chose to live stuck in cycles. They could quote Scripture but would not let the Holy Spirit touch the deepest places of their heart. As a leadHER, frustration can rise when we watch people return again and again to victim thinking rather than stepping into victorious living. Yet, when Jesus calls us to lead, He also strengthens us with an endurance to love others deeply.

Jesus Himself modeled this when He wept over Jerusalem: *As He approached Jerusalem and saw the city, he wept over it and said, "If you, even you, had only known on this day what would bring you peace—but now it is hidden from your eyes"* (Luke 19:41-42 NIV). Jesus longed for His people to know the way of peace, but they refused. As leadHERs, we can feel that same tension and ache in our hearts when others stay bound, even after being shown the way to freedom countless times.

I once ministered to a young woman who had all the biblical head knowledge. She could recite promises, sing worship songs, and even encourage others, but when it came to her own healing, she resisted. She stayed trapped in bitterness toward her parents, ashamed of her past. I prayed with her, fasted, and spent hours in discipleship. For years, I carried a sense of responsibility for her freedom, until one day, the Lord reminded me: *I planted the seed, Apollos watered it, but God has been making it grow* (1 Corinthians 3:6 NIV). That truth was liberating. My role was obedience. I was to plant and water; only God could bring increase. That moment shifted how I lead. I realized that my position is to love, speak truth, and live faithfully. The rest is up to the Holy Spirit.

This epiphany did not mean that I stopped caring, but that I stopped carrying what was not mine. LeadHERship requires knowing where our responsibility ends and where God's begins. Leaning on God has allowed me to face ministry each day without becoming burned out or losing myself. Yes, there have been times when I have needed to rest and refocus, but I have never lost passion. Similar to loving my family, I am deeply passionate about loving Jesus and serving people. People are the purpose.

Leading for Christ is not a job to endure; it is a calling to embrace with joy. By intentionally walking with Jesus, you can continue to carry His fire and passion through every season, every challenge, and every victory. A leadHER's love for God and desire to see lives transformed can multiply through ups and downs. I have found that when I rest in God, the joy of the Lord truly is my strength (Nehemiah 8:10), and that joy continues to fuel me forward with greater vision and renewed passion.

After teaching about being the Bread of Life, Scripture says: *From this time many of his disciples turned back and no longer followed him* (John 6:66 NIV). If people could walk away from Jesus, they can walk away from us, too. As leadHERs, we can choose to allow others' rejection to pull us downward or to fuel us toward the Holy Spirit. Personally, I believe that when a person dismisses me, it does not mean that my love is wasted; instead, my love becomes a spiritual act of worship, igniting a source of passion and fire within my own walk with the Lord.

The call to leadHERship requires us to find balance. If we are not intentional, ministry or any job can easily consume every ounce of our time and energy, leaving our loved ones with leftovers.

Early in ministry, I often said yes to everyone else and no to my own rest and relationships. I thought I was being faithful, but I was actually being unkind to myself and to those closest to me. One evening, I walked through the front door after a long day. The house was very quiet—my husband, Jeff, and children were all tucked in. I was struck by the fact that I had not even sat down with them that day. I was leading everyone else but missing the moments at home, the moments that mattered the most. Holy Spirit immediately called me back to balance. The next morning, I chose to make a small but powerful shift and began scheduling non-negotiable family time. The Lord was teaching me one of the most valuable leadHERship lessons: Commit to the right yes by offering the right no.

The story of Mary and Martha continues to challenge me. Martha was busy serving while Mary sat at Jesus' feet. Jesus said: *"Martha, Martha... you are worried and upset about many things, but few things are needed— or indeed only one. Mary has chosen what is better, and it will not be taken away from her"* (Luke 10:41-42 NIV). In my zeal for ministry, I was often a Martha—busy, but empty. There is a difference between being busy and being productive. Now, I am learning to be both: a Martha with a Mary heart. As we sit at the feet of Jesus, we find the wisdom, strength, and love we need to pour into others. Renewal is not selfish; it is stewardship. When I spend time with Jesus, I return to people refreshed. When I rest, I lead better. When I laugh with my grandchildren, I remember why I lead at all.

LeadHERship means walking the fine line between helping people and enabling them. Scripture calls us to bear one another's burdens: *Carry each other's burdens, and in this way you will fulfill the law of Christ* (Galatians 6:2 NIV). But just a few verses later, it says: *Each one should carry their own load* (Galatians 6:5 NIV). That tension is leadership. Give yourself permission to tell someone, "I can walk with you, but I cannot walk for you."

There have been countless times when I have had to lovingly tell someone, "I can walk with you, but I cannot walk for you." That is difficult when you have a heart that wants to fix and rescue. If we do everything for someone, we are not helping them grow, but keeping them dependent. It is challenging when those we lead choose to remain in a victim mentality, knowing truth, but preferring blame to breakthrough. In those moments, a leadHER must release the individual to the Lord, trusting His love and care for them.

I've shared life with one young woman for more than twenty-five years, watching her wrestle with addiction, self-sabotage, and identity. It has been a long fight—she has lost rounds along the way, but has stayed in to win the fight. Being a leadHER is not just seeing sheep from a distance, but sharing life with them. It means sometimes you even smell like the sheep as you step into the mess. It means speaking truth in love, even when it is hard, and refusing to give up when others might. But it also means learning the importance of boundaries and knowing the right yes and the right no so that you can continue to lead from strength.

Jesus loved people with compassion—He healed the sick and taught the crowds. But even Jesus withdrew regularly to be alone with the Father (Luke 5:16). If Jesus, the Son of God, needed solitude and boundaries, how much more do we? Boundaries are not selfish; they are stewardship. They allow us to love without becoming depleted, to serve without becoming bitter, and to lead without collapsing under the weight of expectations.

One day, I received a call from a young woman who was in a mess of trouble. Some may have seen her as a lost cause, but I saw a daughter who needed someone to believe in her. After praying, my husband and I agreed to bail her out and bring her home with us for several months. She came with pain, habits, and false belief systems that did not disappear overnight. We knew that showing her God's love and His boundaries would allow her to see the basis for true freedom. My over-twenty-year relationship with this friend, who had experienced seasons of freedom and others of bondage, had taught me that it was not my role to fix her, but to walk beside her, exemplifying the love of Christ, while keeping healthy boundaries.

Helping someone find their freedom does not mean that we lose ours. Love without boundaries is not love; it is chaos. As leadHERs, we are to love others deeply while still saying no when needed, giving room for those we lead to grow in their own identity in Christ. Sometimes the most powerful ministry moments do not happen from a stage or a platform but around the kitchen table or sitting on a couch with those whom God has assigned to us.

Still to this day, I have cups of coffee with this woman of God who is thriving in her relationship with the Lord and with others.

I am not the Savior. You are not the Savior. Only Jesus is.

We can walk with people, but we cannot walk for them. We can pray, encourage, and point them to truth, but we cannot live their obedience for them. I've found that boundaries give me the strength to keep showing up with love. They protect my marriage, my family, and my personal walk with the Lord. And they keep me from carrying a burden God never asked me to carry. I often use the illustration of a cup and saucer: When I am filled by the Holy Spirit, people can drink from the overflow of the saucer of my life, but if I let them drink from my cup, I end up drained and dissatisfied. Healthy leadership sets boundaries. My mom has always said, "You can sip from my saucer, but I must stay full in my cup."

LeadHERship is not about climbing a ladder; it is about setting a table. It's not about control; it's about connection. A leadHER doesn't hoard power—she empowers others.

One of the most important lessons I have learned in leadHERship is this: My life is not perfect, but it is purposeful. In the past, I wrestled with the pressure to "have it all together." Jeff and I have a miracle marriage, but leadHERship does not pause when life is messy, and we have had a few messy seasons. In these times, our children were involved in sports, we both had leadership roles to fill, and family and friends needed attention; at times, we were only surviving. We reached out to mentors—people who could pray for us, speak truth in love without judgment, and remind us what the Word says—which allowed us to grow and heal. I learned that I can lead and still be healing, preach and still be growing, be real and still be anointed.

People often look to leadHERs for answers, for stability, and for strength. And while it is true that leadHERship requires strength, it does not require perfection. In fact, pretending to be perfect only builds walls between us and the people God has called us to love.

As a woman who sits on boards, owns businesses, and pastors a thriving church, I have learned that leadHERship is about more than having a seat at the table. It is about shaping the atmosphere of the room. I do not want to simply be a thermometer that reflects whatever temperature is already present; I want to be a thermostat that transforms the atmosphere.

Thermometers read and react, but thermostats set the climate. By carrying the presence of Jesus, I can bring heaven to earth in every space I enter. Whether in a boardroom, a business meeting, or a church service, God has gifted His followers with the ability to shift the atmosphere with faith, love, and vision. LeadHERs are not called to blend in; we are called to set the tone so that others can rise to a higher standard of hope, integrity, and excellence.

Love has a way of knocking the selfishness, pride, and fear out of your heart until what remains is a greater reflection of Jesus. LeadHERship has been that refining fire in my life. It has exposed my insecurities and weaknesses, but it has also drawn me closer to the One who is my strength. LeadHERship will bring both applause and criticism. At times, people have celebrated me, and at times, people have misunderstood or even slandered me. Early in ministry, I let both voices control me. If they cheered, I soared. If they criticized, I sank. But the Lord reminded me, the same crowd that cried *"Hosanna!"* on Sunday shouted *"Crucify him!"* on Friday (Matthew 21:9, 27:22 NIV). If Jesus didn't let the crowd define Him, neither can I.

My security must come from God's approval alone. *Am I now trying to win the approval of human beings, or of God? Or am I trying to please people? If I were still trying to please people, I would not be a servant of Christ* (Galatians 1:10 NIV). Nehemiah reminds us, *"The joy of the Lord is your strength"* (Nehemiah 8:10 NIV). Joy is not optional; it is essential. Joy is what sustains us when ministry is heavy. Joy keeps me laughing with my grandchildren after a difficult counseling session and allows me to preach with fire even when my own heart feels weary. Having joy is a choice, not a reaction; it is not based on circumstances but on Jesus. In both my personal and professional life, joy has been my source of strength.

Leading with love means being Spirit-led and operating with virtue. It means celebrating people when they succeed and standing with them when they stumble, valuing character above charisma and consistency above applause. I often remember my father's words: "Your gift will get you in the door, but your character will keep you in the room." Possessing a talent may allow you to attract followers, but showcasing consistent integrity gives you credibility to lead your followers to something worthwhile.

Being a leadHER includes choosing to stay vulnerable and transparent. I never want to get to a place where I am unreachable or untouchable. Vulnerability builds bridges—when I share not just my victories but also my struggles, people realize they are not alone. Transparency reminds those we lead that growth is a lifelong process. And being open about our journey invites others to keep growing in theirs.

The truth is, no one has it all together. We are all a work in progress. But the good news is that we serve a God who does have it all together, and we can trust Him with every detail of our lives. As the Lord told Paul, *"My grace is sufficient for you, for my power is made perfect in weakness"* (2 Corinthians 12:9 NIV). That Scripture has carried me through many seasons where I felt inadequate. God's strength really does shine brightest in our weakness.

I have found that the seasons where I've been most honest about my struggles—whether in marriage, motherhood, or ministry—were the seasons I've seen God create the greatest fruit in others. People don't connect to a façade of perfection; they connect to the testimony of a life transformed by Jesus. That is why I often say that I don't have a perfect life, but I do have a purposeful one.

As you walk as a leadHER, remember that your calling is not to impress people but to impact them. God did not call you to show off your strength; He called you so you could point others to *His* strength.

Being a leadHER is an amazing calling! But your calling is not about you—it is about God and the future of His kingdom. God created you on purpose, for a purpose. And though He calls you magnificent, your role is to stay humble, vulnerable, and growing. As you do, He will use even your imperfections to display His glory.

I pray that as a leadHER, your greatest desire is to be faithful—faithful to

Jesus, to those God has put in your life to love and care for, and to those you lead. Keeping that order in check will enable you to love deeply without losing yourself.

Not losing yourself is essential—because *you* are God's masterpiece!

Leading with Joy

By DeAnn Alaine

A long time ago, I was a licensed practical nurse. While in nursing school, doing a rotation in the emergency room, a very large man was lying unresponsive on a gurney. I'm 5'1" and was at the time very pregnant; the evil charge nurse told me to mount the man to administer CPR! I wish you could have seen the look on my face, and you can imagine the sight as I gathered my almost 200-pound body to climb on top of a man! I needed a step stool just to get started! Tackling life with joy can be a life-and-death situation. I should mention that the man lived! Woohoo!

Our actions and our words can lead others to joy.

> *Death and life are in the power of the tongue, and those who love it and indulge it will eat its fruit and bear the consequences of their words* (Proverbs 18:21 AMP).

What do you think happens when you are aware of the language you use in your everyday life? We will all bear the consequences of our words: When we speak life, we are partakers of joy! And when we don't, well, that has consequences, too.

From the age of 8, our family culture included going to the movie theater every week! We considered it family time. We would pile into the family van and go to the dollar movie theater in Omaha, Nebraska. It was awesome! But was it really? I saw so many behaviors and attitudes—lust, anger, greed, sexual immorality, and filthy language—all from watching movies! The influence of movies in my life led me to become a professional curser in the third grade. In my head, I would try to make up the newest, worst combination of curse words! Thankfully, the Lord corrected that behavior, and I'm free of that. I don't even know how to think that way anymore! And as a result, my flesh died, and my joy grew because I didn't have to be afraid of "slipping up" in front of my mom! No more concerns of my mouth being washed out with soap; Irish Spring was the WORST!

Now let's tighten the belt a bit more. *But now, put away all the following: anger, wrath, malice, slander, and filthy language from your mouth* (Colossians 3:8 CSB). I consider filthy language to be anything that is the opposite of what God's Word says. For instance, if I talked terribly about myself, that's perverse (or filthy language) because it's contrary to the truth of what His Word says about me! It's not just evidence of low self-esteem; it's dirty. Does Satan love when you criticize yourself? Does he love it when you tear yourself down? Then it's dirty language, and it doesn't belong in your vocabulary! And this is just one example! Joy is killed with negative talk! Conversely, joy thrives in the atmosphere of self-control!

As leadHERs, it's imperative that we protect our testimony (with our mouths) because we are called to a higher standard as we lead others. *Our mouths were filled with laughter, our tongues with songs of joy. Then it was said among the nations, "The Lord has done great things for them"* (Psalm 126:2 NIV). Is the testimony of our mouths a joyful one? We must be careful what proceeds out of our mouths.

Satan, our accuser, hates joy. See, the freer we become, the less control he has. Jesus is the fullness of joy; when we overcome evil, our own joy becomes full, and we get to teach others what the joy of the Lord really looks like! Now that's what leading with joy really is!

. . . .

Janet Berrong

Janet Berrong is a founding member and board member of Women World Leaders. She serves on the board of Florida Faith Alliance, united to fight sex trafficking and bring hope to the vulnerable. A devoted follower of Christ and purpose-driven entrepreneur, Janet leads with compassion, intuition, and faith—empowering women to embrace their God-given identity and live with confidence and grace.

With over 29 years as a licensed health and wellness professional, Janet has dedicated her life to helping others become their best selves—physically, emotionally, and spiritually. She also serves as Chief Operating Officer and Co-Founder of Rainbow of Love, a ministry that brings tangible help and hope in the name of Jesus.

As founder of House of BERRONG, Janet created a lifestyle brand that blends elegance, wellness, and divine purpose—encouraging others to dwell in beauty and walk boldly in faith. A best-selling author in the United States and internationally, Janet finds her greatest joy in sharing the love of Jesus, cherishing her family, and leaving a legacy of light, purpose, and grace for generations to come.

www.HouseofBerrong.com

Giving Your Joyful Yes

By Janet Berrong

God gives every woman—including you!—the potential and opportunity to be a leadHER in His kingdom. But if we don't give Him our focus, listening to His voice and allowing Him to direct our steps, we could miss our calling. That almost happened to me.

Kingdom leadHERship is not about titles, platforms, or applause. It begins with a surrendered heart. It's about knowing who God is and allowing His voice to shape who we are. It's about leading with love, with integrity, with obedience. And most of all, it's about joyfully stepping into the role He created you to fill. Jesus told us, *"You did not choose me, but I chose you and appointed you so that you might go and bear fruit, fruit that will last"* (John 15:16 NIV).

Being a kingdom leadHER is unlike any other form of leadership. It's not a competition—it's a commission. The world may celebrate charisma, influence, and power, but God looks at the heart. He raises up leadHERs who serve, not those who strive for their own glory. Jesus modeled this perfectly when He knelt to wash the feet of His disciples. The Son of God humbled Himself to serve others and taught, *"The greatest among you will be your servant"* (Matthew 23:11 NIV).

Kingdom leadHERship is rooted in humility and sustained by intimacy with God. It flows from our identity in Him, not our performance. It does not seek recognition—it seeks transformation. A leadHER acknowledges her limitations and is open to feedback from God's Word, recognizes the contributions of others, fosters a culture of trust and inclusivity, and inspires others through authenticity, faithfulness, and empathy.

Every call begins with an invitation. God places clues throughout our lives—burdens we carry, passions that stir us, and opportunities directed at us. For me, my invitation to be a leadHER began in childhood. At just 11 years old, my Sunday school teacher trusted me with responsibility. I took attendance, counted the offering, logged records, and delivered them all to the office. This responsibility may have seemed small to others, but to me, it was significant. My service was natural and brought me purpose.

Still, for many years, I battled a sense of unworthiness. I walked through life carrying dreams I was too afraid to act on. I missed many opportunities—doors God opened that I hesitated to walk through. Still, His grace never left me. I believed the lies that I was not good enough, smart enough, and didn't know God's Word well enough. I felt as if all the mistakes I had made in my life cancelled out my calling for Jesus. I had sinned by keeping one foot in the world and one foot in the Word, and I felt as if my wounds and strongholds bound me to sin, which created more separation and feelings of unworthiness. As a result, I never wanted to be out front, because I didn't want the fact that I'm not perfect to be discovered.

Now, I've learned that God does not want perfection; He wants our yes. Because when we give ourselves to Him, He can clean us up and use us as He sees fit.

At the age of 11, God's purpose became apparent to me. In my early 20s, my talents led me to become a successful business owner—it came so early and naturally. However, during my formative years, I had experienced so much trauma and dysfunction that it perpetually pulled me away from my purpose. It took over 30 years to release all the fear and negativity so I could fully walk in God's purpose for my life.

Despite all this, God was always present, regardless of how far I drifted away. And miraculously, 30 years after acknowledging His presence, I clearly heard Him say, "This is your time to rise and be the leadHER I've called you to be. If you say no, I will give this blessing to someone else. But it is meant for you." That moment changed everything. I knew the time had come for me to fully surrender and follow the path God had intended for me. I gave God my yes. Not because I felt ready, but because I knew I couldn't afford to miss His voice again.

I wasn't committing to a role or a title; I was committing to the Lord's work. So I prayed, asking Him to lead me, and I chose obedience over comfort.

During that time, I got a call from Kimberly Hobbs, asking me to prayerfully consider being on the leadership team for a women's ministry God had called her to start. As a result, I became a founding leader of Women World Leaders. God had already been dealing with my heart to go deeper with Him, but I didn't really know what that meant until I got that phone call from Kimberly. I knew in my heart it was my time to step out of my comfort zone and step into the calling God had for me.

Even as I said yes, all my fears and insecurities rose. I would have to be vulnerable and willing to be put on the spot. I had a lack of knowledge in certain areas, but I knew with full faith and trust that God would equip me. It was an opportunity I had to seize and embrace joyfully. My core values were perfectly aligned with Women World Leaders' mission. I was honored and humbled by Kimberly's loving gesture. Being fully aware that she is a woman of faith and prayer, I knew she heard the voice of God telling her to reach out to me.

I soon learned that leadHERship is not without its battles. Scripture tells us the enemy prowls like a roaring lion, and I experienced that firsthand. A year into full ministry, I got sucked back into a toxic relationship that, for decades prior, had a stronghold on me. In that vulnerable season, my eyes drifted, and my focus slipped. The enemy saw an opening and tried to take me off the path God had placed me on.

For a time, I was distracted. I questioned everything. But even in that, God's mercy rescued me. He met me where I was and gently brought me back. Through that trial, I learned that failure is not the end—it can be the refining fire that prepares us for more. My past did not define me. My mistakes did not disqualify me. God used even that time to strengthen me.

> They triumphed over him by the blood of the Lamb and by the word of their testimony (Revelation 12:11 NIV).

That "yes" began a journey I never could have orchestrated on my own. I began serving where God called me; I learned so much about being a servant by being a servant.

Whenever there was a group meeting, I took great pride in being the person who greeted people as they entered. I embraced my role, making women feel warm, many of whom were entering a new place for the first time. They felt the love of being accepted into our Women World Leaders haven. I was the first contact, which helped remove my personal feelings of inadequacy and unworthiness. All because my heart said yes to God. I was doing what God called me to do, and what was in my heart poured out to others. That immediate connection enabled me to build a relationship with each individual.

From there, I said yes to everything God asked of me, big or small. He led me to welcome women into ministry spaces where they could heal, grow, and find their place in God's kingdom. I became the face of Women World Leaders—a growing ministry. I wasn't on stage. I was at the door—literally. I opened my arms, prayed with women, and cried with them. I made them feel safe, seen, and known. That was the beginning of kingdom leadHERship for me. God used my availability more than my ability. And little by little, He entrusted me with more.

As women began to open up to me, trust me, and invite me into their stories, something shifted in me. God began to build my confidence—not in myself, but in Him. I started organizing events, coordinating ministry logistics, and eventually became an impactful leadHER of what was becoming a global ministry.

> But you are a chosen people, a royal priesthood, a holy nation, God's special possession (1 Peter 2:9 NIV).

Kingdom leadHERship doesn't wait for perfection to lead. We are called to lead from our identity in Christ—and that's exactly what God was teaching me. Through every step—ministry, restoration, business—one truth has remained: I cannot lead without the Holy Spirit. The most effective leadHERs are not the most strategic; they are the most surrendered.

> "Not by might nor by power, but by my Spirit," says the Lord Almighty (Zechariah 4:6 NIV).

Every decision I make, I bring before the Lord. I've learned to pause, listen, and obey. Whether it's welcoming a new partner ministry, launching a product, or simply encouraging a woman who crosses my path—I ask the Holy Spirit to go before me.

After restoring me, God told me, "You're ready." He had built a foundation in me through the ministry. And now, He was calling me to expand—into business, into leadHERship, into purpose-driven entrepreneurship. With Him, all things truly are possible.

"Be strong and courageous. Do not be afraid; do not be discouraged, for the Lord your God will be with you wherever you go" (Joshua 1:9 NIV).

Kingdom leadHERship doesn't stop with us. True leadHERs multiply. We are called to pour into others, raise up disciples, and leave behind more than a name—we leave behind people who are stronger because we obeyed.

Being a kingdom leadHER means taking the responsibility to create a legacy and generational impacts so that God's purpose will be felt from now until eternity. Every day, we must plant seeds and care for others so they can flourish and grow; this requires our full attention. We must act as one as we build a unified community of similarly minded and fully committed souls. *And the things you have heard me say... entrust to reliable people who will also be qualified to teach others* (2 Timothy 2:2 NIV).

My calling has led me to give my time and effort to several worthy organizations and causes.

Today, I am still joyfully and actively engaged in Women World Leaders and currently serve on the board of directors. Women World Leaders helps women walk in their God-given purpose, allowing them to share teachings globally through the weekly *Women World Leaders' Podcast* and *Voice of Truth,* their quarterly magazine. In addition, WWL invites writers to share their own God-stories to motivate, inspire, and impact God's kingdom. Each book (such as this one) comprises over twenty authors and has consistently achieved multiple best-seller recognitions in various categories.

My yes to God also includes having the honor of serving on the board of directors for Florida Faith Alliance, which exists to unite churches, communities, and civic leaders in an effort to stop human trafficking through education, prevention, and action. Florida Faith Alliance empowers individuals and organizations to protect children and eradicate trafficking. Under the leadership of Pastor Lynne Barletta, presenters are trained to instruct and educate institutions on how to protect the most vulnerable and recognize telltale signs of potential predators. Her efforts working with local law enforcement have led to multiple arrests and convictions of offenders.

I also serve as the COO and co-founder of Rainbow of Love, a ministry that brings tangible help and hope in the name of Jesus. How does Rainbow of Love bring tangible help and hope? We provide practical care and spiritual encouragement to individuals and families walking through difficult seasons. Whether it's financial assistance or simply the presence of someone who listens and prays, every outreach is a reminder that God sees, provides, and redeems.

Each of these roles is a continuation of my yes to the Lord—a ripple effect of the day I surrendered to God's leadership. I've learned that the most powerful thing we can do is say yes to God. I know this is true because I've lived it. I still live it. And I continue to evolve every day. God's voice has become my calling.

My sense of unworthiness was an anchor that dragged me down for much of my life. Accepting and embracing the essential qualities of being a kingdom leadHER, as outlined in this book, allowed me to achieve the status God had prepared for me and released me from the invisible shackles that had held me. As I said yes to Jesus, He gave me His worth and freedom.

With deep introspection, I created a checklist of what constitutes being a kingdom leadHER. Objectively, a personal assessment was needed. I knew my values, intentions, and heart were always pure, although gone astray at times; I also knew that, at my core, my devotion to God never faltered.

My mind filled with all the key, vital words: love of God, faith, trust, obedience, integrity, surrender, purpose, compassion, empathy, love of others and humanity, forgiveness, commission, transformation, humility.

I spent time with each word: repeating, absorbing, reflecting upon, and dissecting it. Every moment of my life had brought me to this time of introspection. I realized fully that the purposeful life God had intended for me was to enhance the lives of others, uplift their spirits, and guide them to prayerfully embrace God and ask for His favor to guide them to make the right choices in His service, and spread God's Word. Prayerfully and intentionally, I endeavor to follow this call each day.

As I navigated the season God had brought me to, He had yet another blessing to bestow as I followed in His service and He led me to establish BERRONG. My life experiences propelled me to fulfill the vision that is BERRONG—a company that strives to create a legacy and generational impacts that purposefully serve God.

The story of BERRONG, The House of BERRONG, is the meeting of purpose and elegance. BERRONG began with a vision to create a brand that blends luxury with purpose, driven by a deep-rooted desire to offer products that not only stand out in design but also make a meaningful impact.

My journey to founding BERRONG was inspired by my experience as a Licensed Massage Therapist and Licensed Colon Therapist, where I spent nearly three decades walking alongside individuals in their healing journeys. In the treatment rooms, the focus was always on wellness that came from within, empowering others to live healthier and more balanced lives. This experience in holistic health laid the foundation for BERRONG, a brand built on integrity, compassionate care, and true understanding of what wellness means.

But my inspiration for creating BERRONG didn't come solely from my professional experience; it was deeply influenced by the legacy of my grandfather. He was a man of quiet strength who passed away prematurely from heart disease. As a result, he sparked a passion in me for wellness and preventative health that guides everything I do today. His untimely passing reminded me of the fragility of life, and it instilled in me a desire to deep dive to help others care for their health and well-being.

My grandmother, the epitome of grace and elegance, taught me that true beauty lies not just in appearance, but in the way we carry ourselves and treat others. Her wisdom shaped my view of luxury. Not as mere indulgence, but a reflection of how we respect and honor God, ourselves, and those around us.

At the heart of BERRONG is the giraffe, a symbol of vision, elegance, and grace. It represents my aspiration to help our customers look beyond the ordinary and reach new heights in both beauty and purpose.

As BERRONG continues to grow, we remain deeply committed to the values that inspire its creation: offering products that reflect refinement and elegance that encourage a lifestyle rooted in health, grace, and service to others. BERRONG is more than just a brand; it's a legacy of wellness, elegance, and giving back, uplifting and inspiring others, just as I have been inspired throughout my own journey. The joy I carry doesn't come from my accomplishments; it comes from obedience, from walking hand-in-hand with the One who calls, equips, restores, and sends.

God has given us each the potential to be kingdom leadHERs—I am living proof. Despite the fact that I battled feelings of unworthiness and took wrong paths, God never gave up on me. He chased me, sent others to lift me up, spoke to me in His Word, and, little by little, gave me a passion to serve Him and His people. And now here I am—joyfully leading, joyfully serving, and joyfully becoming all He's called me to be.

And I'm telling you: He's calling you, too. Bravely say yes. Say it with joy. Your kingdom assignment is waiting, and you won't want to miss it.

May the God of hope fill you with all joy and peace as you trust in him (Romans 15:13 NIV).

Crista Albritton Meadows

Crista Albritton Meadows lives in Waycross, Georgia. She is a Registered Nurse and has been the Director of Case Management at the local hospital in her town for 26 years.

Crista was a Commissioned Minister with the Assemblies of God for many years. She spent about 20 years ministering as a board member in leadership at her local church, teaching and preaching as the Life Ministries Director, which included small group studies and preaching in the pulpit. She has always been active in women's ministries, including speaking at local ladies' events and conferences.

Crista's first book, *My Brokenness but His Greatness: A Journey of Hope and Healing,* was published in 2015. Much has happened since that time. She is currently writing a new book.

With a deep desire to see emotionally wounded women set free by the power of God, Crista shares her testimony and many years of experience with others. She is currently providing 1:1 mentorship to women and coaching for inner and emotional healing.

Pursuing My Destiny

By Crista Albritton Meadows

As I think about how I stepped joyfully into God's calling for my life, I am quickly reminded of how it all started: Twenty-eight years ago this May, my one and only child was born prematurely. That was the beginning of my spiritual awakening.

I grew up in the church; I was raised to attend church whenever the doors were open. When I was 11, I walked down the aisle to pray the sinner's prayer and was baptized soon after. As far as I knew, I had done everything required to be saved and go to heaven. As I grew up and got married, attending church on Sundays was a natural part of my life. But it was not until my son was born that I received salvation and began a relationship with Jesus Christ.

Within hours of my son's premature birth, I found myself desperate and crying out to God from the bathroom of my hospital room. Due to his premature lungs, my son was quickly put on a breathing machine, and, by midnight, he was transferred to a different hospital that had a higher level of care. Fear of losing my firstborn child gripped me, and in that moment, the scales fell off my eyes; I could see my need for God for the first time in my life. I needed His delivering and healing power for my son.

I quickly realized that even though I had attended church all those years, walked down the aisle to pray the sinner's prayer, and been baptized, I did not have a personal relationship with Jesus. I asked God to forgive me of my sins and give me His power and grace to serve Him and live for Him. And I prayed He would save, heal, and deliver my son. Will came home from the hospital healed after three weeks of hospitalization. I have always believed God has and continues to use my son's birth and life to transform me.

After Will's healing, I began to seek God even more in my own personal time. With a deep desire to know God and His ways, I started watching Christian ministry programs on television. I was like a sponge, soaking up new-to-me truths and revelations about God and His healing and transforming power. Holy Spirit was drawing me closer into a deeper relationship with Him. During this time, I attended a local women's conference where a well-known lady minister was speaking. I was so moved and touched by the power of God operating in her that I thought, *I want what she has.* Despite having been taught that women could not be ministers, I still longed for the power I saw in her.

When Will was a toddler, we joined an Assembly of God church as a family, and I began to grow even deeper in my relationship with Jesus. I received prophetic words that had a great impact on me. I did not understand the gift of prophecy, but I did know that those words ministered to my soul. They brought life, hope, and a new, profound identity and destiny to my life. I hung on every word that was preached, taught, or spoken over me. I found myself coming alive in a new way. I was so hungry for the deeper things of God, and I was open to learning more about Holy Spirit and His gifts and callings.

I so vividly remember the Sunday my pastor approached me after the morning service. Everyone had left the sanctuary when he sat down on the steps of the platform next to the pulpit and asked me to sit beside him. Then he looked at me with such seriousness and asked, "When are you going to start using your teaching gift?"

I was in shock and amazement at his question. I had no idea why he wanted to talk to me, but I certainly did not see this question coming. I do not remember exactly how I responded; I may have been speechless. But I do remember how I felt: validated. I felt seen and valued for one of the first times in my life. There was something in me that the church body needed. And for the pastor to see this in me when I could not even see it in myself gave me such a sense of fulfillment and purpose. This was God's favor on my life.

And Jesus grew in wisdom and stature, and in favor with God and man (Luke 2:52 NIV).

As God's favor on my life increased, He gave me favor with my pastor as well. God was using him to provide me an opportunity to grow into my calling and destiny.

My pastor asked me to start with teaching a marriage curriculum to the adult Sunday School class. I felt so inadequate, but I was willing. I gave God my yes and began with a TV and a VCR on a rolling stand. I would push that cart into the sanctuary on Sunday mornings to teach married couples a marriage video series curriculum.

I told God I was not qualified to teach about marriage—I was not a marriage expert. But I also submitted that if that was how He wanted to use me, I would trust Him and obey Him. I find it interesting now, after many years, that God had me begin teaching with a marriage curriculum, especially since He knew that years later my own marriage would end in divorce. Our God sees the beginning from the end, and He never fails His children. Despite ourselves, He will use us if we choose to obey Him.

Because of that one act of obedience many years ago, when I felt so inadequate and insecure, God continued to refine the gifting and calling on my life as He opened doors for me to teach and preach His Word. I was given opportunities to minister from the pulpit on Wednesday and Sunday nights at my church. Eventually, I was asked to serve in the role of Life Ministries Director, which involved selecting curriculum for, coordinating, and teaching adult Sunday school classes and small groups. Later, I was asked to serve on the church leadership as a board member.

After a few years of being faithful to speak on Wednesday and Sunday nights, my pastor asked me to speak on Mother's Day. I knew this was a divine appointment, but I sure was being stretched out of my comfort zone. I felt honored and blessed to have an opportunity to minister on a Sunday morning—especially on Mother's Day, as God had and was continuing to use motherhood to bring me into my God-given destiny and calling.

God continued to open doors periodically for me to speak at women's conferences and events. I was also able to use my teaching gift on annual mission trips to Honduras, where I would teach youth girls and ladies in the Word of God. I began to learn how to teach with an interpreter and use props to illustrate what I taught.

With all these opportunities, God was preparing, pruning, and refining me. I knew He had a destiny and calling on my life; He created me for more than I had known. I saw how God was using all of these opportunities to teach and develop me. Those were my foundational years of preparation that were training me for what God had next for my life.

After twenty years of ministering, I found myself going through an unexpected divorce. I was devastated and so heartbroken that I did not know how God could ever use me again. I had found so much fulfillment in serving God and pursuing the destiny He had for my life. But now, my life had come to a standstill; all I could do was focus on my own healing. My unanswered questions, "Why God? Why?" remained. All I ever desired was to become who God had created me to be; now I had to accept that my long-held dream of ministering with my former spouse would no longer be a part of my future. My heart was shattered—broken into pieces. I felt like my life was over, and I would never minister again. The divorce was an unexpected detour in my life that led me to tremendous devastation.

So what was next? Where should I go from there? I knew God's plan for me was to be healed and move forward into the destiny and calling He had for my life, but what did that look like now? How could I get up off this floor of devastation and continue the life God had destined me for?

Now, my path looked different from what I had previously believed it to be. That alone was hard for me to wrap my mind around. It was so grievous and felt so impossible. All my dreams and visions were suddenly gone. But God continued to heal me and had even greater ministry opportunities in store than I could have imagined.

My desire and priority over the last four years have been to focus on my own healing journey. I have diligently pursued my inner healing and deliverance to be made whole. In my healing process, I've been led to change churches to receive ministry for my healing over the divorce. Little did I know that within a few short months, God would give me favor once again.

My pastor's wife asked me to facilitate and teach a women's small group study on Sunday nights. I cried tears of joy because of God's faithfulness to me. I had so missed the joy that teaching and ministering to others brought to my life. And now God was blessing me with another opportunity to use my gift in this new church.

The enemy had used my unexpected divorce to make me doubt my gifting and calling; it seemed it was all dead—the ministry, calling, and my destiny. I had grieved the loss of so much all at one time. But suddenly, God was showing me that He had not forgotten me. He was not finished with me. He saw and valued me. I was humbled at this new beginning to use my God-given gift to bless others once again. What I thought was dead was coming back to life in a fresh way. As I began to teach, my healing journey accelerated.

While healing, God has been revealing deeper insights and truths that I would have never known or understood if not for the divorce. I have not seen the complete fulfillment of God's promises for my life, but I know God will bring forth the completion of my destiny in Him. This destiny includes writing another book, teaching women internationally—including via online Zoom calls, and ministering to ladies who have experienced significant loss and grief and need healing from divorce.

The godly connections God has given me over the last four years have been nothing short of a miracle. He has brought new women into my life who have helped my healing process. I now have a new perspective on what ministry looks like for me moving forward. I see God's hand in all the details of my healing journey, recognizing this is pushing me into the God-ordained destiny He has always had for me.

This past Mother's Day, a local church invited me to be their guest speaker. This invitation was very special to me as God reminded me that it would be my first time in the pulpit on a Sunday morning since my divorce. The first time I ever spoke on a Sunday morning, so many years ago, was on Mother's Day. This was another sign of God's redemptive love and power at work in my life. The gifting and anointing God has placed on my life did not die with the divorce. It is more alive than ever. And now that I have received greater healing, I have a greater level of anointing to use for God's glory.

Even when our lives take detours or we encounter unexpected circumstances that we did not see being a part of our narrative, if we desire to pursue the destiny He has for us, He continues orchestrating events for our good and His glory. God's promises for our lives do not change because of unexpected situations. His plan remains the same. Although our journey may change, His destination for our lives stays the same.

Before my divorce, I was pursuing my destiny and the calling of God on my life. The divorce caused me to stop and re-evaluate, heal, and become an even better version of myself, even more like the woman God designed me to be. I am still seeking my destiny—God's calling on my life. Being led by His Spirit, I continue to pursue the purpose for which He created me. The divorce did not stop God's destiny for my life. It has actually fueled my greater desire to pursue who He has called me to be. My desire is to become ALL God has created me TO BE, and TO DO all God has created me TO DO. I know if I BECOME who He has created me TO BE, then and only then can I DO all He has called me to DO.

I believe the JOY of stepping into the calling is to understand the importance of pursuing who God has created us to be. When we work to accomplish the goals not set forth by God, striving in our own power instead of abiding in His, we may perform successfully, but the eventual outcome will be empty and joyless.

To serve God wholeheartedly through our trials, we must give Him all our broken pieces and allow Him to transform us more into the image of Jesus. This process takes time and complete surrender.

> *"I am the vine; you are the branches. If you remain in me and I in you, you will bear much fruit; apart from me you can do nothing"* (John 15:5 NIV).

When we abide in and remain connected to the vine—Jesus—we will produce fruit. Abiding is staying close to God—submitting to His Word, resting in His presence, and seeking to know Him more. We must ask and seek His guidance to change and transform us so we can produce Holy Spirit's fruit.

> *But the fruit of the Spirit is love, joy, peace, patience, kindness, goodness, faithfulness, gentleness, and self-control. Against such things there is no law* (Galatians 5:22-23 NIV).

Being and *doing* are two different principles. For years, all I knew was *doing*, which is performance-based. Through my healing journey, Holy Spirit has and continues to bring me into *being*—allowing Holy Spirit to do the inner work in my soul, which includes my mind/will/emotions—to be more like Him. If I become who He has designed me to be, then I will be able to do what He has called me to do by abiding in Him—staying connected to His presence, His Word, and His ways. There really is no other way to step into your calling joyfully than *to be* with God. Works and performance without God's presence will wear us out, but being who God has created us *to be* will bring great joy to our souls. Out of that place of being *with* Him, we can do more *for* Him.

As you pursue your destiny in Christ, I encourage you to speak God's Word and promises out loud to yourself. *The tongue has the power of life and death, and those who love it will eat its fruit* (Proverbs 18:21 NIV). As you declare God's Word over yourself, claiming His promises as your beliefs, He will empower you to become all He has created you to do to glorify Him on this earth.

In closing, the declaration below was given to me by God several years ago. This declaration empowered me every day to believe that I could become all God had destined for me. I pray that you, too, find your destiny and step joyfully into your calling.

> *I am a daughter of God.*
> *I am an heir with God and a co-heir with Jesus.*
> *My mind is set on things above, and my heart desires the greater things of God.*
> *My body is whole and healthy, in Jesus' name.*
> *My emotions are aligned to the Spirit of God.*
> *My ways will glorify my Father in heaven.*
> *And my life will produce the fruit of the Spirit.*
> *I will advance the kingdom of God, and I will see a harvest of righteousness.*

I am chosen by God to lead.
I am empowered by Holy Spirit to lead.
I will lead from the heart of the Father.
I will lead with integrity.
I will lead with the authority given to me by Christ.
In Jesus' name. Amen!

Leading with Expectation

By Stacy Jo Coffee-Thorne

Have you ever stepped into a moment where nothing looked promising, but something inside you kept whispering, "God is about to move"? That whisper is expectation. It is faith in motion. It is the confident belief that God has already been working behind the scenes long before the evidence appears. A leadHER who carries expectation walks with anticipation that God's goodness is preparing the way, opening doors, and aligning the details. This kind of leadHERship does not flow from perfect circumstances; it flows from a heart anchored in the faithfulness of God.

Expectation is not wishful thinking; it is rooted in the character and promises of God. Hebrews 11:1 (NIV) says, *Now faith is confidence in what we hope for and assurance about what we do not see.* Expectation is this kind of assurance. It is the willingness to take God at His Word and trust that what He has spoken will come to pass. LeadHERs who carry this kind of faith draw others into it. Hope rises, and they begin to see possibilities where they once saw limitations.

Leading with expectation also means leading with prophetic vision. God often reveals things to our spirits long before we see them with our eyes. He gives glimpses, whispers, and impressions of what is coming. He shows us the potential in people before they see it in themselves. He breathes ideas into our hearts that feel bigger than our abilities. Habakkuk 2:3 (NIV) says, *For the revelation awaits an appointed time... Though it linger, wait for it; it will certainly come.* LeadHERs who carry prophetic expectations do not give up during delays. They hold the vision with confidence, trusting that God's timing is perfect.

A powerful truth about faith is that we do not fight for victory; we fight from victory. Jesus has already conquered the enemy, and the promises of God are already settled in heaven. Expectation comes from this revelation. When we lead with expectation, we are not begging God to move, but we are standing in agreement with what He has already declared. We speak His Word with confidence, and we believe His promises even when the natural circumstances have not yet aligned. This posture changes the way we pray, the way we lead, and the way we stand in the face of obstacles.

Romans 15:13 (NIV) says, *May the God of hope fill you with all joy and peace as you trust in him, so that you may overflow with hope.* When hope overflows in a leadHER, it impacts everyone connected to them. People begin to rise higher, faith begins to stir, and rooms that once felt heavy become places of possibility. A leadHER who carries expectation becomes a carrier of hope, and hope is powerful. Expectation shifts the atmosphere around us!

There have been many moments in my own journey when God asked me to believe long before I could see anything. Whether it was stepping into a new assignment or trusting Him with provision, the Holy Spirit stirred expectation before the evidence ever appeared. I learned that living with expectation means leaning into what God is doing behind the scenes. It means choosing to trust His voice above my own logic and believing that His promises are worth waiting for.

Expectation also strengthens endurance. When you expect God to finish what He started, you do not quit. You dig deep to find the energy to keep sowing and believing that His promises will come to pass, even when the process feels slow. You stand firm, knowing that the God who called you is the God who will see it through. Ephesians 3:20 (NIV) declares that God *is able to do immeasurably more than all we ask or imagine.* A leadHER who believes this leads with anticipation, not anxiety.

Leading with expectation is a kingdom mindset. It is believing that God's Word is true, His promises are active, and His power is already moving on your behalf. It is waking up with the quiet confidence that God is working even when you cannot see it.

So, lead with expectation. Lead with eyes that see beyond the now and faith that rests boldly in God's promises. Lead, knowing that it is already done, and the best is yet to come!

. . . .

Lori Nolan

For the past two decades, Lori Nolan has been a beacon of hope for people seeking holistic health solutions grounded in faith and integrity. She is a published author and speaker; her first book, *The Balanced Life Method: The 7-Pillar Blueprint to Lasting Health and Wellness,* launched in June 2024. Through the innovative Balanced Life Method, Lori empowers people to uncover the root causes of imbalance and embrace lasting transformations.

After spending years in the fitness industry and health coaching in the medical space, Lore recognized that the soul and spirit of a person must be healed before the body can be. In 2017, Lori Nolan Health, LLC was formed, and God gave her the 7-pillar approach.

Whether through personalized one-on-one coaching, dynamic group workshops, or impactful corporate wellness programs, Lori redefines what it means to live well. Rooted in a commitment to faith and personalized care, her brand inspires people to reclaim their health, guiding them toward sustainable wellness and a renewed sense of purpose, the way God intended according to His Word.

Restored Identity

By Lori Nolan

We all have a tremendous, purposeful call on our lives! God had each of our destinies written before the world began... what a revelation to get hold of. But pursuing our purpose and calling often requires us to seek healing from life's adversities. The good news is that God, our great healer, is always available, and when we allow Him to heal us, we will also experience spiritual and intellectual growth.

I always knew my purpose was to help people, even when I was young. I was very empathetic and compassionate growing up, and I still am today. But to become a kingdom leadHER, I had to embrace health and healing for myself. I want to share my story with you with the hope that it will offer encouragement to anyone questioning or wondering about their own life.

I grew up in a wonderful, loving Christian home with my parents and my younger brother, and attended Christian school. Around the fourth grade, I accepted Jesus into my heart, which I know only because my mom kept the note my Sunday school teacher sent home to let them know. From the outside, my family life seemed wonderful—we were the perfect little Christian family. But that wasn't really the case.

During my entire childhood, I was abused by a family member. I told my mom when I was about 9 years old, but since my dad was a new Christian, my mom thought it best to keep it from even my father. At that time, those things were not brought into the light. My mom said she would handle the situation, and for the next decade, my mom, the family members involved, and I kept this secret. When the truth came out, like it always does, my father was shocked and had his own battle to deal with psychologically. By the grace of God, my parents worked through their personal issues surrounding this and are still happily married today after 60 years.

Fast forward to my college years when I became the "worldly" party girl. I went to college, but didn't really want to be there. I didn't have much direction and struggled with anger, anxiety, self-worth, and the fear that no one would ever love me, even though my parents loved me and I'm blessed to have the best earthly dad. I didn't know my identity in Christ and had no idea how much my heavenly Father loves me.

I wanted to be married young and have a family of my own, so that's what I did. I got married at 21, had all three of my children by the time I was 31, and was divorced at 34. I then picked up right where I left off at age 20, acting out and looking for love in all the wrong places. I was so broken.

One night, I was suffering from enormous guilt and shame, begging God to please help me. I knew I was at the bottom of the barrel, and I needed His hand to pull me out, and that is exactly what He did. Deuteronomy 31:6 says, *Be strong and of good courage, do not fear nor be afraid of them; for the Lord your God, He is the One who goes with you, He will not leave you nor forsake you* (NKJV).

I was trying to piece my life back together while struggling to work and be a single mom. My heart broke every time my kids were shuttled back and forth from their dad's house to mine. That's when I became very vulnerable, and the enemy told me the biggest lie: I needed a man to complete my family. He made me believe that I couldn't be a single Christian mom and asked me, "How would that look to others?" Soon, I fell prey to the smooth talk of a man I barely knew. Though he ended up being abusive in every way, I still married him. I had no self-worth, was suffering with shame, and did not know the full love of God.

Being in that marriage put me and my children through almost ten years of agony, until we finally divorced. I had memorized Jeremiah 29:11 and said it often: *"For I know the plans I have for you," declares the Lord, "plans to prosper you and not to harm you, plans to give you hope and a future"* (NIV). But I wondered how that verse could possibly be true with the messes I kept getting my life into. The enemy had a plot to take me out and keep me out, but, praise God, the enemy always loses.

Starting the next chapter of my life in my early 40s, I pressed into my relationship with my heavenly Father and rededicated my life to Jesus. Up to that point, I felt like I knew God and was saved, but I had no real relationship with Him. Jesus took me into the wilderness with Him to begin my healing process; it was the most beautiful and peaceful time of my life. I wish I could say that after that I was fully healed and knew my worth and value in Christ, but I didn't. However, I did become fully surrendered, making Him Lord of my life.

I ended up marrying again—to the man I am married to now. It's been said that broken people attract broken people, but God is so merciful and loving, and He has a perfect plan for each of our lives. Unfortunately, that doesn't mean we won't go through pain and, most importantly, the refining fire. That's what the past thirteen years have been for me, a refining process. If you know the story of the silversmith and the spoon, you'll remember how the silversmith holds the metal in the fire while all the dross (the impurities) falls away. He knows precisely when to take the metal out of the fire: when he can see his reflection in it. God does the same with each of us. He uses fire to burn off our impurities so we can reflect who He is.

Over the course of the past 13 years, God has done so much with me. I went back to school for Integrative Nutrition, then started my own health coaching practice. That is where my purpose and my calling were truly birthed. I've been blessed to work with so many brilliant practitioners in the field and learn an abundance of knowledge.

My passion has always been to help others, especially when it comes to their health and wellness. My grandmother and mother instilled that love of all things wellness in me when I was young, but God had to teach me that being healthy and well meant so much more than just having a nice physique and good physical health.

About four years ago, we moved from New York to Florida; God was about to teach me something that would forever change my life. He introduced me to so many wonderful, godly people who taught me about inner/emotional healing. All the years I spent in the fitness and medical industries, I had never looked at the spirit and soul of a person. I learned to heal the body by fixing the symptoms, only to have them keep returning. But God showed me that I needed emotional healing. My heart had been very broken since I was abused when I was young, and from that, I developed self-worth issues.

I am all for good Christian counseling, but though I spent years in therapy trying to get help, I still didn't know how valuable and loved by my heavenly Father I was. There are some soul wounds—injuries to your mind, will, and emotions (heart)—that only God can heal. I had never learned about the power of the name and the blood of Jesus, nor about the authority that we as believers have over all the schemes of the devil. But God began teaching me all about that to ensure I understood that I can operate from a place of victory. I don't have to try to attain victory; in Christ, I already have it.

If you look at my life, there have been so many valleys and dark times that it's truly miraculous I am here today doing what I am doing. My earthly father was always my biggest fan and cheerleader; he still is to this day. And knowing that my heavenly Father had my purpose planned before I was ever conceived truly amazes me. The enemy tried to steal that when I was young and attempted to rip my family apart, but he failed at both!

God used even the most painful times to get me to where I am today. He makes beauty from ashes, Scripture tells us, and believe me, I've had some seasons in my life that were true ash piles. I wondered how God could ever use all I did and went through for good—sometimes I still do—but I trust His Word, and He is faithful to it. Romans 8:28 says, *And we know that all things work together for good to those who love God, to those who are called according to His purpose* (NKJV).

I took a spiritual gifts assessment at church, which revealed my gifts are Leadership, Encouragement, and Prophesy. Those gifts came from God; they certainly weren't manufactured by me. Today, I can absolutely see how those three tie into the calling God has given me to be a leadHER in His kingdom. I have a passion to see people healed from the inside out, and I want people to know how much health and wellness mean to God. He wants your soul to be healthy, so your body can follow.

> *Beloved, I pray that you may prosper in all things and be in health, just as your soul prospers* (3 John 1:2 NKJV).

I used to have very distorted and broken thinking about who I was and what I thought I deserved. I felt guilt, shame, and worthlessness due to the choices I had made. But that's not who God said I am.

> *I will praise You, for I am fearfully and wonderfully made; Marvelous are Your works, and that my soul knows very well* (Psalm 139:14 NKJV).

For so many years, my soul didn't know that I was fearfully and wonderfully made, even though I had read that verse thousands of times and wanted to believe it so badly. It wasn't until I went through my own inner healing that Jesus restored what the enemy stole, my *identity*. Now I know that I am His daughter, a princess of the King, and He calls me *Special.* I have value and worth that are priceless to Him... as we all do!

Years ago, I was coaching a lovely Christian woman who was suffering from the same symptoms God had healed me from. She was in the same spot I was for all those years. At that time, sadly, I didn't know about inner/emotional healing—I could only pray for her and help coach her memorize Scripture and use her words to create life. Looking back, there were many people I worked with who needed greater guidance than I could offer at the time. I believe that is why God is now calling me to another level in my coaching career.

God gave me seven pillars to use as a coaching tool in my business, and then He asked me to write about it to get it into the hands of others. Now, He is asking me to "get out of the box" and step up to the next level to help others receive emotional healing.

This is a HUGE calling! Don't think for a second that the enemy hasn't tried to whisper those old lies to me, because he has. But when we receive emotional healing, we learn how to hold onto that health through Jesus so we don't fall back into the trap of the devil. He's a liar and a thief and will always try to steal everything good from us, including our healing. But I hold onto the amazing experience I had with Jesus when I went through my emotional healing; the visions and images He gave me are emblazoned in my heart and mind.

Still, I've had many conversations with the Lord about this next season that He is asking me to step into. Maybe you've experienced the same thing. Questioning if you can do what He has called you to without messing up. Wondering if you're qualified or competent enough. God has repeatedly assured me that He called me, and therefore, He will equip me. I now understand that I had to walk through that process myself so I could help others.

Another lie from the enemy was that my life needed to be perfect for God to be able to use me. Let me tell you, many areas in my life are not restored yet. But although I still have unanswered prayers and this has been one of the most challenging areas in which to trust God, I continue to wait, always hoping in Him. Not being perfect does not delay us or disqualify us from the plans and purposes God has ordained for us. When He says we're ready, it's up to us to step into that anointed calling. God is never early, and He's never late. Even though you might be waiting on God to answer some very big prayers and even perform the impossible in your life, get active and work together with Him! Doing so will undoubtedly increase your faith and hope.

As kingdom leadHERs, we all have a call on our lives—whether in our homes as wives, moms, or grandmothers, in the workplace as CEOs or employees, or in ministry. We are women leaders, and we need to lead others to Jesus, no matter where we are. God put amazing gifts and talents inside you—things that are unique and special and given for a specific purpose. He asks you to steward those gifts wisely. As you do, God will keep promoting you, giving you missions that will further impact His kingdom.

If you haven't, I encourage you to spend time alone with God and specifically ask Him to reveal your gifts and how He wants you to use them. His direction will help propel you forward and give you clarity about the next steps He has ordained for your leadHERship calling.

And if you've never experienced inner/emotional healing, please pray about it. God may reveal some wounds in your heart that need to be addressed. People tend to think that just because they have never gone through something catastrophic like abuse, losing a loved one, or divorce, that they don't have soul wounds, but that's not true. We all have been wounded, even if it was from being bullied, losing a pet, or experiencing embarrassment. Jesus hung on the cross to heal all our wounds. He bore all our griefs and carried our sorrows.

Surely He has borne our griefs And carried our sorrows (Isaiah 53:4 NKJV).

Our God loves you and wants you to be whole and healed, both emotionally and physically. You may need to continue to seek emotional healing as seasons in life go on and new challenges arise. That's totally normal. Not until the day we step into glory and He wipes away all our tears will we finally be eternally perfected. What a glorious day that will be! But that doesn't mean we shouldn't start now.

Looking back now and reading Jeremiah 29:11, I know what it has meant to me over the years. So many times, I wanted to believe that God had a plan and purpose for me, but my circumstances told me the opposite. Thankfully, our circumstances change, but God's Word never will. I can say with all my heart that I know and believe that God's thoughts for me are good, He has thoughts of peace and not evil (no matter what's happening around me) to give me a future and a hope. Halleluiah! I've had to learn how to speak life over the situations in my life. It's easy to fall into negativity and speak the whispers of the enemy. We must be very intentional, and I encourage people to find several Scriptures (your sword) that pertain to you and your situation, and sharpen it daily. When the enemy comes to try to derail or distract you from your kingdom purpose, say those Scriptures out loud using the authority you have in Christ.

I praise God that the enemy always loses! I praise God that He spared my parents' marriage and restored it from a lie. I praise God that He protected my life, and no weapon formed against me could prosper. I praise God that He makes a way for all of us to heal and be restored and made new. I praise God that He has called me to help others and walk their journey to health, freedom, and wholeness—what a privilege it is to do His work.

And I praise God that He put this book in your hands. I pray my story will give you hope on your path to being the leadHER God has called you to be.

> *Now may the God of hope fill you with all joy and peace in believing, that you may abound in hope by the power of the Holy Spirit* (Romans 15:13 NKJV).

Alana de la Cruz

Alana de la Cruz is a multi-talented singer, #1 international best-selling author, transformational speaker for women and teens, entrepreneur, and founder of SOLWIN (Shining Our Light Women's International Network). Her Christian women's TV network airs on ROKU TV and all major streaming TV platforms, sharing global messages of hope, healing, and faith.

A two-time survivor of domestic violence, Alana's life is a powerful testimony of resilience and divine restoration. Her mission is to help women and teens recognize their worth, embrace their identity, and walk boldly into their God-given purpose. She is passionate about healing the soul—mind, will, and emotions—through inner transformation and spiritual growth.

Alana also serves as the Austin Director for She Leads Texas, a faith-based organization empowering women leaders across Texas with purpose, power, and prayer. She leads monthly gatherings that cultivate relationships, civic engagement, and spiritual growth.

Everywhere she goes, Alana plants seeds of healing, courage, and faith, leaving others inspired by the deep love of their heavenly Father.

Contact Alana via email: alana.delacruz@solwin.tv

God Equips the Called

By Alana de la Cruz

As we examine the essential qualities for success in leadHERship and business, we must give ample credence to the importance of resilience and perseverance. Even the Word of God clearly exhorts us to have perseverance: *And let us not grow weary of doing good, for in due season we will reap if we do not lose heart* (Galatians 6:9 NKJV).

Every woman in a leadHERship role encounters unique challenges and obstacles that test these pieces of "equipment"—resolve and determination. Somewhere along the way, we are bound to discover that we have been gifted with this equipment and will experience God's presence as He continues to develop and refine these qualities in us. Despite this, we may not realize that these traits are the exact tools we need to walk out our calling from God.

Very early in my life, God allowed me the privilege of an accidental discovery that He had inherently equipped me with resilience and perseverance. By happenstance, I learned that resilience and perseverance were not just learned traits—they were ingrained in my very being—a gift from God that was present in my DNA from a young age.

I vividly remember the moment when I first discovered my ability to press through and reach my own goals. I was just 7 years old, living in a small neighborhood. While all the other kids learned to ride their bikes with ease, I was left behind, struggling and relying on training wheels. Instead of feeling sorry for myself or shrinking down in comparison, I made a bold decision.

One morning, I approached my dad and asked him to take off my training wheels. I had set a goal for myself that I was determined to achieve: I would ride my bike without training wheels by sundown, when I had to be back in the house. I set my face like a flint toward that goal, with my strong-willed, 7-year-old mind. My only thought that day was: *I WILL RIDE MY BIKE WITHOUT MY TRAINING WHEELS LIKE THE BIG KIDS!*

I didn't want the process to take long; I didn't want to struggle for days or weeks. I wanted to be able to ride my bike like the rest of my friends, and I wanted it to happen quickly.

With no friends or family around to cheer me on or offer encouragement, I set off on my mission, not pitying myself. With so much courage and determination built up inside of me, I surely didn't mind if I had an audience or not. As I fell off the bike time and time again, I didn't give up. I didn't need anyone else to motivate me or push me forward; I was completely self-motivated, confident in my abilities, and determined to succeed despite any challenges I faced.

Hours passed. The sun began to dip below the horizon. But I refused to give up.

Finally, just before dusk, I did it. I rode my bike with just two wheels, a triumphant smile on my face as I pedaled around the neighborhood. I had achieved my goal through sheer determination and perseverance, and I knew at that moment that I was capable of overcoming any obstacle that stood in my way.

Years later, when I faced challenges and difficulties starting my own business, God brought me back to this indelible memory, reminding me that the same resilience that had carried me through the trials of learning to ride a bike would take me through any trial in life. He showed me that the same determination and perseverance that had been present in me as a child were still alive and well, ready to be called upon in times of need.

As women called into leadHERship, we must learn to tap into the resilience and perseverance God has placed within us. We must draw on the strength and determination that allowed us to overcome challenges in the past and use them to propel us forward in our current endeavors. Just as I refused to give up when learning to ride a bike, we must refuse to give up when faced with obstacles in our professional and personal lives.

Isaiah 40:31 reminds us, *But they that wait upon the Lord shall renew their strength; they shall mount up with wings as eagles; they shall run, and not be weary; and they shall walk, and not faint* (KJV). We can work to develop perseverance as we wait on the Lord, trusting that His timing is perfect.

As I reflect on my journey of stepping into my God-calling, I am reminded of the moment God first spoke to me about it back in 2004. I was with a friend eating at a Thai restaurant when God decided to show up unexpectedly, swiftly, and powerfully. His glory manifested upon me with such strength that my face almost landed on the plate of food when the waitress placed it in front of me. As my face lay prostrate on the table and my body limp under the power of God, I heard the audible voice of God speak. He said, "Your women's ministry will expand and broaden to women in Hollywood. Worldwide, worldwide, worldwide... television!"

At that time, I was just a newborn in the Lord, unsure of what He meant by worldwide television or even how to begin a women's ministry. But I held onto His words with all my heart, knowing that I had an undeniable, powerful encounter with the living God. I had received a word from God that would change the trajectory of my life forever.

Habakkuk 2:3 declares, *For the vision is yet for an appointed time; though it tarry, wait for it; because it will surely come, it will not tarry* (KJV). God's promises don't expire. They mature and come to fruition in His divine timing.

Fast forward to 2020—the pandemic hit, and my life hit the restart button. After being laid off from my job and unable to continue my princess party business due to the shutdown of events, I found myself at a crossroads, unsure of what to do next.

In that moment of uncertainty, God spoke to me powerfully once again, telling me that it was time to start a Christian women's internet TV network. I was convinced that He had chosen the wrong woman, but He reminded me of the words He spoke to me back in 2004 in that Thai restaurant. He pointed out that "Worldwide, worldwide, worldwide" stood for www or "internet" television and that He could only reveal it now since back in 2004, there was no such thing as YouTube, ROKU, or any streaming TV devices.

This revelation only further convinced me that my calling to start an internet TV network was certain. As crazy as the calling had sounded to my ears, I bowed before my Lord and Savior and, with fear and trembling, accepted the call.

> Being confident of this very thing, that He who began a good work in you will carry it on to completion until the day of Christ Jesus (Philippians 1:6 KJV).

As soon as I said yes, JOY began to pour into my heart; it was as if I could hear all of heaven rejoice simply because I said YES to my call.

This was a huge leap of faith. I began by holding Jesus' hand and not once ever letting go as I stepped out of the boat and onto the water. Within weeks of saying yes to my call, the enemy swooped in to try to abort the mission before it even had a chance to launch. However, God had already seen the beginning from the end and prepared me for this pivotal moment when I nearly quit.

Every day for a week, the Lord had spoken to me while I was in the shower—each time showing me the same 20-second vision. In the vision, I was wearing a beautiful red-carpet dress as I sat at a table at an awards ceremony. An announcer got on the microphone and said, "And the award goes to... SOLWIN TV!" I then saw myself reacting and walking up to the stage to receive the award in tears. Every time the Lord showed me this vision, my heart would tell Him, "Lord, this is all well and good; however, I don't want the accolades of man. I am not looking to be seen. I am only doing this for You and Your glory to be seen and known."

After the seventh day of seeing the vision, I had a phone call with a woman who declined to become part of our initial launch. Although the call began innocently, unbeknownst to me, I was entering into the lion's den where the lion was waiting to devour me. It was a sudden covert attack by the enemy, who began unleashing the bombs overhead. I was picked apart, judged, persecuted, and then told that God could never and would never bless me personally because of my past, and He could not and would not bless SOLWIN.

I hung up, absolutely stunned, heartbroken, and crushed into a million pieces. I truly looked up to this woman who had befriended me in a short period of time. She had a past similar to mine, and we had comparable talents. Confusion rushed in. Questions began to bombard my head. *Am I not capable of leading these women? God needs to use someone more worthy of this calling. I must have heard wrong... God wouldn't dare use me. Why would He give this important task to me? I am completely UNQUALIFIED!*

I felt dirty and stained, and all the shame of my past came rushing over me like a tidal wave. I felt like God could not and would not use me because of my past. The enemy used the unthoughtful words of this woman to speak layers of lies over me, and I believed it so much that immediately after the phone call, I told God out loud, "I QUIT!"

When I said this, I meant not only that I quit my calling, but that I quit Christianity altogether. For a brief moment, the enemy had me in a weak spot, deeply convinced of his barrage of lies—that I could never be good enough for this calling, nor my walk with God, and never would be.

But just as soon as I said it out loud, my heavenly Father's voice boomed as large as a city, speaking back to me audibly: "NO! YOU WILL NOT QUIT!"

I broke down crying, sobbing on my small desk in my bedroom. I was upset that God Almighty wouldn't even let me quit!

As I wept, images of the repeating seven-day shower vision began to emerge from my spirit like little bubbles of encouragement popping up in my devastated mind. The Holy Spirit whispered, "Remember what I showed you?" I began sobbing even harder.

Each bubble that rose was loaded and supercharged with God's love and hope for the future. Each time I accepted one, it would explode in my heart with God's joy and forgiveness toward the person who had spoken such negativity over me. I could feel myself getting a bit stronger minute by minute. I was experiencing the ministry of the Word of God—the JOY of the Lord truly is OUR STRENGTH!

> We are hard-pressed on every side, yet not crushed; we are perplexed, but not in despair; persecuted, but not forsaken; struck down, but not destroyed (2 Corinthians 4:8-9 NKJV).

Needless to say, I was pressed but not crushed, persecuted but not abandoned, struck down but not destroyed! My mind and my heart reverted to YES in that moment, and I have been forever faithful to His calling ever since that day.

And we know that all things work together for good to those who love God, to those who are the called according to His purpose (Romans 8:28 NKJV).

As I continued on through the early years of building an internet TV network, I faced countless obstacles and challenges. There were moments when I felt like giving up, when I doubted I had the strength to carry on all the responsibilities of both the business and everyday life.

So much sacrificial love, time, and energy have been poured into my calling, both behind the scenes and from front and center stage. But through all the ups and the downs, God has been faithful to walk through this journey with me. He brings a constant reminder of the resilience and perseverance that He had placed within me from a young age.

Just as I had refused to give up when learning to ride a bike, I now refuse to give up on my God and my God-given calling to expand my women's ministry through streaming television. I've tapped into the strength and determination God has instilled in me, knowing that with His guidance and support, I can overcome any obstacle that stands in my way.

Along the way, I also realized that perseverance isn't just about holding on in the moment—it's about keeping the long-term vision front and center. God equips us with patience and faith to see beyond the current struggle. The bike I once rode without training wheels was small compared to the monumental challenges God called me to lead through, yet the principle is the same: trust in the process, hold steadfast in faith, and keep your eyes on the divine destination. Every leadHER, every woman, every person called by God will face times of uncertainty, criticism, and exhaustion—but these moments are not signs to quit; they are confirmations that God is training and equipping us to rise above. Perseverance often comes with a deep awareness that even when human eyes cannot see a solution, God is already orchestrating the outcome. It is in those quiet, unseen moments that God strengthens our spirit and renews our hope for the journey ahead.

As I look back on the challenges I have faced and the victories I have achieved, gratitude for the resilience and perseverance God has gifted me fills me. I am reminded that He equips the called; all we have to do is say yes to His plan for our lives. He qualifies us to see the miraculous happen.

As women in leadHERship roles, let us stand firm in our faith, knowing that God has equipped us for such a time as this.

> *"For if you remain silent at this time, relief and deliverance will arise for the Jews from another place, but you and your father's house will perish. Yet who knows whether you have come to the kingdom for such a time as this?"* (Esther 4:14 NKJV).

Let us press on, confident in the knowledge that God's plans for us are greater than anything we could ever imagine.

If you remain faithful to the calling He spoke to you many years ago, and you never give up, no matter what the enemy may throw at you, He truly will do exceedingly, abundantly more than you could ever ask or think in your life! Clinging in faith to that truth will empower you to walk with greater resilience and perseverance. It's an upward cycle.

> *Now to Him who is able to do immeasurably more than all we ask or imagine, according to His power that is at work within us* (Ephesians 3:20 NIV).

> *Let us hold fast the confession of our hope without wavering, for He who promised is faithful* (Hebrews 10:23 ESV).

Resilience and perseverance are not just traits that we can develop—they are gifts that have been given to us by a loving and caring God. And when we lean on Him and trust in His plan for our lives, we can be confident that we will have the strength and determination to overcome any challenge that comes our way.

> *The one who calls you is faithful, and he will do it*
> (1 Thessalonians 5:24 NIV).

Let us embrace the resilience and perseverance equipment that God has placed within us, and let us use it to overcome the challenges of leadHERship and business. With God's strength guiding us, we can achieve great things and make a lasting impact for the sake of His kingdom.

Psalm 138:8 declares, *The Lord will fulfill his purpose for me; your steadfast love, O Lord, endures forever* (ESV).

Whatever the Lord has called and purposed you to do, you can be certain that He has and will equip you. So, just say yes, and move forward confidently with the resilience and perseverance He has so graciously gifted you!

Leading with Boldness

By DeAnn Alaine

I have never had a shortage of boldness.

In 2013, I was taking acting classes in Atlanta, Georgia. One Sunday, I had the opportunity to visit Buckhead—an expensive area in Atlanta. My hubby has seen a sprawling home for sale on the internet, so I decided to check it out. When I arrived at the edge of the property, the gate was open, so I took the chance and drove up to the 20,000+ square foot home. I got out of my car, walked up to the beautifully crafted, double-door entrance with pillars on each side, and knocked. A gentleman came out from a different entrance to greet me. I told him why I had shown up, and he welcomed me into his home to meet his wife and proceeded to take me on a 2 1/2-hour tour—I didn't even see the entire home!

Boldness with legs can be a very powerful tool. However, it can also be incredibly dangerous! Let's take a look at the boldness of one man in Gethsemane the night Jesus was betrayed.

> Jesus said, "My friend, go ahead and do what you have come for."
>
> Then the others grabbed Jesus and arrested him. But one of the men with Jesus pulled out his sword and struck the high priest's slave, slashing off his ear.
>
> "Put away your sword," Jesus told him. "Those who use the sword will die by the sword. Don't you realize that I could ask my father for thousands of angels to protect us, and he would send them instantly? But if I did, how would the Scriptures be fulfilled that describe what must happen now?" (Matthew 26:50-54 NLT).

Later in this story, Jesus miraculously attaches the man's ear back to his head—but the slashing never needed to happen in the first place!

Clearly, there are different types of boldness. Let's look at a different situation.

> Herod was delighted at the opportunity to see Jesus, because he had heard about him, and had been hoping for a long timeto see him perform a miracle. He asked Jesus question after question, but Jesus refused to answer (Luke 23:8-9 NLT).

What a stunning example Jesus gives us of being bold under pressure! Of all people, Jesus could have said whatever He wanted, yet He boldly remained silent!

Was Jesus always quiet in His boldness? Nope. Jesus had just healed a demon-possessed man who was blind and mute. When the Pharisees heard about the miracle, they criticized Him; Jesus knew their thoughts and publicly called them out. *"You brood of snakes! How could evil men like you speak what is good and right? For whatever is in your heart determines what you say"* (Matthew 12:34 NLT).

Boldness is a trait common to leadHERs. LeadHERs tend to be innovators and seek wisdom and courage to boldly go in the direction God has called them, rather than simply following the crowd.

On the flip side, allowing boldness to take over without the practice of self-control can cause even a leadHER to get into verbal trouble. When we choose boldness without the direction of His Holy Ghost, we can do great damage to people who support the cause we lead!

Personally, I have learned that, although I am a bold, Irish leadHER, I cannot be the General of Joy who spouts out verbal ear-slashing garbage to people around me and then tries to justify it! Being a bold leadHER—as God has called us—requires sensitivity training! We must learn to be sensitive to His Holy Ghost to know what kind of boldness to apply.

When I spoke to the couple at the Buckhead mansion, God had me share with them about the Lord and heaven. My testimony met them where they were. My act, which may have seemed impetuous—even an invasion of someone's privacy—was really a bold adventure designed and led by His Holy Ghost.

Let's always seek God's wisdom as we strive to lead boldly where He would have us go—so we don't inadvertently cut off someone's ear!

. . . .

Roberta Kay

Roberta Kay is a pastor, entrepreneur, investor, and certified financial and life coach whose heart is to empower women to become all they were created to be. A widow and proud mother of two amazing young adult sons, Roberta has walked through her own seasons of loss, healing, and restoration. Out of those experiences, she has discovered her true calling—to equip women to rise in faith, walk in freedom, and lead with courage, even when they don't feel qualified.

She is the founder of Roberta Kay Ministries, where she blends biblical truth, personal testimony, and practical wisdom to help women reset, refocus, and reignite their faith. With over 20 years of experience as the owner of the largest preschool on Florida's Treasure Coast, Roberta brings entrepreneurial insight and leadership experience into her ministry and coaching. Her mission is simple: to inspire women to embrace God's call, step into leadership with confidence, and live with clarity, courage, and joy.

For prayer requests, more information, or to connect, please email Roberta Kay at connect@robertakay.com or visit www.robertakay.com

Leading When You Don't Feel Qualified

By Roberta Kay

Since you are reading this book called *Kingdom LeadHERship*, I'm going to assume you are hearing a call from God to lead. That can be a daunting position to be in when you feel unqualified. If that's where you are, be encouraged! God is working in your life, preparing to unfold an incredible plan—all you have to do is say, "Yes."

Growing up, my family was, well, let's just say, not ideal. But God chose my situation just for me, and He used every one of my steps to mold me into the leadHER He created me to be. When I was a child, no one ever focused on my potential, my goals and dreams, or even my future success. I did not have any role models grooming me to run a business or succeed in life. If you had told my younger self that one day I'd be leading a ministry, building schools, and encouraging women to rise up in their calling, I would have laughed, and maybe even cried. There was no way that I would have been able to see myself accomplishing anything. I felt unworthy, invisible, and unseen. But God...

Mine is a story of how God took a little girl from a small town, born into dysfunction and abuse, and slowly uncovered the leadHER He had already planted inside her. It's a story not of my strength, but of His. I love what Paul wrote in 2 Corinthians 12:9-10. *And he said unto me, My grace is sufficient for thee: for my strength is made perfect in weakness. Most gladly therefore will I rather glory in my infirmities, that the power of Christ may rest upon me. Therefore, I take pleasure in infirmities, in reproaches, in necessities, in persecutions, in distresses for Christ's sake: for when I am weak, then am I strong* (KJV). Without the power and strength of Christ, I would never have become who I am today. And if He can do it for me, He can surely do it for you.

I grew up in a lower-middle-class family in a small, country town. Both my parents worked very hard. My mom was a waitress at a nearby diner, and my dad was a carpenter. I knew they loved me, but things were far from what a home should be. My dad was a raging alcoholic and was verbally and physically abusive to my mom. My earliest memories are tinged with chaos, confusion, fighting, and broken promises. Because of the fighting, fear gripped my soul at an early age. I was terrified of people, failure, leaving my bedroom at night, and simply of being seen.

Fear and insecurities haunted my life in almost every area. At times, I would freeze, unable to speak, which happened especially when others were mistreating me. At school, I was always embarrassed. Finances were tight at home, so my mom made a lot of my clothes. They were not very fashionable, and were often too short as I grew faster than she could sew. I felt ashamed and didn't know how to stand up for myself or say "No," so I allowed things to happen even when I didn't want them to. I often had a feeling deep down that I shouldn't do something, but I listened to others instead of trusting the voice of God or the nudging of His Spirit. Unfortunately, I carried that teenage response into my adulthood. I hadn't yet learned to honor that quiet knowing inside me.

I struggled to see myself as anything valuable. My father would humiliate me, calling me stupid. He would take anything I said about what I wanted to do or become, and basically let me know that I didn't have a chance. And I believed him. I thought I had nothing to offer and that I could never become anything or have anything. That lie became a lens through which I saw everything.

I was drifting, without purpose, without promise, and without hope. I constantly compared myself to others—even in high school, everyone else seemed so put together. Their lives seemed whole; mine felt fractured. Their future seemed promising; mine felt impossible.

Even after I gave my life to the Lord, the enemy had a way of whispering reminders of my past: "You'll never be enough." "You'll never measure up." "You'll never do anything worthwhile."

Looking back, I see that God was already writing my leadHERship story even in the mess. He had been placing seeds in me all along—even when I didn't recognize them.

As a little girl, I took over a paper route and grew it. I added neighborhoods, managed schedules, and collected payments—unknowingly building business skills. Then there was the backyard fair I created: I charged admission and sold tickets to games I had made up. I even recruited neighborhood kids to help. I was organizing, leading, and marketing at 12 years old.

Still, I felt useless. Trauma, fear, and low self-worth had grown deep roots within me.

My teen and early adult years were complicated. With such low self-esteem and the lies that constantly tormented me, I couldn't see the good. I worked in great atmospheres and had such potential, but I didn't understand that God was opening doors for my success. I taught dance classes and kept the books for the studio. I worked for IBM in the personnel department. Still, I didn't recognize my gifts and accomplishments; all I could see was that helpless, fearful, and insecure little girl. All I felt inside was pain. And I fell into a deep drug addiction.

My addiction added another layer of shame. I couldn't stop the spiral. I began attending college for business and dance, where I was one of the top cheerleaders. But I continued reaching for the drugs and alcohol to cover up my fears. Just one and a half semesters in, I was injured during a cheer flip, causing me to drop out. No one else knew it at the time, but I had missed so many classes due to the drugs and alcohol that the injury was almost a blessing. Unfortunately, this left even more scars, which I thought proved that I was never going to make it in life.

My parents moved to Florida, and I reluctantly followed. That was God's design. My father had stopped drinking, and things were looking better for my parents. Unfortunately, my drug addiction hadn't stopped. After moving, I worked for an investment company in the operations department, but I was still so lost, running with all the wrong kind of people. It was a nightmare that I didn't know how to escape. But God began to move on my behalf like never before. He found me in my lowest place and pulled me out. Through the prayers of others and an invitation to a small Bible study, my life took a drastic turn for the better. I gave my life to Christ, and the healing process began.

After my salvation, everything began to shift. God sovereignly delivered me from drug addiction and smoking as He began healing me from the inside out. He was moving fast! But I was still so fearful. I couldn't even say hello to people or look them in the eye. God began to place me in different ministries—first, with the babies, then the children's ministry. I had no idea what He was doing, but He sure did.

A pastor asked me to share my testimony at a boy's prison, and I just said yes, even though I was so scared. I had never spoken in front of anyone, and now I was supposed to address about 400 teenage boys in a juvenile detention center. I will never forget that day as I took my first step onto the stage and literally felt God take over. That shy little girl stayed behind the curtain as I stood there and shared with those young men what the Lord had done in my life. I gave the altar call for them to receive Christ, and nearly every one of them came forward. Soon after that day, I was asked to become the youth pastor and the administrative secretary of a soon-to-be-established church.

I couldn't believe what God was doing through me. I was helping build a church from the ground up. The things He was teaching me were amazing. We didn't have Google or smartphones back then. But I had a direct line to the Father, who began to speak to me and give me the courage to say, "Yes."

I was still terrified, but I was obedient. I just kept asking the Lord for His wisdom and strength, and each small yes added a brick to the foundation God was building in me. I started leading from behind the scenes—handling logistics, schedules, and budgets, encouraging youth, and managing the office, books, and events. God was pulling out the leadHER in me, and I didn't even know it.

Years later, I married a pastor and started a small preschool at my father-in-law's church. Then, in 2002, my father-in-law, who was aging and burdened, pleaded with my husband and me to take the reins of the church. So, despite caring for our own two toddlers, we took on the ministry, committing to rebuild the congregation that had been through several painful church splits and was on the verge of bankruptcy. We expanded the preschool, using its growth to help financially support and sustain the church, and I became a senior pastor. It was a leap of faith and obedience rooted in faith that God would provide.

Kidzone Preschool Academy became one of the largest preschools on the Treasure Coast of Florida. Life was good, and we were watching the Lord do miracles almost daily. We had built a church and a K-12 school in St Marc, Haiti, as our mission work, and we were ready to expand the ministry and plant other preschools in different states. In 2013, we headed out to Arizona to begin the expansion.

Then, in 2015, the unthinkable happened. My husband became gravely ill with liver cancer and passed away on January 11, 2016. I never thought I would be a widow at 50 years old. I was now a single mom, trying not only to survive but also to be there for my two teenage boys, who were just 14 and 15 years old. They were trying to navigate one of the toughest seasons of their lives, and I was doing my best to hold everything together—parenting, pastoring, running the preschool, and leading. All while working through my own pain.

Within two weeks after my husband passed away, my father died unexpectedly (my mom had passed away a few months before my first son was born). And then, on top of everything, just one month later, our preschool lost one of its programs due to an administrative issue, causing us to suffer a substantial financial loss. We were in trouble. All of our advisors said we'd be bankrupt in six months. "Sell the school," they said. "Close the doors." "Walk away." I was exhausted—spiritually, emotionally, and physically. I felt completely alone and so inadequate.

But God spoke to me and told me, "Don't sell." Every day, He gave me the next step. I didn't have a five-year plan, but I had a five-minute prayer. I would say, "God, what do I do today?" And He would answer.

Due to my husband's illness, we had been unable to personally manage the facilities or oversee the operations for the previous three years, and what happened in our absence was heartbreaking. The buildings and the grounds of the preschool and church site, along with another property the church owned, had been utterly neglected. From multiple broken air conditioning units to destroyed plumbing, a failed lift station, and other major structural concerns, everything needed attention, and we required finances to repair it all. Somehow, God kept providing.

One of the most powerful miracles during that time was with a property we owned in Tennessee. The pool needed extensive repairs; the estimate was $30,000, money we didn't have. But God brought a dear couple who had heard about the need to donate the full amount. It was a beautiful sign that I was not alone and that God was still providing.

During that same season, God was using me to pour into our teachers. As He was strengthening me, I saw Him work in them, too. Some began to believe, many for the first time, that God could use them in greater ways, and many were set free from things holding them back. It was beautiful to see God move in such powerful ways. He was literally changing lives before my eyes.

Through pouring into those women and seeing God move, Roberta Kay Ministries was birthed. What started there inside the preschool grew in my heart; I knew I wanted to empower others to become all that God created them to be. I recognized all that God had done and was doing in my life, and now I was seeing Him do it in others' lives, too.

God was moving powerfully, and everyone, including members of the church, was commenting about how strong I was. However, I knew I was not working in my own power; the strength they were seeing was God's. Yet even with all the signs, wonders, and miracles I was experiencing, that little voice kept roaring at me: "You can't do this." "You're not smart enough." "You're going to lose it all." Unfortunately, I began to believe those lies.

Looking back now, I can see so clearly: My low self-esteem caused me to doubt what God was already doing through me. Although I gave Him praise for everything, I was unable to see that He was using me. He was leading me daily, giving me the wisdom and the strength I needed. And though I had the answers, I didn't trust myself to lead. Instead, I was leaning on others' voices more than trusting the still, small voice of God within me. That was the lesson!

When God places YOU in a position, know that He will speak to YOU. Others may have opinions, but God will give direction to those He has positioned. He doesn't need our wisdom, our resources, or our resume; He just needs our YES, our obedience, and our faithfulness to do His will.

I'm so grateful I said YES! When everyone else was advising me to sell, God said, "No, it's not time." I am thankful for those years of pain, when I learned to surrender to God and trust His timing—and His timing was perfect. Around mid-2019, the Holy Spirit began to nudge me with the instruction that it was time to put the facility on the market. I didn't understand it. I argued, "But God, this is our income. It's doing well. We only have one more year before we will be able to obtain the program funds again. Why would we walk away now?" He didn't give me the reasons why, He just said, "Trust me."

Reluctantly, I chose to trust Him and put the property on the market. The preschool typically served 300 to 350 students, but by the end of April 2020, right before we closed on the sale, we were down to 45-50 students due to COVID-19. And that is when I saw the hand of God. He knew a year before what was going to happen. We don't see what God sees. And we don't always understand His ways. His Word tells us that His ways are higher than our ways. We have to learn to trust Him and follow His voice.

Since then, God has opened up a whole new world for me with Roberta Kay Ministries, where I am able to do what I love: Encourage others in their faith by helping them see that God is doing above and beyond all they could ask or think. We are all called and equipped for a beautiful future. Your past does not disqualify you; it has prepared you for your next chapter. Every trauma, loss, mistake, and challenge becomes fertile soil where God will grow something remarkable.

Looking back, I can see that as I walked the many roads of my journey, God was making me into a leadHER even though I felt completely unqualified. Being a leadHER doesn't come from a title, a healthy family background, or living a life of privilege. It isn't about having it all together or always making the right decisions. And being a leadHER isn't reserved for the best speakers or the most confident personalities. No—being a true leadHER is about saying YES to God and trusting Him to use your life—even, or maybe especially, the broken parts.

If you feel unqualified to lead, you are starting in a great place. Feeling unqualified means you'll have to rely on God—and that's what faith is all about. When you fear you aren't enough—smart enough, good enough, prepared enough, strong enough—remind yourself that it's not about what you can do, it's about what God wants to do through you. As Paul wrote in Philippians 4:13, *I can do all things through Christ who strengthens me* (NKJV).

If God is calling you to lead, and you don't know where to begin, start by saying "Yes." He will meet you there. Then, He will lead you, guide you, and cause all things to work together for your good and the good of those He has called you to lead (Romans 8:28)! As a follower of Christ, you are already a leadHER—because He lives in you. And, make no mistake, He has created you to do great things. In Him, you are qualified.

So, rise up, leadHER. It's your time to shine!

Heather Cockrell

Heather Cockrell was born and raised in South Carolina, but Birmingham, Alabama, became home when she relocated with her job over 25 years ago. There, she met her husband of 23 years, Duane; they have been blessed with three amazing children—Alex, Danielle, & Denise.

Although Heather has been in the corporate world for over 30 years, she discovered her true calling as a women's empowerment coach through serving in numerous women's ministries and pursuing ministry leadership training at Highlands College.

Heather is a coach and mentor with a passion for enabling women to discover and embrace their true God-given identity and empowering them to step into the unique calling God created them to fulfill for such a time as this! Through this passion, God birthed Sister to Sister, Heather's one-on-one coaching and women of faith networking ministry.

You can contact Heather at mysistertosister.life@gmail.com and find her and Sister to Sister on social media or at www.sistertosister.life.

Discovering Your Kingdom Purpose

By Heather Cockrell

Do you feel God calling you to do more, but you aren't sure what? Do you listen to sermons and podcasts or read books about people "discovering their purpose" or "walking in their calling" and wonder how they figured it out, what steps they took, and how God revealed their calling to them?

That was me a few years ago. I saw many people at church, on social media, and at ministry conferences who seemed to be doing exactly what God had created them to do. They were flourishing and making an impact in God's kingdom—how did they know what to do? Did they just wake up one morning with a divine revelation? Did they hear a celestial "ding!" and the light bulb just flipped on? I felt like I was the only one trying to figure it all out.

I used to constantly jump into church and ministry projects because there was a need to fill and I knew I could help. Time and time again, I volunteered for various activities, teams, and projects, thinking maybe I'd discover my one true purpose for being on earth; perhaps I would finally know what God was calling me to do and who He was calling me to be. I had no doubt He was calling me, but what exactly was He calling me to do? I served at church and in my community, went to ministry leadership school for two years, led women's Bible studies, and helped launch a new women's ministry. I ended up tired, stressed, and burned out. Why was this? I was doing the Lord's work—being the hands and feet of Jesus. I couldn't help but wonder, *Why do I feel so worn down? What's wrong with me?*

Don't misunderstand, God used every single bit of my work. I made godly relationships, prayed with people, and spoke truth to others. I served my community and those in need and saw God do miraculous things. Along the way, I discovered some things about myself and especially about how amazing God is. Still, I felt like there was so much more that He wanted me to do. But what? And how was I supposed to figure it out? I had done ALL the things I felt called to do and still hadn't discovered the answer.

Looking back now, I see that I was on a journey to discover my kingdom purpose. God was preparing me with every single step, teaching me to walk in the Spirit—to discern the right steps from the wrong ones and recognize His confirmation to continue or His wisdom to stop. God used my pain, missteps, and misunderstandings for His glory, eventually making the confusing crystal clear. Unexpectedly, what excited me, gave me peace, and encouraged me were not the things I was good at or had mastered, but those paths that were new and uncomfortable, that stretched my confidence and strengthened my faith. This journey to my kingdom purpose has been one of the most rewarding parts of my life.

I cannot fully articulate what it means to be an active part of building God's kingdom while walking out your unique calling; it is an incredible experience, which may feel difficult and, at times, even painful. On my journey, the Lord revealed some steps that allowed me to discover my unique purpose and calling for His kingdom, which I'd like to share with you.

TO FIND YOUR KINGDOM PURPOSE...
DEVELOP A RELATIONSHIP WITH GOD

The first fundamental and foundational discovery I made on my journey to discovering my purpose in God's kingdom began with developing a relationship with Him.

Growing up, I didn't learn about God having a purpose or calling for His children, and I never heard about having a relationship with Him. My religious environment was strict, with a lot of people doing things in the name of God while talking about rules, doctrine, and consequences. I saw people say one thing, but do another, and I wanted nothing to do with it. I saw misguided religion, which skewed my view of God and persuaded me to stay away from Him for most of my life.

Later, when I finally got so buried in my own sin and shame, I became desperate enough to seek out the true God instead of the god I had fabricated. I was desperate to know Him, to hear from Him, and for Him to tell me how to fix the mess I had created.

You see, I had been unfaithful to my husband—and not just with anyone; I had an affair with the husband of my best friend. When my husband found out, my whole world started crumbling around me. I didn't know how to fix it, nor how to fix what was so broken inside me that had caused me to commit this horrible betrayal. I cried out to God and told Him I would do anything; I would go anywhere—even back to that religion I swore I would never return to. I just needed Him. And I needed Him to tell me what to do.

God was right there when I opened my heart to Him. He had always been there, just waiting on me. When I cried out to Him, not only did He restore my marriage, but He also redeemed my friendship with my best friend and saved my family. My husband and I have now been married for 23 years and have three beautiful children. Only God!

"You will seek me and find me when you seek me with your whole heart" (Jeremiah 29:13 NIV).

No matter what or who has kept you from having a deeply close and personal relationship with God, know that He is waiting for you. For me, it was misguided religion; perhaps you've been wounded by a human relationship, a career, or the loss of a dream. Is there something you thought you were born to do or someone you thought you were destined to be with, but instead that something ended up leaving you less than satisfied or even broken-hearted? The pain I endured changed everything for me: my goals, my thoughts, and my perspective about myself and everything around me.

Having a relationship with your heavenly Father is the single most deeply satisfying and fulfilling thing possible. God created relationships, and He wants to have one with you! All you have to do is set your eyes on Him and speak to Him, inviting Him to be a part of your life. Take that first step, ask Him to direct your steps, and before you know it, you will be seeking Him with your whole heart in everything you do.

LEARN TO COMMUNICATE WITH GOD

The second crucial step in discovering your kingdom purpose is communicating with your Father. Communication is the key to any healthy relationship, so listening for and discerning the Creator's voice is paramount to walking out the purpose He has for you.

God speaks to each of us differently because He created each of us uniquely. He knows you better than anyone does, so He knows what method of communication resonates best with you. You only need to take the time to listen to hear His voice.

"Be still, and know that I am God" (Psalm 46:10 NIV).

God speaks through His Word. Sometimes I will see or hear the same Scripture multiple times in the span of a few days or weeks. Or I'll get chills when I'm reading a particular story in the Bible. Frequently, I will read a verse I've read many times in the past, when it suddenly comes alive to me in a new way. If you are open to listening as you read God's Word, the Holy Spirit will always reveal what He wants you to know. Open your heart by praying, "Lord, what do you want me to know as I read your Scripture? How do you want me to apply it?"

God also speaks through worship. For over a year, I was in an almost impossible, toxic work situation. I had been with the same company for 30 years, so the decision of whether to stay or go wasn't an easy one. I prayed for direction for months with no answer. One day, while I was in the middle of singing and worshipping, I heard, "It's done. Trust my timing." I knew God was referring to my job. In that moment, peace washed over me. Anxiety and stress were suddenly replaced with calm confidence. I did my part and started applying and interviewing for jobs. I asked God to open the right doors and close the wrong ones. Six weeks later, I was offered a new position at a different company. That job came with a salary increase, less responsibility, and a work/life balance I hadn't experienced in decades.

At times, God speaks through dreams and visions. Through the years, I've heard of famous songs, inventions, and even art that came to creators in dreams. Some of my friends have very vivid dreams that they have seen come to fruition or that they fully understand months or even years later. God has yet to speak to me through dreams, but He has given me visions from time to time when I am fully awake. Rarely do I understand what they mean in the moment, but He reveals them in time.

God speaks through His people. Early in my walk with Him, I was praying about which women's Bible study to attend. It was going to be my first study as a part of the first church I joined in my adulthood, so it was a big step for me, and I wanted Him to choose it. Over the course of two weeks, I had no less than ten people suggest that I join the same study! After hearing that same suggestion so many times, there was no doubt in my mind that God was speaking through other people; so, of course, I signed up. That Bible study was life-altering. It helped me heal from so many of my past hurts and mistakes, was one of the most powerful experiences of my life, and introduced me to three of my closest and most trusted friends.

When I was first listening for God's voice, I was so unsure of how to discern His thoughts from mine. But as I practiced—studying His Word, listening with my heart in worship, and seeking the guidance of other trusted Christian sources—and asked God for clarification, His voice has become clearer. One of the greatest joys I've had is learning to discern my heavenly Father's voice. To be able to hear His direction and revelations, receive His wise guidance, bask in His love, and laugh at His humor is priceless!

Once I learned to recognize my Father's voice, I could ask Him all kinds of questions, and my prayer life changed drastically. Now, when I pray, I always praise Him, thank Him, and ask Him for what I need, but I find that asking specific questions bears so much good fruit and honestly is fun because it's interactive. It's a dialogue. He answers in His time, not mine, and I'm 1000% good with that!

ASK HIM

When a mentor asked me, "Who does God say you are?" I was dumbfounded and a bit embarrassed to realize I had never even *thought* to ask Him. I felt silly, but since then, I've realized that many others have never asked Him either. Why is that? Why do we not ask the One who created us, who He created us to be?

To accept my true identity in God, I had to get rid of the false identities others had spoken over me. I prayed and I asked my Father to reveal to me any false identities I had taken on. These came quickly to mind, and they weren't pretty: liar, cheater, and adulterer were among the worst. Those were things I had done in my past, but they are not who I am and certainly not who He created me to be. Then I prayed and asked God to crucify those false identities in the mighty name of Jesus. When I did, I had a vision of Jesus ripping up that list and throwing it over His shoulder! Then He looked directly at me and said, "Done!"

Next, I prayed and asked, "Father, who do YOU say I am?"

I was going to write down every word so I didn't forget anything I heard. With my pen hovering over a piece of blank paper, I waited. Seconds went by, and I didn't hear anything. Then... bam! The words started flooding into my mind: daughter, mother, coach, servant, leader, builder, warrior.

Then the unexpected happened: I heard "gardener," and I had a vision of being in a garden with tall flowers that had the faces of people on them. I was walking from flower to flower, watering them with my watering can. The other roles weren't much of a surprise, but "gardener" had me stumped. It was a term I never would have considered part of my identity, and I wasn't clear in the least what God's expectations were of me in that role. So, of course, I asked Him!

"Father, what does a gardener do for your kingdom? What does it look like for me in this season?"

Understanding my kingdom purpose has changed my dialogue with my heavenly Father. As our relationship deepens and my understanding of Him grows, He continues to reveal additional aspects of my purpose, guiding my assignments. Once you know who God created you to be, you won't want to be anyone else!

For we are God's masterpiece. He has created us anew in Christ Jesus to do good works, which he prepared in advance for us to do (Ephesians 2:10 NIV).

God has created each of us with spiritual gifts and abilities, and we are called to exercise those gifts. As followers of Messiah, we have the same fundamental purpose and calling: To love and glorify God, love His people, and make disciples. But how we do that, how we walk that out individually, is unique to each of us because we are all created differently—with a specific set of gifts and talents.

> We have different gifts, according to the grace given to each of us (Romans 12:6 NIV).

One way God reveals our kingdom purpose is through our spiritual gifts. Do you know what your spiritual gifts are? The first time I took a spiritual gifts assessment, the results dumbfounded me. High on my list were Pastor/Shepherd and Exhortation. *Huh? I don't want to be a pastor,* I thought. *I don't like public speaking, and I'm not sure how many Scriptures I can actually recall to counsel or inspire anyone!*

As I began to start walking out what I felt the Lord calling me to do from season to season, I began to have opportunities to exercise my gifts, and I felt the confirmation. My preconceived notions were not how God intended me to use the gifts He had given me! Two activities I am most passionate about now are speaking God's truth to support and encourage people going through difficult times (exhortation and pastoring/shepherding). I don't stand on a stage or speak to large crowds; I help individuals as God brings them into my life.

I have a personal relationship with my Creator, I listen to His voice, and because I asked, He's told me about my true identity in Him and guided me to exercise my spiritual gifts.

WALK IN FAITH

The last and final step in the journey to my kingdom purpose was to walk forward in faith. I began taking one step at a time, following His lead.

Walking by faith means being willing to start walking even when you don't know exactly where you're heading. If we had all the answers up front, where would faith even come in? The more we walk by faith, the more beautiful and exciting the process becomes, and the deeper our relationship with Him develops. As God confirms each step, the more confidently we become in walking out our calling.

God told me I was a coach and a gardener for His kingdom. I am now coaching people and planting seeds of His truth via several different avenues, but I started out with one small step.

As opportunities arose, I prayed for God to direct my steps, to open my eyes to see and my ears to hear the Holy Spirit. I assessed if I had peace or anxiety about getting involved in a new ministry or project, and when I needed more confirmation before saying yes, I asked for it. I didn't rush in based on my own thoughts, but I took time to pause and pray. Did I take a few wrong steps along the way? Absolutely. But that's OK. God turned me left, right, or had me step back, and I learned valuable lessons along the way that I applied as I continued taking steps forward and growing in spiritual maturity. God can do more with the right motivation and a wrong step than with no step at all.

Our walk with God is an ongoing journey and adventure! But when we travel with the Creator of the universe, what could be more exciting? All good things come from Him, so we know that whatever He has for us will be levels above anything we could possibly imagine for ourselves.

So, what are you waiting for? Be brave! Seek a relationship with God, listen for His voice, ask for His guidance, and then walk forward in faith as you rise into your kingdom purpose!

For God has not given us a spirit of fear, but of power and of love and of a sound mind (2 Timothy 1:7 NKJV).

Leading with Forgiveness

By Stacy Jo Coffee-Thorne

Forgiveness is one of the hardest choices we will ever make, yet it is also one of the most freeing. As leadHERs, we carry responsibilities that stretch us, but nothing weighs us down more than bitterness. Unforgiveness may start small, but if left in our hearts, it becomes a quiet poison. It steals our clarity, drains our joy, and limits our capacity to lead with compassion and strength.

In Reviving Recovery: Unbound, the ministry I lead alongside my husband, Allen, this truth is woven into nearly every lesson. Healing cannot occur when unforgiveness is still taking up space. We can talk through our pain and process our wounds, but if our hearts remain tied to resentment, we will keep circling the same hurt. Forgiveness is not pretending something did not happen; it is choosing to no longer allow that grievance to control us.

For many years, I misunderstood forgiveness. I thought it meant minimizing the pain I felt or being ready to reconcile. But forgiveness and reconciliation are not the same. Reconciliation takes two willing hearts. Forgiveness is between you and God—it is your decision to release someone into His hands, saying, "Lord, this hurt is too heavy for me. I give it to You."

Jesus spoke very directly about forgiveness. In Matthew 6:14-15 (NIV), He said, *"For if you forgive other people when they sin against you, your heavenly Father will also forgive you. But if you do not forgive others their sins, your Father will not forgive your sins."* Those words are not meant to scare us, but to remind us that forgiveness is not optional. It is a spiritual requirement. Jesus is not trying to place a burden on us; He is trying to free us from one. Jesus knows that unforgiveness blocks His healing work in our hearts.

Ephesians 4:31-32 (NIV) echoes this truth: *Get rid of all bitterness, rage and anger, brawling and slander... Be kind and compassionate to one another, forgiving each other, just as in Christ God forgave you.* Bitterness is heavy. Forgiveness is freedom.

There have been times in my own journey when forgiveness felt impossible. Betrayal cut deep, and words brought real pain. But every time I brought the weight to Jesus, He met me and whispered, "Let Me carry this." And when I finally released it, the peace that followed was undeniable. Forgiveness did not change the past, but it changed me. It allowed me to lead with softness instead of hardness, clarity instead of confusion, and compassion instead of defensiveness.

As leadHERs, if bitterness fills our hearts, it will seep into our words, decisions, and relationships. But when forgiveness fills our hearts, freedom follows. A forgiving leadHER is a healed leadHER with God's power to help others heal. People are drawn to leadHERs who have walked through pain and chosen grace instead of hardness.

Forgiveness is not weakness; it is strength surrendered to God as we trust Him with what we cannot fix. When we forgive, we don't let someone off the hook, but we place them into God's hands as we choose freedom for ourselves.

Take a moment to pause with the Lord. If He stirs something in your heart—whether a memory, a person, or a pain you have been holding onto—know that He is inviting you to lay it down. Freedom begins the moment we choose to forgive.

If you are ready to release the weight of unforgiveness and walk in healing, I invite you to pray this prayer with me:

Heavenly Father,

Thank You for the forgiveness I have received through Jesus. You have shown me mercy and grace beyond what I deserve. Today, I ask You to search my heart and remove any trace of unforgiveness that keeps me bound. I choose to release every hurt, offense, and disappointment into Your hands.

Heal what has been wounded and fill those places with Your peace. Teach me to lead from a heart that is free, compassionate, and full of grace. Let my life reflect Your love and forgiveness in every word and decision.

In Jesus' name, Amen.

Sylvia Meade

Sylvia Meade lives in North Palm Beach, Florida, and is a full-time realtor. She lives with her husband, Brian, and has two boys: Caleb, 30 years old, and Christian, 28 years old.

Raised as a devout Catholic, Sylvia accepted Christ when she was 14 years old. Watching her father drive away when she was 6 years old caused deep-rooted hurt in her life, leading to many extreme ups and downs. However, Christ has brought healing, and she has overcome many issues throughout the years.

Sylvia was raised by a single mother who always made Christ a priority in their life. Her mother taught her to be giving and to keep faith and family as her highest priorities. She also taught her that you have to work hard for what you want and to never compare yourself to others because, ultimately, our main focus should be our identity in Christ.

Marred to Radiant Princess

By Sylvia Meade

Marred: damaged or spoiled; rendered less perfect, attractive, useful; scarred, bruised, defective, inadequate.

Radiant: flawless, perfect, beautiful, sufficient, graceful, rebuilt, sound, strong.

Although we each have experienced obstacles and challenges in our lives, God has a plan. Every woman has that tiny seed inside of her that, in its due season, will flourish and bloom if she surrenders to God. I pray that my story will inspire you to take the first step to begin to fertilize and water that seed so you can live the life that God has created for you to live! As a daughter of the King of the universe, I invite you to awaken the princess within!

Sometimes when we look at a princess, all we see is her exterior appearance; her external world. As we admire her beauty, clothing, and jewels, we don't realize that becoming a princess did not happen overnight. The journey to radiance begins from the time we are in our mother's womb.

*For you created my inmost being; You knit me together in my
mother's womb... Your eyes saw my unformed body; all the days
ordained for me were written in your book before one of them
came to be* (Psalm 139:13,16 NIV).

The circumstances that mold and shape us throughout our lives, and the
family and DNA we are born with, are all facets of our journey to becoming
a princess at God's appointed time.

I want to share with you my own journey, which, along the way, did not
seem to be one of becoming a princess. However, everything God allows
to happen in our journey of life is all part of His divine plan for our calling,
the specific gifts He has imparted in us, and the plans and purposes He calls
us to fulfill. I hope you will learn from the various lessons I've encountered
on my journey. Who knows? These lessons may be invaluable nuggets
that eventually will be part of *your* crown. You see, a beautiful jewel is not
initially radiant without going through an intense heating process, and the
shine and radiance of each jewel of your crown will not appear until its
appropriate time, which will come when your refining process is complete.

So, how did my journey begin? I was born an only child; however, my
cousins were like my brothers and sisters. In the first seven years of my life,
I lived well. I had a nanny, beautiful clothes, and attended Holy Rosary
Catholic School in New Jersey. I was always with my father; he and I were
very close.

When I was 4 years old, my family moved to Florida, where my mother and
father owned a small hotel. I went to a private school, and everything was
beautiful in my life. I quickly learned, however, that life was not at all as it
seemed. My father began having affairs, my parents fought, and one day,
without explaining anything to me, I watched my father drive away. This
moment threw my life into a negative downward spiral; I knew he had left

me, and he would not return. Time passed. There was no communication at all, not even a call on my birthday. My mother finally accepted the fact that my father would no longer be helping her with my upbringing, financially or otherwise.

For a while, my mother tried to manage the hotel on her own; she really believed she could. But then three men stormed in on Christmas Eve with guns, tied me up, left me alone in a back room, and took all the money in the safe. My mother soon sold the hotel, and we moved to the Dominican Republic, where my parents were from.

My father's leaving was my first experience of deep and hurtful rejection, and the armed robbery compounded my belief that really bad things happen when someone decides they no longer want to be in your life. This was forever imprinted in my mind subconsciously.

Another incident has remained with me that also added to my feelings of rejection. When I was in the 4th grade, our class was to exchange Secret Santa Christmas gifts. I happened to pick the name of a girl I admired very much. I was so excited that I told my mother I wanted to give her my most treasured favorite doll. I asked my mother to sew a new dress for the doll, brushed her hair perfectly, and wrapped her as beautifully as I possibly could. I could not wait for my doll's new owner to unwrap and discover this precious gift!

Upon receiving the package, the girl eagerly tore the paper off. When she saw what lay inside, she slammed the doll down on the floor and said, "How dare you bring me a used present!" Shortly thereafter, the class went out to the playground, and I wouldn't go. I stayed in the classroom by myself and cried and cried. Rejected again.

That is when the nuggets began the arduous heating process. The hurt that I witnessed my mother experiencing because of my father's public infidelity and watching him drive away to never return completely changed my countenance and existence. The men who stormed in with guns left an imprint of fear within me. I became angry and resentful as thought patterns of unworthiness grew in me. I also developed a mistrust of men after seeing my dad have affairs and leave his family. Jealousy, insecurity, and destructive behavior began to manifest. As a result, I became obsessed with gaining approval from others, longing for acceptance. I started creating a wall to shield me from further hurt, interacting with everyone from a safe distance. And the incident with the doll caused me not to get too close to girlfriends, because friends can cause hurt and disappointment.

However, as I've grown and faced these issues, I've learned that the longer we remain in hiding, the more power we give the destructive voices in our lives. As leadHERs called by God, we must bring any destructive voices—including secrets and unhealthy thoughts—into the light so we can experience freedom. God's Word is full of promises to us. As we immerse ourselves in the Bible, we are *transformed by the renewing of [our] ...mind* (Romans 12:2 NIV).

Although I continued to build my belief that bad things just happen to me all the time, there were positive influences that created happy memories. Church and faith were important to my family; during my time in the Dominican Republic, one of the most impactful things I experienced was watching my grandfather, a devout Catholic, walk up and down the streets with his Bible, sharing God with everyone. His actions laid the groundwork for my strong faith.

Additionally, I would sleep with my grandmother, and when she awoke before sunrise to pray, I would watch her. That memory has been invaluable to me. As an adult, I've come to realize just how precious those pre-dawn moments were. I didn't know it then, but God was showing me intricately how He works. For every trial and tribulation He allowed into my life, a heaping dose of goodness and mercy offset it!

Although my life in the Dominican Republic was, for the most part, good,

I did continue to harbor resentment and anger towards my father. His town was three hours from where my mother and I lived. I couldn't get over the anger I felt from his abandonment. One day, he came to pick me up for a visit, and I screamed that I did not want to go, but my mother made me go with him. His infrequent attempts to see me, combined with the fact that he had a different woman living with him the few times I did visit, added even more to my anger and resentment.

> But the pot he was shaping from the clay was marred in his hands; so the potter formed it into another pot, shaping it as seemed best to him... Then the word of the Lord came to me... "Like clay in the hand of the potter, so are you in my hand" (Jeremiah 18:4-6 NIV).

When God allows rain into your life, He also provides sunshine. Sometimes, it's not easy to see, but it's always there. He wants us to learn lessons from our trying times. To become the leadHERs He has called us to be, we should work toward discovering the root of our behaviors, positive or negative. Each experience molds and shapes us into the women God calls us to be.

We must uncover the root of our behaviors to begin the healing process, to experience freedom and clarity, and to begin the life that God has called us to live.

As I grew, I began to feel, for small moments, that God loved me and desired the best for me. However, I continued looking for affirmation from everyone around me. The wall I continued to build around me fueled destructive thought patterns. Additional negative experiences with men fueled my mistrust and anger. I had yet to discover that forgiveness brings freedom and healing.

You see, we each have a choice. I encourage you to choose today to take the steps necessary for complete freedom so that God can give you the life that is rightfully yours!

> "Therefore everyone who hears these words of mine and puts them into practice is like a wise man who built his house on the rock. The rain came down, the streams rose, and the winds blue and beat against that house; Yet it did not fall, because it had its foundation on the rock" (Matthew 7:24-25 NIV).

My mother and I returned to the United States to live in West Palm Beach, Florida. I continued to battle internal anger and resentment fueled by my father's actions. I didn't want to trust any male figure in my life. At the age of 14, I began to drink and go to parties secretly—I became very creative at lying to my mother.

I even went as far as trying cocaine with a boy I liked; thankfully, that was only a one-time thing. I did not like how it made me feel. I was just trying to be accepted by this boy who, deep down, I knew did not even care about me. This destructive behavior was a product of the low self-esteem I had developed.

> Be alert and of sober mind. Your enemy the devil prowls around like a roaring lion looking for someone to devour. Resist him, standing firm in the faith, because you know that the family of believers throughout the world is undergoing the same kind of sufferings (1 Peter 5:8-9 NIV).

I subconsciously continued to choose men who made me feel like my father did. However, I finally came to know who Christ was and recognize that God made me feel so loved and whole; this was something I didn't feel anywhere else in my life. I understood that the enemy was doing everything possible to attack me and keep me down, and little by little, through God's Word, I gained the strength to get back up stronger than before.

I clung to God and His Word because I knew that the only way I would fulfill the true calling on my life from God was by claiming His promises.

> *In God, whose word I praise,*
> *in the Lord, whose word I praise—*
> *in God I trust and am not afraid.*
> *What can man do to me?*
> *I am under vows to you, my God;*
> *I will present my thank offerings to you.*
> *For you have delivered me from death*
> *and my feet from stumbling,*
> *that I may walk before God*
> *in the light of life.*
> (Psalm 56:10-13 NIV)

To be a kingdom leadHER, we must intentionally forgive those who have hurt us, releasing destructive emotions. Forgiveness is not a response to someone else's regret or repentance; as Christians, we forgive because God has forgiven us. By forgiving those who have hurt us, we can discover our own freedom, healing, and happiness. We cannot position ourselves for a life of greatness while harboring ill feelings and unforgiveness toward others.

Take time with God, asking Him to identify who you need to forgive. Then, whether that person is still alive or not, I encourage you to write them a letter—for your eyes only—releasing every feeling and thought. Even if the person who would theoretically receive the letter has no idea that your ill feelings exist, tell them you've forgiven them. Purge your feelings and release the bitterness that has been holding you back. I wrote a letter to my father and didn't hold anything back; it was a powerful breakthrough that catapulted me toward becoming a kingdom leadHER!

Sister, I want you to know that God has a hope and a future for you

(Jeremiah 29:11)! To become a radiant princess and kingdom leadHER, I had to determine to embrace the precepts of God, immerse myself daily in His Word, and put on His full armor (Ephesians 6:10-17). I attended intense weekend retreats that helped me get to the root of my issues, and, with the Lord by my side, I slowly began to see myself as God sees me: His radiant, beautiful, and confident daughter. I sought the Lord, even when I didn't feel like it, and He began to break me free of those strongholds and heal my broken heart. God showed me that the lessons from my past helped to build my character, and what happened to me did not define me. He assured me that the hope and future He had for me was waiting—I just had to keep my eyes on Him. And that is true for you, as well.

God uses each season of challenges to refine us. He knows and has ordained your future as a kingdom leadHER, even as He allows challenging seasons to mold and shape you for the future He has prepared.

When I was bullied in middle school and mistreated by young men, yet continued searching for the Lord in the middle of it, God was working in me so I could become a kingdom leadHER! Even though I could not see a future and everything seemed dim, I remained focused on God's Word and my faith. I never doubted God. His Word reassured me that I had a purpose, that I was loved, and that I had a future. God also sent people along the way to lift me up, hold me accountable, and speak life into me. I will treasure those gifts forever.

God instilled in me a determination to rise above. So I began attending retreats and leadership conferences, reading leadership books, and surrounding myself with leaders I could glean and learn from.

I share all of this to say that although you may not be able to see beyond the dark tunnel you are in, persevere. I persevered, and it prepared me for the wonderful husband and life I have now. God provided me a man who had been in the Army for over ten years and wasn't afraid to push me out of my comfort zone. God saw the work I had done on myself, and He knew when

I was ready to meet my Boaz—the man who would walk with me hand-in-hand as we serve God together.

My prince arrived 22 years ago! My future husband walked into a restaurant where I was having dinner with a friend. When I had dreamed of him, I prayed that God would bring me a tall, Christian man who enjoys boating, fishing, and diving, and is a businessman who is not afraid to work with his hands or put on a tuxedo! And yes, my prince is all of that! I met him after being divorced for close to four years, and he helped raise my two boys to be gentlemen, college football players, and live beautiful, successful lives.

Through my perseverance in prayer, the study of God's Word, and journaling, God allowed me to become a strong Christian mother. As a result of God's grace to me and my children, both my sons have become leaders in their own lives.

This is why, my dear sister, I was eager to share my story with you. I want you to know that you are a beautiful princess and daughter of the Creator of the universe. Hold your head high knowing that God, your King, has your back!

As I look at my life now and consider what I had to overcome, I see God's hand and great love for me woven throughout every year of my life. My life is so blessed. I have a wonderful husband who loves me so much, and I have two handsome, healthy boys.

I am a princess in God's kingdom....

You are a princess in God's kingdom....

So straighten your crown, my sister, and get ready to lead like royalty!

Anita Cordell

Anita Cordell is a dynamic leader whose life's work bridges faith, business, and storytelling. As a multi-award-winning actress and producer with over 100 commercials and 65+ films to her credit, Anita uses her creative voice to bring light to dark spaces and truth to the screen. She is also a successful Realtor and the founder of Yellow Brick Group, where she advises and equips to build legacy through homeownership.

Anita is also the author of *Rinse, Reflect, Repeat,* a bestselling devotional. This unique book guides readers through the Bible alphabetically in a year. She also uses her daily devotions to host the *Rinse, Reflect, Repeat* podcast. Anita is a passionate speaker, motivating her audience to rise to greatness, fulfilling God's purpose for their lives. Through every platform—from real estate to film, from writing to speaking—Anita champions faith-filled leadership with boldness, integrity, and purpose.

She is available for interviews, panels, speaking events, film opportunities, and faith-based coaching. You can purchase her book, explore her podcast, or connect with her at: anitacordell.com

Superpower LeadHERship Trait

By Anita Cordell

Just by the mere title of this chapter, I can only imagine you are looking for the reveal of a superpower trait that will launch you to Wonder Woman status as a leadHER. Perhaps you are even envisioning your arms raised out to your sides while you perform a quick circular twirl in a back alley, and then, voila, you are transformed into the Wonder Woman leadHER you so desire to be.

Maybe in your mind's eye, you have even donned your red corset with the golden eagle emblem on the chest and your blue shorts accented by a golden belt. Don't forget the long and thick golden bracelets on each wrist to shield the oncoming bullets thrown at you and the lasso to catch the bad guys.

While you are at it, go ahead and grab that tiara, because you will need it to remind you that you are truly a wonder of a woman, despite life challenges.

Hello. My name is Anita Cordell, and I'm an entrepreneur. I've been self-employed, running a real estate business since 2001. In 2006, I launched my film and commercial acting career, and then, in about 2010, I added public speaking appearances, making me a multi-faceted business owner. Oh, and as of the fall of 2024, I also became an award-winning author when my 365-day devotional, *Rinse, Reflect, Repeat*, was released.

Did I mention I'm a mom of four (including my son-in-love), Mae Mae to four beautiful grandchildren, a proud wife, a retired pastor's kid, and a dog mom of three amazing pooches? In my spare time, I try to keep any surviving plants alive in my home by not forgetting to water them, and I am learning the new art of throwing pottery on a wheel. My continued hope is to master the creation of ceramic pieces that have some functional form. Full confession, though: I seem to supernaturally find a way to kill more plants than I keep alive, and I create ceramic pieces with all kinds of dents, curls, bumps, and misfortunes. I guess each piece has its own flavor of "Anita personality." (Yes, you have my permission to laugh out loud.) These ceramic mistakes give ample opportunity for show and tell—with lots of giggles along the way.

I'm not here to portray visions of my business grandeur or show off accolades and awards. I'm not even here to tell you all the how-tos of being a *wonder* of a woman. Yes, keeping God right by my side is truly the number one trait that leads to the wonderful aspects of my businesses and leadHERship roles. Yes, there are essential attributes I try to master as I live out my life with purpose and intention. But instead, I want to share a superpower you might not deem worthy to place on the shelf next to all the other Wonder Woman features we strive to master.

This particular trait is not as glamorous as some. In fact, we might not even want to admit we have it—it's warped, has dents in it, and, just like my flawed pottery pieces, is not one we care to show off. And yet, recognizing and harnessing this trait is part of the process of becoming a woman who can confidently grab her tiara. Facing it is vital to living a life of leadHERship. So I'd like to encourage you to consider proudly putting this battered trait on the shelf next to the characteristics you *purposefully* study and reflect on.

The trait I'm talking about is... drum roll, please... FEAR.

I can see you now. You are scratching your chin and, with a tilted head and squinty eyes, glaring at me with a look that says, "Wait, what? You're listing fear as something to glean from as you're developing into a leadHER? How can being afraid help me become the Wonder Woman God created me to be? How is having this trait a good thing?"

Now, before you immediately turn the pages of this chapter and jump to the next one, or close this book entirely, thinking I'm shady, give me your ear. We often give our ears to influencers of all sorts—podcasters, authors, pastors, teachers, leaders, and friends seeking opportunities for new ideas, words of encouragement, or even to better ourselves through critiques. So please lend it to me for a bit as you hear me out.

There are roughly 365 verses in the Bible that address fear—one passage for every day of the year. Several of those verses tell us, "Do not fear," so that must mean God knows we *will* fear. In fact, might I propose that this trait could rear its head daily? We can experience often-hidden fear in the form of anxiety or a more visible fear that occurs when we face a life-threatening situation. Regardless of how big or small, fear is a part of our lives more often than we would probably like to admit.

So, how is this a good thing? How does God use fear for leadHERship growth? While it is not something we desire, I would like us to acknowledge that we all have this trait and begin to view it with a fresh set of eyes—as a piece to a puzzle. We can value fear because it can propel us forward—IF we let it.

I attended college as a single mom, having never married my daughter's father, which compounded the usual challenges of receiving a higher education. Boy, those stress migraines are something I still remember to this day. I was figuring out college life and classes while navigating day care for my daughter, budgeting, and handling everything in between.

To add to my stress, after I graduated, my daughter and I changed churches.

We began attending Sheffield Family Life Center, an inner-city church that helped me grow in a deeper fashion on my journey of faith. However, as a pastor's kid, the fear I faced at leaving my dad's congregation was extreme. Though our move was life-changing, my challenges continued.

I had just $25 each week in my budget for eating out. So, each Wednesday night, our treat was McDonald's drive-through on the way to serve in the youth ministry at Sheffield. Every other meal was hot dogs, mac 'n cheese, cereal, waffles, and a few special crockpot dishes. I knew exactly how much my paycheck would be every two weeks, and every dollar had a name to it—from how much I tithed, to my rent, gas, groceries, and utilities. I carefully watched my spending, tracking it all on a spreadsheet.

In about 1998, after I had been a member of the church for several years, Sheffield launched a building campaign to expand the church. We were prepped as a congregation to begin praying about how much we could pledge over the next year toward the building fund. This pledge was above and beyond our tithe and was an act of faith. The building project was a way for us to activate a modern-day tabernacle building. Just like Moses asked the Israelites to bring supplies to help build the tabernacle, we were asked the same.

I began maneuvering dollars around on my budget spreadsheet to cut money in one category to apply toward my building fund pledge. I tweaked it, modified it, and tried to stretch my dollars, committing to spending less in the coming year in order to fulfill my pledge promise. I finally figured out a way to give about $80 extra a month, making my pledge about $1000. That was a lot for me. New to tithing and budgeting, I was hopeful that I could make it work, but I was not at peace. Something about the number did not sit well with me. It was as if God was telling me that there was another number He wanted me to consider. I knew what that number was deep in my heart, but my fear of the number God gave me was nearly crippling; I did not want to think that the voice prompting me was real.

With just seven days until the church's big celebration kick-off, my conversations with God regarding the amount of my pledge seemed to be never-ending. Each week, I had sat in church wondering if I had heard Him right. The number in my heart just seemed illogical and almost stupid. My mind raced.

Anita, what are you thinking?

Anita, you have a daughter to take care of!

Anita, are you sure you are hearing God?

Repeatedly, questions entered my mind. I was consumed with wanting to obey God's voice. The fear I was experiencing was two-sided: On one hand, I was afraid of being disobedient to the Lord. On the other hand, I was terrified of making this astronomical commitment that He was guiding me to. How could I win? I really felt like I was in a lose-lose situation; the fear of disobedience and the fear of financially going under were lingering over me.

I clearly remember the morning of the pledge day. A massive tent had been put up where the new building would be erected. Several thousand chairs were lined up for the congregation, and the stage was prepped for the worship team and the church staff. A special guest was brought in to encourage us as a congregation to hear from God and to stay committed to our pledges.

I grabbed a pledge card and, still wondering what to write, sat down. Fear welled up in my heart. After the worship time came to an end, we heard an incredible sermon, and then it was time— time for each of us to write on our pledge card the amount we would promise to pay in the next year toward building the new sanctuary.

Lines began forming as people got up from their seats, walked to the front of the makeshift church, and placed their pledge cards in the buckets lined up at the altar.

I looked down at the pledge card in my lap, grabbed my pen, and wrote the number I felt God had been talking to me about for several months.

<$10,000>

My mind reeled. *$10,000? Yes. That's right.*

I wrote $10,000 on my pledge card. Was I afraid? Absolutely. But what I was MORE afraid of was NOT putting that number on the pledge card. I was MORE afraid of NOT obeying.

My fear of missing God's voice and not stepping out in faith propelled me to write that number.

Facing fear, I embarked on a year-long journey of paying off my pledge. It was a journey of doing everything I could to keep my word to the church. That first night, I lay in bed knowing I had obeyed God, but fearing the unknown and trying to trust God more deeply.

In the coming months, every spare dollar I obtained went toward my pledge. I had made just a tiny dent when my annual review came up at work. In the next few months, I didn't just get one raise, I got THREE. Yes. THREE RAISES.

I started seeing a shift in my faith that led to anticipation and excitement. About ten months into the year, I had miraculously paid off almost one-third of the pledge. Can you believe it? Money just kept appearing. But while I had a good chunk paid off, I began getting concerned that I wouldn't see my promise through.

My new fiancé, Nathan, paid his pledge off and started helping me pay mine. We were down to about three weeks before the total was due, and I had exactly $5000 left to pay. I had no idea how I would finish it or what God would do. That is, until one night about two weeks before the final day.

Nathan, returning to his home, found an envelope taped to his door. Inside the envelope was a check.

Yep. You guessed it. For $5,000!

The check was intended to go toward our honeymoon, but we both knew God had provided it for the pledge. Did the fact that we gave the money to the church make the giver of the check upset? You bet. But we knew we had to obey God by faith.

You can't grow if you don't become okay with getting out of your comfort zone, and many times, getting out of our comfort zone means that we must face our fears. Fear—even a fear of growing—can keep us in our comfort zone, causing us to become complacent. But God wants so much more for us. When we face our fears, He strengthens us with His strength, growing us in ways we can't begin to imagine.

When we face our fear, we grow into the purpose for our lives. Stepping out in faith gives God the opportunity to mold us.

We all have "fearful" tendencies—the question is: Do we live in fear, or do we face it? We all have different fears; mine are different than yours, and yours are different than mine. So, if fear is what holds us back, why are we afraid to face it and study it so we can grow? I would propose that we don't face our fear because of, well, fear. It's a vicious cycle.

You may think that because I made a wild financial leap of faith, I have made sound financial decisions as a leadHER. Unfortunately, that is not the case. Not four years after this pledge and faith journey, Nathan and I became a bit zealous and forgot to stay humble.

It was 2003. I distinctly remember walking into a courtroom with my husband, my head hung in embarrassment.

I was more embarrassed by this moment than my 6th-grade choir concert, when I peed in my underwear. I was dead center on the stage, in the middle of all the rows of bleachers, and couldn't slip out. My nerves got me, but I was too afraid to make a commotion in front of hundreds of parents and family members. It was easier to stand there and let it all out. So, I peed on the metal bleachers while belting out the songs. Thank you, Mom, for making me an ankle-length dress for this event.

Back to my story.

My husband and I were standing in front of a judge, filing for bankruptcy for our real estate business. I was just two years into being a realtor. I was supposed to be a trusted advisor for my clients. I would pick them up and drive them all over Kansas City, answering questions on home buying. Then, I would drop them off and cry the whole way home. Each day I showed homes, I repeated this scene.

As we walked into that courtroom, I prayed that none of my clients would see me. The choices that got us there were nothing shy of pride and naivety; we entered into a bad partnership with the wrong investor, who took advantage of us and our zealousness. If we had been fearful of the RIGHT things, we would not have had to endure a life-changing pause on our entrepreneurship endeavors. If we had feared the LORD more than we feared missing out, we probably would have saved ourselves a lot of tears. But instead, our choices caused us to go through hardship.

Many times throughout my life, I have encountered that ugly trait called fear and have been forced to decide whether to live under its control or seek God's wisdom and power to face it. I've realized that when I run and hide, I'm actually hiding something much greater than the fear; I'm hiding the wonder of a woman God made me to be.

Facing and conquering our fear with God's power not only gives us victory over the battle, but it also allows us to grow. Linking arms with our heavenly Father and looking fear right in the eyes allows our faith to blossom.

Fear threatens to hold us in our comfort zone, but when we look past the fear to God's strength, it becomes a tool that can catapult us to victory.

So, as I gaze on my shelf and cheer on those other Wonder Woman traits of leadHERship, I also thank fear. For facing my fear is what has made me trust God more, lean into Him more, and sharpen the other glorious traits that allow me to lead myself and others as we face this life together.

Even though the Bible tells us not to fear, and it's not glamorous to admit failure, reflecting on the fear we've encountered and the actions we have taken to avoid or face it helps us develop into the women God has called us to be. I know this firsthand.

Thanks to fear, I have grown more equipped to serve God—stronger and closer to Him than ever. And isn't that what being a Wonder Woman is all about?

Leading with Gratitude

By DeAnn Alaine

Have you noticed that the word "attitude" is within the word gratitude? I know it's not spelled perfectly, but still!

I've heard that phrase, "Have an attitude of gratitude." Oh, blah, blah, blah, give me a break! We all know how important it is as a leadHER to have an attitude of gratitude. But the reality is, sometimes I want to have a bad attitude! Sometimes I want my flesh to win! This may be a shocker, but sometimes I want to throw my computer out the window of a 7th-floor building during PMS because I don't have any chocolate around! My body is in its 50s, but my skin acts like it's 14! AND I haven't even begun that particular seasonal change yet! Some say I should be grateful for that, but I get tired of sore boobs and having to practice self-control up the yin yang! GRATEFUL?!?!, Shnarfdeeshnangle!

My beloved husband should be grateful to have lived through 15 years of estrogenic changes! Thankfully, he is.

Let's talk about Lot's wife. You'd *think* she would be grateful that two angels would come to rescue her and her family from Sodom to save them from utter death, but nooooo, she was too busy missing her friends, her favorite heels, and her Longaberger basket collection. She did the only thing she was told not to do and, as a result, became the most exclusive salt block on the planet! I'll bet the horses of that region had plenty of gratitude for that nice piece of salt.

Then the Lord rained down burning sulfur on Sodom and Gomorrah—from the Lord out of the heavens. Thus he overthrew those cities and the entire plain, destroying all those living in the cities—and also the vegetation in the land.

But Lot's wife looked back, and she became a pillar of salt (Genesis 19:24-26 NIV).

Then you've got the Israelites. They'd been slaves for 400 years, then were miraculously delivered. Yet when they got stuck between a rock and a hard place, were they grateful for their deliverance? No! They gave in to fear because they wanted a different leader who would lead them BACK to Egypt!

> All the Israelites grumbled against Moses and Aaron, and the whole assembly said to them, "If only we had died in Egypt! Or in this wilderness! Why is the Lord bringing us to this land only to let us fall by the sword? Our wives and children will be taken as plunder. Wouldn't it be better for us to go back to Egypt?" And they said to each other, "We should choose a leader and go back to Egypt" (Numbers 14:2-4 NIV).

Sometimes I learn what NOT to do when I read my Bible. But as we all know, learning is not the same thing as application.

In looking at gratitude, I realized there are times when I am grateful but don't take note of it or say it out loud. I wonder, how would things look different if I chose to be intentional about giving thanks out loud with my mouth? When we give thanks out loud, it pivots our heart into a better position. It shifts our mindset from the knowing of gratitude to the application of gratitude!

The next time you get together with your board members or your team, start with a "Greatness Gratitude Session" and see how it changes the atmosphere! The "Greatness Gratitude Session" is when everyone at the table says how someone else showed greatness in a tough situation, or greatness in a skill, or is thankful for someone who used the greatness in them to do something for someone else.

As leadHERs, we experience working with many different personalities, so having an attitude of gratitude isn't just a good thing; it's a necessity. If it's been a while since you've practiced gratitude *out loud* and you're feeling a little rusty, thank God for indoor plumbing and that you have clothes made of fabric instead of frocks made of leaves!

And when someone is near you who thinks totally differently and maybe talks in such a way that tempts your flesh to be rubbed the wrong way, shove gratitude in your flesh's face and thank God that that person is created in the image of our Savior, even if they don't resemble Him in any other way.

It's easy to take for granted what God has given us. Let's be intentional about recognizing that we have so much to be grateful for and lead the way in offering our gratitude!

. . . .

Kelly Williams Hale

Kelly Williams Hale is a speaker, author, and life coach. She is passionate about Jesus and encourages others to deepen their personal relationship with Him. Her teaching and online courses help Christian women walk in their unique calling to bring God glory.

Partnering with the Holy Spirit, Kelly teaches women how to be courageous and confident in Christ. Her speaking topics include spiritual growth, emotional resilience, and leadership.

Kelly is happily married (third time's a charm!), a mom of three—each born a decade apart—delivering her youngest at 44 years old. Kelly is living proof that our mess truly becomes our message and past mistakes don't define future success.

To connect with Kelly, you're invited to join her Facebook group, *Sisters Who Shine,* or visit thebebravelife.com

Learning to Listen and Lead

By Kelly Williams Hale

For years, I heard people casually mention "hearing from God" in conversation, and I really didn't get it. *What does that even mean?* I'd wonder. *Like, is there an audible voice?* I was genuinely confused about how this whole divine communication thing worked. That all changed one day in 2006.

I attended a conference called She Speaks, hosted by Lysa TerKeurst, speaker, author, and founder of Proverbs 31 Ministries. I knew deep in my spirit that God had called me to speak, so I went to North Carolina on a wing and a prayer—a true leap of faith. I spent the weekend surrounded by women who also knew they were messengers for the Lord, using their voices for His kingdom. That's where I heard Him. I was awakened from a fairly deep sleep with these words ringing in my spirit: "My grace is sufficient."

Now, let me paint the picture of where I was spiritually at that time. I was just getting back into the Bible, beginning to understand how much Jesus loves me and discovering who God really is. For so long, I'd imagined Him as this imposing figure in the sky—lightning bolts shooting from His fingertips when I'd make a mistake. But God was revealing Himself to me as someone who loves me. Not a judge waiting to condemn, but a Father delighting in His daughter.

When I heard "My grace is sufficient" in that hotel room, it wasn't an audible voice, but a sense. A thought that popped into my head—randomly. Nothing I had been actively thinking about. In fact, I was sound asleep!

Sometimes when we imagine hearing from God, we will second-guess ourselves. *Was that really God? Or was that just me?* Maybe you've felt like He hasn't heard you, so you assume you can't hear Him either. But instead of assuming, we can simply ask the Holy Spirit, "Lord, was that You?" Then be still and wait.

The challenge for me is in the being still part! But when we quiet ourselves and pay attention to what pops into our head—thoughts that align with Scripture and thoughts that feel like truth landing in our spirit—that's often the voice of God.

Here's the thing: God speaks to each of us differently, based on our relationship with Him and our unique personality. Some people receive legit visions—wide awake, seeing things happening in the spirit realm. Others hear from God through photos or pictures, whether physical images or mental ones. I've learned that God often speaks to me through other people—when I'm listening to a podcast, hearing a message at church, or just having conversations with friends. His voice can be heard in so many ways.

When you know, you know. And yet... we can overthink it, can't we? *Oh my goodness, was that from the enemy? Did God really say that, or was that just me.*

Here's my hack: if what you hear lines up with Scripture and aligns with God's will and His character, then it's God's voice. The thought that popped into your head? That's Him. The Bible says we have the mind of Christ (1 Corinthians 2:16 NLT).

I remember my son Dallas telling me he wanted to start praying with his girlfriend (which was awesome!), but he didn't know what to pray. Then a thought came to him: the Serenity Prayer. I told him, "Dallas, that was God! He was speaking to you, reminding you of that prayer." That's what God does—He brings thoughts to our minds that we weren't actively thinking. If it aligns with His Word, it's from the Lord.

Now, I need to tell you something important: Just like God knew us before we even made it to planet Earth, the enemy also has spiritual knowledge of the anointing God placed on our lives. Wild, right? What's happening in the spirit realm is real and active.

> *You saw me before I was born. Every day of my life was recorded in your book. very moment was laid out before a single day had passed* (Psalm 139:16 NLT).

However, the enemy cannot access our thoughts. Let me say that again— the enemy does not know what we're thinking. He only responds to what we speak out loud. We give him ammunition when we say things that aren't aligned with God's truth. We must be mindful of the words we say.

> *The tongue has the power of life and death* (Proverbs 18:21 NIV).

We all have a calling on our lives. Satan wants to hinder that. He'll try to make us doubt, to make us think we misheard God or made the wrong decision. But Romans 8:28 says: *And we know that in all things God works for the good of those who love him, who have been called according to his purpose* (NIV).

We have a purpose. We have been called. And God will take even our missteps—when we hear His voice but don't take action, or when we mishear Him and it was actually our own thoughts or emotions—and He'll work it together for good. Even when we make a decision that wasn't quite right, we're still moving in the right direction. We can pause and say, "Okay, God, I thought You told me to do this. I might have misheard You."

We're in a constant state of sanctification. It's a process. We may have heard Him correctly, but things didn't work out the way we thought they would. God knows we're human. He'll allow our mistakes because they will often sharpen us. Refine us. If we're willing, our lessons will expose what needs to be excavated and worked out, for His glory.

> *You were taught, with regard to your former way of life, to put off your old self, which is being corrupted by its deceitful desires; to be made new in the attitude of your minds; and to put on the new self, created to be like God in true righteousness and holiness* (Ephesians 4:22-24 NIV).

Another Scripture just popped into my mind (see how He does that?): *No weapon formed against you will prosper* (Isaiah 54:17 NKJV), which means there *will* be weapons formed—but they will *not* prosper.

When you're wondering if you're hearing His voice, remember that He speaks uniquely to you. And remember that even in our uncertainty, He will guide us, refine us, and work everything together for our good and His glory. *Your* voice matters, sis. He's calling you to use it.

Okay, story time. It's a little embarrassing, but I think you need to hear it.

Last summer, my boss quit. She was the Creative Services Manager. I'm a graphic designer. Almost as soon as I heard the news, I heard God's voice—clear as day—telling me to apply for the position. Get your resume together. Update your portfolio. Apply.

There are five other designers on the team who would potentially report to me. I'd been a manager before. I love developing people and helping them grow. But there was another component to the job: working with other departments and their managers, navigating how to get creative work through the company. And, to be honest, I did not want to do that.

I was afraid. Afraid of the additional responsibility. Afraid of losing the freedom I had working from home. It just felt like too much.

And you know what I did?

Nothing.

I knew it was God. I absolutely knew. But I didn't apply.

I have to tell you something: There are consequences when we disobey. And I have been living out those consequences for the past year. We hired a new manager from outside the company—someone with no connection to our team. It became clear very quickly that this was not a good fit.

I've been with my company for nearly nine years. We were a family. It wasn't long before I began hearing about challenges my coworkers were having, and something rose up in me—a pressing desire to advocate for them. Not for myself, mind you. I've always been someone who goes with the flow. My approach is: My job is to make your job easier. I'm a good employee, diligent, working with excellence. I probably overdo it because I'm so grateful to work from home! But when I heard my teammates struggling, something shifted.

The new manager seemed lovely. She was made in the image of God, after all. And probably wonderful in other contexts. In fact, after the team interview—where she said all the right things—I said, "I love her!" I tend to give people the benefit of the doubt. I want people to succeed. I wanted the best for her. But the reality was not lovely. The past year has been a masterclass in initiating difficult conversations, learning to respectfully challenge decisions, and advocating for others even when it's uncomfortable.

God used my disobedience to develop my leadHERship.

Let that sink in. My willful choice to ignore His voice became the very thing He used to grow me. He took my wrong decision and is using it to refine me. As I mentioned earlier, He's exposing traits in me that need to be excavated and worked out.

I know things are going to change—I feel it in my spirit. This job isn't forever, and God has been preparing me. That's what He does. He takes our disobedience, allows us to face the consequences, and then uses it all for our good if we're willing to receive His correction.

Here's something unexpected: I'm learning so much about the spiritual realm through this situation. About how evil is real, about how spirits can attach to situations and people. But *God has not given us a spirit of fear, but of power and of love and of a sound mind* (2 Timothy 1:7 NKJV). And Jesus said, *"You have heard that it was said, 'Love your neighbor and hate your enemy.' But I tell you, love your enemies and pray for those who persecute you"* (Matthew 5:43-44 NIV). I have had the opportunity to pray for this woman, to love her regardless, to look at her through the lens of compassion.

It has grown me. Refined me. Sharpened me.

None of it is wasted. Bad decisions, wrong choices, even disobedience—it can all be used for God's glory. In fact, God probably knew I wasn't going to apply. He already knew I would disobey. And He had a plan even for that.

Here's a beautiful plot twist: Last December, I discovered that a coworker I'd never really connected with—one of the reasons I didn't want the job— had been radically saved. She was sharing Jesus with people! And I heard God whisper: "If you had taken that job, I would have worked it all out."

He already had a plan. He would have handled the relationship I was worried about. God is such a good, good God, and He really does work all things out for our good. I'll be honest—this year has been difficult to navigate. It's been uncomfortable. It's required love. This journey has taught me about loving people who treat you badly. It's taught me about operating in love when the world has gotten so divisive that people are afraid to share their opinions. I've been afraid to share my thoughts in so many scenarios because of fear—fear of being misunderstood, fear of not being liked.

But here's what I'm learning: I don't have to prove anything to anybody. I know my intentions. And, more importantly, God knows my heart. Dear sister, we don't have to "prove anything." We can release the need to show people how good we are, which, unreleased, can lead to being taken advantage of, walked over, and taken for granted.

God is breaking that off me. He's teaching me to use my voice to stand up for myself—and to advocate for others. And He's using my disobedience—my refusal to apply for that job—as the very classroom where I'm learning these lessons.

None of it is wasted. Not a single moment.

The power of our testimony—good, bad, and ugly—is exactly how we show up in our calling. God uses our mistakes and our lessons to develop our leadHERship. Our stories are meant for His glory.

Each of you should use whatever gift you have received to serve others, as faithful stewards of God's grace in its various forms. If anyone speaks, they should do so as one who speaks the very words of God. If anyone serves, they should do so with the strength God provides, so that in all things God may be praised through Jesus Christ (1 Peter 4:10-11 NIV).

We are all leadHERs in God's kingdom. Every single one of us. Our leadHERship will be unique, because we are unique. Our calling is meant to serve others *and* edify the body of Christ. The Lord has given me a voice to encourage others and share my testimony. He's also given me the gift of graphic design to help other people share their testimonies through their unique stories.

For we are God's masterpiece. He has created us anew in Christ Jesus, so we can do the good things he planned for us long ago (Ephesians 2:10 NLT).

Before I embraced my gifts, I operated with that crazy "proving energy"— feeling like I had to show everyone I was a good person, constantly clarifying what I meant, trying to make everyone understand my heart. It was exhausting. It's still an area of growth for me. Our sanctification is ongoing.

But here's what I've learned: If I'm going to share truth, I'm going to share what God is telling me to share. And if I decide not to, there *will* be consequences. My strength comes from the joy I have in the Lord, and I know it's going to carry me. God promises it will, because He's calling me to share truth more boldly, not to be afraid or discouraged. He recently asked me: "Do you trust me more than you're worried about being misunderstood?" Yes, Lord. I do.

That's a little frightening. But also exciting. Because I don't have anything to prove anymore.

One last story. My cousin, Stephanie, went to heaven about a year ago— after my new boss started working with us. I didn't really understand how much her passing affected me until just a few months ago. We weren't close growing up, but we developed a friendship over the past ten years. She was the first woman, girlfriend/cousin, I'd lost. And it affected me deeply.

When we lose people, it hurts our souls. There's pain. And grief. The Bible says there's *a time to weep and a time to laugh, a time to mourn and a time to dance* (Ecclesiastes 3:4 NIV). In other words, there are seasons in life.

An unforeseen benefit of my year of "refining" is that I've become more involved in ministry. I work closely with the Women World Leaders ministry, formatting books (this one, for example!) and designing *Voice of*

Truth magazine. By His grace, the Lord has allowed me to use my creative gifting for His glory. I am humbled by the opportunity to reach women who are hungry for the Lord.

Recently, I helped launch a teaching series called Inner Healing, using both my design skills and social media expertise. It was incredible—deep, biblical training about healing our souls. When we accept Jesus, the Holy Spirit comes to live inside us, and our spirits are secure. But we also have a soul—our mind, our will, our emotions—and that part of us can be wounded and experience trauma.

It was the fourth and final class that impacted me most. In an instant, the Lord showed me what He created me to do: guide and empower women on their healing journey. As someone who's "been there, done that," I know the transformational power of a relationship with Jesus. Who He is and the hope and encouragement He offers. The abundant life that's available—the life Jesus died for.

Life isn't meant just for us just to survive. We don't have to wait until we get to heaven to experience peace and joy. The kingdom of God is here now, and we get to walk and experience a healed and whole life with Jesus. The Holy Spirit living inside of us equips us to walk in power and authority against demonic spirits and the evil in the world.

"You are the light of the world—like a city on a hilltop that cannot be hidden" (Matthew 5:14 NLT).

I don't know exactly what's next on my journey. Perhaps I'll leave my safe, secure 9-to-5 and step out on faith. I'm sure it'll be super uncomfortable. Whatever it is, I will definitely say yes next time, though! I will say yes to obedience. When God says it's time, I'll be ready. The past year has been preparation—particularly in growing my leadHERship and discipline.

Just this week, a book I helped design and format launched. I've been working with this client on his story—God told him to write it years ago (he finally OBEYED!)—and it's been such an honor to help him get this message out into the world. His wife passed away from cancer, and the book chronicles her journey and the lessons God brought him through. It's powerful.

I've always said that sharing our story is God's gift to us because we impact the world through our testimony. Nobody can dispute what God has done in our lives. It's indisputable, undebatable. It's our experience, the truth of what God has done, that makes us. The lessons have led us to where we are today.

Revelation 12:11 says that we overcome the enemy by the blood of the Lamb and the word of our testimony. Four years ago, when the Lord brought that Scripture to mind, I shared a very dark secret the enemy was holding over me—my abortion. I wrote a chapter for another Women World Leaders' book, sharing that story. It wasn't at all what I intended to do, but I heard God's voice. A thought that popped into my head—that didn't come from me—and aligned with Scripture and truth. And I obeyed. That moment really was the impetus to where I am today. Helping other people format, design, and get their testimonies published.

When we make our plans, sometimes God has different plans for us. You want to make God laugh? Tell Him your plans. Don't worry—He has better plans. God has a sense of humor; I'm so thankful for that.

Friend, as you continue your journey, remember: God will ask you to do things that are uncomfortable, and there will be consequences when we don't obey, but He works all things together for good. So step joyfully into the calling He has for you, sis. Use your voice. Use your gifts. Share your testimony.

That's kingdom leadHERship.

Shelsea Becker

Shelsea Lyn Becker is a visionary leader, comedic speaker, ministry founder, creative director, and media host. She is a dynamic, faith-driven leader whose calling bridges humor, creativity, media, and discipleship. As well as being an award-winning comedic speaker known for her quick wit, Hill Country, Texas charm, and down-to-earth storytelling, she is the founder and visionary of LYN (Love Your Neighbor) Ministries, Inc., a 501(c)(3) nonprofit dedicated to equipping, empowering, and uniting women in biblical truth.

Through the SheWill Conference, Girls' Weekend God's Way Retreats, producing music, media, and building community, Shelsea's mission is clear: to see women healed, discipled, and released into their God-given callings.

https://linktr.ee/lynministries

My Visionary Calling

By Shelsea Becker

There I was, sitting in the Alamodome in San Antonio, Texas. Big, pregnant, and sweating through my maternity top, I was convinced I might give birth right there in the middle of the women's conference.

Although I was keenly aware of the precious life God was growing in me, the baby who would soon enter the world, I was unaware of another miracle He was preparing me to birth. God had begun weaving His marvelous plan into my life long before that moment.

PROPHETIC BUS

Something stirred in my spirit when I heard about a massive conference coming to Texas six hours away. It was an unshakable nudge that said, *You need to get women there.*

So, I did what any bold-but-nervous young woman would do—I reached out to the women's pastor at our church. She was one of the first examples of godly leadHERship I witnessed: humble, confident, never intimidated by other women's gifts. Instead of shutting me down, she made room. She must have seen something in me that I couldn't yet see in myself. That's the kind of leadHER you want to find—someone who speaks life into you and doesn't clip your wings before you learn to fly.

The pastor gave me the green light, and I started planning. I felt deeply convicted that we needed a bus. I didn't want women splitting off into cars and cliques, but united and connected. I knew the Holy Spirit was pressing this on me, and I couldn't shake it.

We didn't have the budget for a bus, so everyone said no. Undetermined, I prayed. And when that didn't seem to move mountains, I prayed harder. I called up Nanna Howdy—a godly woman whose life motto was "Call it all joy"—and we dropped to our knees in my living room; still, nothing. Days passed. Then weeks. I had over 30 women registered, hotel rooms booked, and still no bus.

Then one ordinary day, I was staring out my window when my neighbor pulled into his driveway—in a full-sized charter bus. I hollered out loud. I hit the door giggling like a kid on Christmas morning. *That's my bus,* I thought. And sure enough, when I asked him, he said yes. He had just bought it "for fun" and was more than happy to drive our group to San Antonio and back.

That moment was more than a transportation miracle—it was a prophetic confirmation. That was the first time I truly stepped into my calling as a visionary. I had seen the bus before it ever existed. Others said no. God said, "Wait." I saw it in my spirit before it was parked in the driveway.

TAP ON THE SHOULDER

I was sitting in the Alamodome at that conference—belly full of baby and laughing so hard I thought I might go into labor—when God did something I'll never forget.

Chonda Pierce was on stage, cracking jokes like we were at a comedy club instead of a church conference. I didn't know you could be funny and Christian. I was mesmerized. She wasn't just telling jokes—she was telling truth through laughter, and I felt something in me shift. That laughter cracked something open. It healed a part of me I didn't even know needed healing.

Then, right there—surrounded by thousands of women—I felt a tap on my shoulder. I knew it was the Holy Spirit. And I clearly heard Him whisper, "That will be you one day," as if He were pointing to the stage, to the sea of women laughing and leaning in, to a moment full of Jesus and joy and sisterhood. I looked around, thinking, *Umm... You sure You got the right gal?* After all, I had barely gotten us there. The whole bus miracle wiped me out, leaving me exhausted. *Leading women? Getting up on stage? No, thank you.*

Still, I couldn't deny that whisper, so I just kept it to myself. But God doesn't whisper without follow-through.

That night at dinner, our church group was seated at one long table—the kind where you have to shout to get the salt passed. From way down at the other end, I heard someone call my name.

"Shelsea!"

I looked up. "Yes, ma'am?"

It was our pastor's wife—soft-spoken, deeply discerning, the kind of woman who never says anything just to fill space. She smiled and said loud enough for the whole table to hear: "I can see you on that stage one day."

I nearly choked on my dinner. Wide-eyed and stunned, I asked, "Wait... what did you just say?"

Calm as ever, she repeated herself. "I see you up there. That's you."

And then—get this—the entire table started nodding in agreement. Like they'd known all along.

I hadn't told a single soul what the Holy Spirit whispered to me just hours earlier. But God confirmed it at the dinner table. He used someone I respected to say what I wasn't ready to admit. My heart was racing. I was flipping out on the inside.

But I knew.

God wasn't just planting a dream—He was calling me to it. And in His kindness, He made sure I didn't mistake it for a passing thought.

> *"By the mouth of two or three witnesses every word shall be established"* (2 Corinthians 13:1 NKJV).

He knew I would question it, so He confirmed it. It was a stake in the ground—the moment I realized that the God who gave me visions was also writing me into the vision.

> *Faith is the substance of things hoped for, the evidence of things not seen* (Hebrews 11:1 NKJV).

MY CALLING

I didn't know I was stepping into my calling. Honestly, I didn't even know what my calling was. Apostle? Visionary? Those were titles reserved for someone more qualified, more seasoned. I had no one to model it for me, no blueprint for how to walk it out. All I knew was that throughout my life, I felt different—like I didn't quite fit. Like I was out of step with everyone else.

While other kids were trying to blend in, I was imagining. Daydreaming. Creating, planning, designing. I thought it made me odd. Turns out, it made me called. What I once thought was "too much" was actually the groundwork for a kingdom assignment. The vivid pictures I carried in my spirit as a young girl would one day become blueprints for God to gather women, form community, and cultivate healing through worship and a discipleship conference.

I didn't know that seeing the bus in my spirit—and then believing for it until it literally showed up in my neighbor's driveway—was me walking in my calling. But that moment, as simple as it seemed, was God revealing what He had already placed in me: vision, faith, leadHERship, and the ability to mobilize people toward a purpose.

A visionary is someone who sees and hears from the Lord concerning the big picture. The mission. The divine strategy. A visionary carries the "what could be" and receives insight into what God is building—often before anyone else can see it.

This calling operates in the role of a biblical apostle—someone sent with authority to build, establish, and lead. Apostles don't just dream; they mobilize. Like generals in an army, they are entrusted with direction and deployment. They lead people, not based on their own ideas but by Spirit-led strategy.

To walk in a visionary calling is to learn how to recognize and trust God's voice, even when others don't see what you see. It's being faithful to carry what's not yet visible and move forward as if it already is. If you're going to be a visionary, you must know the voice of the One who gives the vision.

And that's exactly what He began teaching me—how to hear His voice.

"My sheep hear My voice, and I know them, and they follow Me" (John 10:27 NKJV).

I practiced listening—writing my prayers in a journal, then sitting in silence. When I felt a whisper in my spirit or a Scripture rise up in me, I'd write that too. Day after day, I repeated this rhythm. Learning to discern the voice of God was the foundation of everything.

It amazes me how the little projects I once thought insignificant were actually giant stepping stones in my journey. God walked me through small leadHERship tasks first. One by one, He gave me assignments to build my confidence—not in myself, but in His voice. What felt small at the time was preparation for something much greater. Each task, each "yes" built my trust, obedience, and confidence.

Never despise small beginnings—God often starts in the seemingly ordinary to prepare us for the extraordinary.

LEADHERSHIP

Besides being a visionary, God called me to leadHERship. In fact, God calls and anoints all Christians to lead for His kingdom in some capacity, and every leadHERship role He ordains is necessary and sacred.

There are many styles of leadHERship, and just as many arenas in which to lead. Some lead within the walls of their homes, raising children, stewarding peace, and shaping the next generation. Others lead on a national scale, influencing culture, policy, and movements. Some lead within the church, and God positions others in the world. Each of our leadHERship paths is different, but no matter the platform, leadHERship is holy ground.

I've learned that I am a visionary-style leadHER, called to operate on a national level outside the traditional church walls. But I didn't start there. I began with the small, seemingly insignificant assignments that God used to train, test, and transform me.

If you had told my tenth-grade self that one day I'd be leading a team of strong, Spirit-filled, alpha-type women on a women's conference national tour, I probably would've wet my pants. I was terrified to talk to people. But looking back, I can see that the lioness leadHER was always in me. I remember trying out for the high school dance team and actually making it. Although I was scared out of my mind to perform, I did it scared. Before every halftime show, I'd stand on the sidelines whispering to myself, "This will all be over in three minutes. Can I be brave for just three minutes?" It wasn't the dancing that scared me—it was the people watching.

One night, my worst fear was realized: During a basketball game routine, when we were supposed to drop from standing into a right-legged split, my mind went completely blank. I just stood there—frozen—while the rest of the team dropped to the floor. I couldn't hide. Everyone saw. And in that moment, I had a choice: cry or keep going. So I pivoted—I turned my mistake into a cheer and sold it like it was choreographed that way. When the team stood up, I joined back in like nothing had happened. I didn't know it then, but that was a defining moment. I learned I can do hard things—and I didn't die.

That was my first glimpse of leadHERship: problem-solving under pressure, adapting, and staying in the game. LeadHERship isn't about perfection; it's often about responding when things don't go as planned. Can you pivot? Can you find a solution in the chaos? That's the stuff leadHERs are made of.

Today, I lead a team of powerhouse women with diverse backgrounds—from different cities and denominations—all bound by one Spirit. They are strong, grounded, and bold leadHERs; I am a leadHER of leadHERs. I never would've known how to lead them if God hadn't first asked me to coach junior high volleyball.

On paper, I wasn't qualified to be a volleyball coach—I had zero experience. And it was a job I honestly didn't want to do. But after weeks of wrestling with God, I applied. Somehow, I got hired. My reluctant yes became an award-winning season. Then I moved up to Junior Varsity at the high school, then Assistant Varsity, and eventually became the Varsity Head Coach. Coaching a group of young girls who were still figuring out their identity wasn't always easy; some days felt like herding cats, and other days were pure harmony. But in the chaos and the chemistry, God was sharpening my leadHERship skills. I learned both the intricacies of the game and how to see and anticipate what others couldn't.

I also learned to lean into the Holy Spirit to meet each girl—to recognize where she belonged, see her strengths, and build her up. Riding the bench was nobody's purpose. My job was to call out each girl's worth and teach her how to spend time with God before she even touched the court. I coached to the level of the strongest player, and the others rose to meet her. I saw what it meant for a body to move in sync, for each part to do its job—a picture of the Body of Christ.

> For as we have many members in one body, but all the members do not have the same function so we, being many, are one body in Christ, and individually members of one another (Romans 12:4-5 NKJV).

During that coaching season, I was in a coffee shop when God downloaded the entire structure of what is now known as the She Will Conference. In 45 minutes, He gave me the itinerary, speaker list, theme, price point, and flow of the entire event. It would be a one-day women's discipleship conference with God's Word as the main event. The heartbeat would be women championing women, discipleship training, and community building.

WEIGHT OF THE CALL

Many times I wanted to quit—even before I ever really started. I had every reason not to say yes: I had no money, no job, and no clue what I was doing. But I said yes anyway. And that yes has cost me—time, talent, treasure, and more tears than I can count. I haven't taken a paycheck in eight years. Every dollar goes back into the ministry. Who else clocks in for eight hours a day with no paycheck? I once asked God if I could quit and move to the Florida Keys. His answer? "You can—but you'll end up doing the same thing: gathering women and teaching My Word." That's when I knew—this calling isn't just what I do. It's what drives me. It is what brings me joy.

I don't always get it right, though. In fact, there are days it feels like I take two steps forward and five steps back. There have been hurts—some light bruises, some deep wounds. But through it all, I've learned the power of humility. I've had to be quick to apologize, own my mistakes, and ask for forgiveness. Just as important, I've learned to forgive—even when no apology comes. Unforgiveness clogs everything, jamming the creative, spiritual, and relational flow. Forgiveness is foundational. It is essential to lead well.

An effective leadHER isn't born, but privately allows God to build within her the strength to lead through chaos, uncertainty, and fear. Three pillars uphold me in leadHERship:

1. *Sit with Jesus. Daily.* Not to study, journal, or run through a prayer list. Just to be. I call this time my Linger Lounge—a space where I linger in His presence, engaging all five senses. I look and listen, usually in nature; I immerse myself, often in water, and I tune in to Him as I appreciate the wind, the quiet, the colors, the fragrance of blooming flowers, and the birdsong. God is all around; sit with Him. Stillness builds spiritual sensitivity.

2. *Know His Word.* If you want to understand the character of God—how He moves, speaks, responds—then you have to study Him. Jesus only did what He saw His Father doing. That's the posture of a true kingdom leadHER. God isn't stingy about revealing Himself or sharing His wisdom with us; it's all in His Word. LeadHERship without the Word will lead you into burnout and prevent breakthrough.

3. *Die to self.* A leadHER isn't born selfless; she must die to herself daily. If your mission is to self-promote, can you really care about those you're leading? Whose heart are you stewarding—yours or those God entrusted

to you? One of the hardest parts of leading is laying down what you want for the good of the whole. And that doesn't happen on a stage, but in private, daily conversations with the Lord. When God asks us to care for His people, He holds us accountable. That's heavy—but it's also holy. And the only way to carry that weight is to let the Holy Spirit lead us first.

Kingdom leadHERship begins with Jesus' instructions, *"Seek first the kingdom of God"* (Matthew 6:33 NKJV). It is rooted in a desire to edify and empower the body of Christ. Godly leadHERs give their team the credit and shoulder the blame. They work to be consistent and faithful as they pray for their team, bolstering and supporting them toward victory.

I never imagined God would use a vision of a bus, a whisper in a crowd, or a volleyball coaching job to position me to lead a ministry full of Spirit-led women that spans cities and seasons. But that's the beauty of a kingdom calling—it unfolds in layers, not leaps. God has a way of turning our obedience into holy assignments. Every stretch, setback, confirmation, and commission we encounter is an Invitation to partner with God.

Will you seek God's voice, follow His Word, and lead with His heart? Will you commit your yes to Him as you lean into sacrificial love and Spirit-empowered grit? Into growth that requires pruning? Into people who require grace? And into moments so full of purpose and presence that joy overflows? That is what He is asking. And trust me, if you say yes, you won't regret a moment.

The Lord announces the word; the women who proclaim it are a mighty throng (Psalm 68:11 NIV).

Leading with Excellence

By Stacy Jo Coffee-Thorne

For a long time, I thought excellence was about flawless execution and the kind of success others could see. But the more I've walked with the Lord, the more I've realized that excellence is not about performance, but it is about presence. It is not about doing everything right; it is about doing everything as unto the Lord himself. True excellence starts in the quiet places where no one is watching. It begins when we decide that everything we touch will reflect the character of the One we serve.

Colossians 3:23-24 (NIV) says, *Whatever you do, work at it with all your heart, as working for the Lord, not for human masters, since you know that you will receive an inheritance from the Lord as a reward. It is the Lord Christ you are serving.* When our leadHERship and our daily efforts are offered to God first, the weight of other people's opinions begins to fade. Excellence becomes an act of love toward Him who called us.

Leading with excellence means bringing our best into everything we do, not for recognition, but out of reverence. Whether it is managing a business, leading a ministry, raising a family, or serving in our community, the standard should always reflect His goodness. Excellence is stewardship. It means being faithful with what we have, where we are, and with who He's placed around us.

Excellence is not only about what we produce; it is also about how we treat people. Kingdom excellence has a tone that sounds like kindness, grace, and humility. It means honoring others even when we disagree and choosing to speak life even when opinions differ. Philippians 2:3-4 (NIV) says, *Do nothing out of selfish ambition or vain conceit. Rather, in humility value others above yourselves, not looking to your own interests but each of you to the interests of the others.*

That verse reminds us that excellence is relational as much as it is operational. The way we lead people matters just as much as the goals we seek to accomplish. The highest form of excellence is not found in polished presentations or perfect plans, but in the fruit of the Spirit we demonstrate. If our words cut others down, if our tone breeds division, or if we lead without compassion, we have missed the heart of excellence altogether.

There will be moments in leadHERship when you don't see eye to eye with someone and it's tempting to push harder, to prove a point, or to walk away frustrated. But excellence calls us to respond in love, to listen before speaking, and to extend the same grace we've been given. Sometimes the most excellent thing you can do is hold your peace and let your humility speak louder than your opinion.

Excellence is not easy and often costs us something. Sometimes it requires longer hours, more patience, or more humility than we may want to give. It could mean biting your tongue when you could easily justify your frustration or apologizing when pride would rather wait for someone else to apologize first. But true excellence is formed when we choose to honor God through our conduct and character, not just through our accomplishments.

God Himself is excellent in all He does. Psalm 8:1 (NIV) proclaims, *Lord, our Lord, how majestic is your name in all the earth! You have set your glory in the heavens.* When we lead with excellence, we reflect God to the world around us. Our excellence points others to His goodness.

Excellence is not about perfectionism or performance; it is about obedience and offering our best to God, no matter how small the assignment seems. It is working with integrity, leading with humility, and treating others with love. It is remembering that how we handle *people* matters just as much as how we handle *projects*.

LeadHERship that honors God is marked by excellence and love. Whatever God has placed before you today, do it wholeheartedly, do it graciously, and do it unto Him. Let your leadHERship reflect integrity, humility, kindness, and love. Because when you lead with excellence, you build more than earthly success; you build eternal impact.

- -

Afterword

As you finish reading these final pages, our prayer is that something deep within you has been awakened. Not just an idea or an inspiration, but a holy stirring.

Each chapter in this book was born from the lived experiences, battles, breakthroughs, and victories of women who dared to say yes to God in their own unique corner of the kingdom. These women did not write from theory; they wrote from testimony. They wrote from the frontlines of faith—where calling collided with real life, joy had to be chosen, surrender led to strength, and God proved Himself faithful again and again.

And now, beloved leadHER, the mantle is extended to you.

Stepping into your God-given assignment is not always comfortable. It often requires courage, resilience, refinement, and a willingness to walk by faith when the path ahead isn't fully clear. But joy—kingdom joy—is not dependent on circumstances. It flows from knowing Whose you are and why you were created.

You were born with purpose. You were designed with intention.

You carry gifts that heaven entrusted to you because your generation needs what God has given you.

Joy is not the absence of pressure; it is the presence of Jesus in the middle of it. And when you lead from that place, you lead differently. You live differently and love differently. You step into your calling, not with heaviness, but with the confidence of one who knows the King has gone before her.

Kingdom LeadHERship: Stepping Joyfully Into God's Calling is more than a compilation; it is a chorus. Every voice, every chapter, every story has joined together to declare a single truth: God still calls His daughters to lead, rise, build, minister, influence, and shine.

Being a kingdom leadHER is not about having a platform; it's about having the right posture. It's not about a title; it's about transformation. It's not about being perfect; it's about being surrendered.

You are not called to lead alone. You are part of a global sisterhood of joyful warriors; women who were once where you are but now stand on mountain peaks because they refused to stop climbing. These women are here to cheer you forward as you step into your own God-designed destiny.

As you set this book down, may you pick up:

- A renewed commitment to deep joy
- A sharper clarity
- A Holy-Spirit-infused boldness to walk out your assignment

Whether your leadership unfolds in ministry, the marketplace, your home, or the quiet spaces where no one else sees, know that heaven sees. And heaven celebrates your yes.

May you go forth strengthened, equipped, and empowered to lead with grace, courage, wisdom, and above all, joy. Because in God's kingdom, joy is not optional; it's a weapon.

Joy breaks heaviness.

Joy fuels perseverance.

Joy helps you keep your eyes fixed on Jesus—the One who calls, equips, and goes before you every step.

Our prayer is that as you close this book, you will hear God whisper what every daughter of the King needs to hear: "You were made for this."

Step boldly. Step faithfully. Step joyfully into your calling.

The kingdom is waiting for your leadHERship.

.

More WPP Anthologies!

Like the mighty bison that charge directly into approaching storms, true leaders do something extraordinary—they run toward the chaos. The stories in *Unstoppable Leaders* feature faithful men who discovered that God's strength is perfected in weakness. And how ordinary challenges become extraordinary breakthroughs when faced with Biblical courage.

Faith Unchained: Climbing to Freedom by God's Grace is more than a book; it's a lifeline for weary hearts ready to rise. On these pages, you'll discover powerful testimonies from women who have walked through fire and found freedom. The words within don't present a quick fix; they offer hope and healing.

The stories and teachings in *Restoration* will fill you with hope as you witness God's steady and sure hand at work. Although we may feel like we've lost everything, we can stand strong, knowing God will bring beauty from the ashes of our lives. There is no need to despair—God's restoration will begin the moment you give your heart and circumstances to Him.

Men, families, communities, and countries must be on guard as courageous and battle-ready warriors. Men of God are each commissioned to be vigilant conquerors, prepared to lead the fight to overcome evil. The valiant authors in *Fit 2 Fight* share how they have overcome using the weapons that ensure victory no matter what we face.

God longs for you to have ferocious faith grounded in His unwavering love. Get ready to be encouraged as you open the pages of *Unshakable: God Will Sustain You.* Through true stories written by faithful and resilient women, you will witness God's sustaining power available to those who rely on Him.

The authors of *Unseen: You Are Not Alone* share their struggles of feeling isolated and unnoticed and detail how our awesome God helped them overcome every obstacle to find what truly matters: Him. These stories and devotional teachings shed light on the truth of your significance and value. You are never alone!

Despite all the adversities we face throughout our lives, God is the source of our hope. As you read the pages of this book, you will see how God brings *Hope Alive* to every person who is yearning for a reason to go on. Like a broken tree in a dark place is primed for new growth, God can use the rich soil of your dark place to prepare new life to sprout in you.

The authors of *Miracle Mindset: Finding Hope in the Chaos,* have experienced the wonders of God's provision, protection, and guidance. These stories and teachings will ignite a spark within you, propelling you to encounter the marvel of God's miracles, even in the chaos.

Life is full of storms and rough waters. The stories in Navigating Your Storm: By United Men of Honor will give you the ability to see the light of God and navigate your storm victoriously.

With Joy Unspeakable: Regardless of Your Circumstances, you will learn how joy and sorrow can dance together during adversity. The words in this book will encourage, inspire, motivate, and give you hope, joy, and peace.

Surrendered: Yielded With Purpose will help you recognize with awe that surrendering to God is far more effective than striving alone. When we let go of our own attempts to earn God's favor and rely on Jesus Christ, we receive a deeper intimacy with Him and a greater power to serve Him.

United Men of Honor: Overcoming Adversity Through Faith will help you armor up, become fit to fight, and move forward with what it takes to be an honorable leader. Over twenty authors in this book share their accounts of God's provision, care, and power as they proclaim His Word.

Embrace the Journey: Your Path to Spiritual Growth will strengthen and empower you to step boldly in faith. These stories, along with expertly placed expositional teachings will remind you that no matter what we encounter, we can always look to God, trusting HIS provision, strength, and direction.

Victories: Claiming Freedom in Christ presents expository teaching coupled with individual stories that testify to battles conquered victoriously through the power of Jesus Christ. The words in this book will motivate and inspire you and give you hope as God awakens you to your victory!

WPP's Mission

World Publishing and Productions was birthed in obedience to God's call. Our mission is to empower writers to walk in their God-given purpose as they share their God story with the world. We offer one-on-one coaching and a complete publishing experience. To find out more about how we can help you become a published author or to purchase books written to share God's glory, please visit: worldpublishingandproductions.com

Don't Let Misunderstanding Win empowers you to transform the interactions in all your relationships, shifting them from adversarial to win/win partnerships. Stop being driven by a scarcity mindset, and begin living from a place of abundance.

From the award-winning, bestselling *I'm Sober... So Now What?* series, comes *Unity in Recovery*—a powerful next step for anyone seeking deeper healing after addiction. This book goes beyond staying sober and explores what it means to live in true connection—with ourselves and with others.

Who Is Able? The Dana Louise Cryer Story is an incredible journey of tremendous pain, pierced by tumultuous circumstances and filled with twists and turns. God's incredible love transforms this true-life survival account into a miraculous outcome of total freedom. This book will leave you breathless and in tears at what only God can do.

At seventeen, Audrey Marie experienced a sudden and relentless excruciating firestorm of pain. *Chronically Unstoppable* tells of her true-life journey as she faced pain, developed strength, and battled forward with hope.

The world has become a place where we don't have a millisecond to think for ourselves, often leaving us feeling lost or overwhelmed. That is why Max Gold wrote *Planestorming!*—a straightforward guide to help you evaluate and change your life for the better. It's time to get to work and make the rest of your life the BEST of your life.

Riley Rossey is not your everyday bullied student, but one who discovers how to utilize his talents to assist other shy and picked-on individuals. Journey with Riley as he meets bullying head-on and becomes a God-given blessing to so many in *The Bullied Student Who Changed All the Rules* by Robert M. Fishbein.

www.ingramcontent.com/pod-product-compliance
Lightning Source LLC
Chambersburg PA
CBHW071709120626
46550CB00001B/162